D1455345

THE SIMON & SCHUSTER

POCKET GUIDE TO BEER

6TH EDITION

MICHAEL JACKSON

A FIRESIDE BOOK
PUBLISHED BY SIMON & SCHUSTER, INC.

Michael Jackson's Pocket Guide to Beer, 6th edition

To my late father, Jack Jackson
born Isaac Jakowitz, Yorkshire, 1909–84

Acknowledgments

Countless brewers worldwide, and their national organizations, have helped me in my researches over the years, and I thank them all. My further thanks for help with my most recent work to:
Larry Baush, Stephen Beaumont, Eugene Bohensky, Vince Cottone, Tom Dalldorf, Stephen D'Arcy, Erich Dederichs, René Descheirder, Alan Dikty, Sarah and Phil Doersam, Jim Dorsch, Pierre-André Dubois, Drew Ferguson, David Furer, Gary and Libby Gillman, Geoff Griggs, Brian Harrell, Erik Hartman, Bob Henman, Hans J Henschien, Graham Howard, Japanese External Trade Organization (JETRO), Eric Källgren, Nirbhao Khalsa, Alan Knight, Konishi Brewing, Jim Krecjie, Graham Lees, Lars Lundsten, Rob Maerz, Bill Mezger, Steve Middlemiss, Mikko Montonen, Multilines, Hans Nordlov, Ryouji Oda, Barrie Pepper, Chris Pietruski, Bernard Rotman, John Rowling, Rüdiger Ruoss, Silvano Rusmini, the late Dr Hans Schultze-Berndt, Todd Selbert, Conrad Seidl, Willie Simpson and his many beer-loving friends, Ritchie Stolarz, Peter Terhune, Unto Tikkanen, Anastasy and Jo Tynan, Derek Walsh, Przemyslaw Wisniewski, Kari Ylane

… and everyone else who helped me, or shared a beer, on the road.

FIRESIDE Rockefeller Center
1230 Avenue of the Americas
New York, NY 10020

Commissioning Editor Sue Jamieson
Executive Art Editor Fiona Knowles
Editor Lucy Bridgers
Designer Geoff Fennell
Researcher Owen Barstow
Production Anne Childers

The author and publishers will be grateful for any information that will assist them in keeping future editions up to date. Although all reasonable care has been taken in the preparation of this book, neither the publishers nor the author can accept any liability for any consequences arising from the use thereof or from the information contained therein.

Manufactured in Malaysia

10 9 8 7 6 5 4 3 2 1

Library of Congress Cataloging-in-Publication Data is available

ISBN 0-684-84381-1

CONTENTS

INTRODUCTION

A BEWILDERING CHOICE

Ever more beers beckon from the shelves of shops, the tap-handles of pubs and restaurants: Czech lagers, German wheat beers, Belgian Trappist ales, British pale ales, American microbrews. Which is the best ... or the beer for the mood or moment? How will it taste, and where can it be found?

Not only are more beers becoming available beyond their own shores, more breweries are opening in almost every country. Many of the newcomers are small, but their beers may deserve big reputations. Most breweries are making more beers than they once did, often in revived or new styles: from beers made with hot rocks to chocolate stouts and cherry brews.

This is a guide for the shopper, pub-goer, holidaymaker and business traveller. It reviews famous brews and little-known delights, from Adelaide, Australia, to Anchorage, Alaska, from Toronto to Tokyo.

Some demand consideration here simply because they are so widely available, others because they are so distinctive. Many are available outside their own country, others (especially those made in brewpubs) may be very local indeed.

The selections for every national chapter have been revised in this new, expanded edition. There is more detail on Scandinavian beers, and for those of Japan and Australasia. There are more than 650 new or revised tasting notes.

MICROBREWERIES

Once, all breweries were "micro". Germany, especially Bavaria, never lost those village taverns that brew their own beer, make their own bread, butcher their own meat. Britain was down to a handful of "homebrew houses" when they were rediscovered by the consumerist Campaign for Real Ale in the early 1970s. By the middle of that decade, a new generation of small breweries was springing up in Britain, and the movement quickly spread to the United States. After military service in Britain, Jack McAuliffe returned to his homeland and started the New Albion Brewery, in Sonoma, California. This later gave rise to the Mendocino County Brewing Company, which is still thriving. At that time, there were about 40 brewing companies in the USA. Two decades later, there are more than 1,200. Today, parties of German brewers visit the USA to study microbreweries.

Within the new generation, the terms have become blurred, but a restaurant that makes its own beer is usually now known as a "brewpub". This distinguishes it from a "microbrewery", which exists primarily to serve other people's pubs. Next up the size scale is the old-established local or regional brewery, and finally the national, or global, giant.

Some beers are created by entrepreneurs who have no brewery of their own. These people hire time at established breweries to have their own products made, usually under the supervision of a technical consultant. These entrepreneurs are known as "contract brewers". Often, their technical consultants are retired brewers, many of whom spent their working lives being obliged by their employers to make ever-blander beers. Now, they have emerged from retirement to make beers that they really like.

IS SMALL BEAUTIFUL?

There will always be a bigger market for bland beers, but they should not be allowed to wash away the more interesting choices for the discerning drinker. Large brewers have the skills to make distinctive beers, but sometimes their brew-kettles, and their marketing ambitions, are too big for specialities. Faced with the mass-market might of the giants, the smaller brewer should exist to specialize.

Food and drink are central to the quality of life. A good beer is a sensuous pleasure. The ever-present enemies of that pleasure are cost accountants who seek to cheapen its ingredients or make it faster; Head Brewers who want to collude in the interests of "science"; and marketing men who would render beer more "accessible" at the risk of persuading consumers that they should be drinking pop.

Once again, with no economies of scale, the smaller brewer does better to make traditional beers and hope that consumers will pay a fair price for them. The evidence is that they will.

WHAT MAKES A GREAT BEER?

Wine is more vulnerable to the mercies of soil and weather, but beer is the more complicated to make. The barley must first be malted and made into an infusion or decoction, the enigmatic (and none too hardy) hop added as a seasoning, and the whole brewed before it can be fermented, matured and conditioned.

In carrying out these procedures, the brewer is seeking to impart (in aroma, palate and finish) his own balance between the sweetness of the barley malt, the herby dryness of the hop, and the background fruitiness of the yeast used in fermentation. These characteristics are immediately evident in a fresh beer, especially one that has not been pasteurized (this process, unless it is carried out with the greatest of care, may merely deaden the beer to the ravages of travel and time).

The balance will be weighted differently according to the style of the beer, but it must always be achieved. A chef may intend one dish to be delicate, another to be robust, but each must have its own balance. After balance comes complexity. A wine-maker knows that each style is expected to have certain features, but beyond those there should be the individuality of its own character. Each time the drinker raises a glass of fine wine, new dimensions of aroma and palate should become apparent. So it is with a fine beer.

Any fine food or drink is enjoyed with the eyes and nose as well as the palate. The more individualistic beers, especially of the darker styles, can have a great subtlety of colour; most styles will present a dense, uneven "rocky" head if they have been naturally carbonated in fermentation, rather than having been injected with carbon dioxide; a properly carbonated beer will leave "Brussels lace" down the sides of the glass after each swallow. A good beer should be poured gently down the side of a tilted glass. A final, upright, flourish may contribute to its appearance, but the formation of a good head should not rest on the beer's being dumped violently into the glass.

Conventional beers are intended to be clear though excessive refrigeration can cause a "chill haze" in a good-quality, all-malt brew. The haze should subside once the beer reaches about 45°F (7°C). Conventional beers are also at risk of general deterioration (though they will not necessarily succumb to it) from the moment they leave the brewery. They are intended for immediate drinking, and not for keeping.

Brews indicated to be conditioned in the cask or bottle will contain living yeast. Unless the beer is poured carefully, the palate will have a "yeast bite", but the sediment is not harmful (in fact, its health benefits are quickly apparent). Very strong bottle-conditioned brews will improve with age.

Bottle-conditioned ales naturally have a very fruity aroma. In any beer, an unpleasant aroma reminiscent of damp paper or cardboard indicates oxidation (quite simply, the beer has gone stale). A cabbagey or skunky aroma means that the beer has been damaged by supermarket lighting or by being left in the sun. Beer is a natural product, and does not enjoy rough treatment.

STRENGTH

This is not a measure of quality. The ideal strength for a beer depends upon the purpose for which it is intended. A beer that is meant to be quenching, and to be consumed in quantity, should not be high in alcohol. The classic example, the Berliner Weisse style, has around 3 percent alcohol by volume. A typical premium beer, whether in Germany, Britain or the United States, might have between 4 and 5 percent by volume. A strong "winter warmer" may typically have between 6 and 8 percent. Although there are specialities of up to 17 percent, beers of this strength are hard to brew, and to drink in any quantity. At these levels, alcohol stuns beer yeasts to a point where they can no longer work, and the residual sugars make for heavy, cloying brews. There are, of course, wines of this strength, but they are not consumed by the half-pint.

Alcohol by volume is the system most commonly used to describe the strength of wine, and it is the simplest rating to understand. In some countries, including those of the European Union, beer is labelled according to alcohol by volume. With changes in the law, this may become the convention in the US. Most legislation concerning strengths of beer in the US is written in alcohol by weight. Since water is heavier than alcohol, this produces lower figures. In several brewing nations, the authorities were traditionally more concerned to tax what goes into the beer: the malt, wheat or other fermentable sugars. This is variously described as density or original gravity. Each of the older brewing nations developed its own scale for measuring this, the German Plato and similar Czech Balling systems being the most commonly used. In those countries, drinkers are inclined to be less familiar with alcohol content than with gravity.

The two do not have a direct relationship, since alcohol content is also a function of the degree of fermentation. The more thorough the fermentation, the higher the level of alcohol produced from a given gravity. The less thorough the fermentation, the fuller the body. Alcohol content and body are quite different, and in this respect opposed, elements of a beer.

THE MALTS

As grapes are to wine, so barley malt is to beer the classic source of fermentable sugars. The barley is malted (steeped in water until it partially germinates, then dried in a kiln) to release the starches that are then turned into fermentable sugars by infusion or decoction in water in a mashing vessel. This process is parallel to that carried out in the first stages of production of malt whiskies. In addition to deciding the pro-portion of malts to be used to achieve the desired density, the brewer is also concerned with their origin.

Certain varieties of barley are grown especially to be malted for the brewing industry. Among them, those that are grown in summer are held to produce cleaner-tasting, sweeter malts, though there is some debate on this. Some brewers also feel that inland, "continental" barleys produce better results than those grown in maritime climates. With varying harvests, there are differences in the quality and availability of barley, and the brewer has to account for this in the fine detail of his mashing procedure, its durations and temperatures. He will also adjust these according to the precise character he is seeking in his beer. They are among the hundreds of variables, and thousands of permutations, that contribute to the final character of every beer.

The traditional malting barleys are of varieties that have two rows of grain in each ear. Six-rowed barley is also used, though it produces a huskier, sharper character in the beer. Traditionalists stick to two-row barley but some brewers claim to seek the character they find in six-row varieties.

To the consumer, the more immediately obvious influence is the way in which the barley has been malted. There are many different standard malting specifications, each intended to produce a different result in terms of both colour and palate. As to colour, the more intense the kilning of the malt, the darker the beer. In palate, the character of the barley and the way in which it is malted can impart tones that are reminiscent, for example, of nuts, caramel, chocolate, espresso or licorice. These variations in malting differ in the moisture of the grains at the time of the kilning, as well as in the cycles of temperature and duration.

Depending upon the style of beer being produced, the brewer may use only one or two different types of malt, or as many as seven or eight. He may also use a proportion of unmalted barley, sometimes highly roasted, as in the case of dry stouts like Guinness. German and Belgian "white" beers are made with a pro-portion of malted wheat. So, naturally enough, are Weizen beers (it means wheat, after all). Belgian lambic beers use a proportion of unmalted wheat. One or two highly specialized beers use other grains. Less traditional grains include proportions of rice and corn, both used to lighten beers, and the latter especially for its low cost. Also for reasons of cost, and to boost alcohol in expensive strong beers like American malt liquors, cane sugar may be used. In Belgium, candy sugar is used in strong Trappist monastery beers. In Britain, milk sugars are used in sweet stouts.

In a cheap beer, barley malt may represent 60 percent of the mash, and corn or other adjuncts the rest. In Bavaria, barley malt and wheat are the only fermentable materials allowed. Elsewhere in Germany, the same goes for domestic beers but not for exports. A few other countries have similar laws, the closest being those of Norway and Greece. Within the EU, a country may insist that its own breweries work within a "Pure Beer" law, but it cannot block imports for failing to conform.

The Hops

Early wine-makers lacked the knowledge to produce by fermentation alone products of the quality they sought, so they employed seasonings of herbs and spices, creating the forerunners of today's vermouths and of patent apéritifs like Campari. Distillers, faced with similar difficulties, used a spicing of juniper and coriander to dry the palate of their product, thus creating gin. Liqueurs like Chartreuse have a similar history of development. In the same tradition, early brewers used tree-barks, herbs and berries.

Juniper and coriander are still used in a handful of highly specialized beers, but the hop eventually became the standard choice. The hop is a climbing plant, a vine, that is a member of the same family as cannabis. In ancient times, its shoots were eaten as a salad, and in Belgium they still are. Its cone-like blossoms can have a sedative effect, and are used in hop pillows. The cones also produce tannins that help clarify and preserve beer, and resins and essential oils that are the principal sources of aroma and dryness.

This dryness, or bitterness, is a part of the flavour balance of beer. An especially hoppy beer is a marvellous apéritif because its bitterness arouses the gastric juices. Brewers have their own scale of Units of Bitterness. Some very bland beers have as few as 12 Units of Bitterness; one or two tasty classics have over 50. A very hoppy beer will be full of earthy, aromatic, herbal, flavour notes.

Since all hops contain elements of both bitterness and aroma, the same variety may be used for both purposes, but this rare. Each variety of hop is usually identified as being ideal either for bitterness or aroma. A brewer could use one variety, but is more likely to use two or three, even seven or eight. He may put hops into the kettle once, twice or three times. The early additions are to provide bitterness, the later ones to confer aroma. To heighten aroma, he may even add blossoms to the hop strainer, or to the conditioning vessel. This last technique is known as "dry hopping". At each addition, he may use only one variety, or a different blend of several. He may use hop oils or extracts, or the whole blossom, in its natural form or compacted into pellets. There are many varieties of bittering hop, but few that enjoy special renown. Aroma hops are the aristocrats.

In continental Europe, the classic is the Saaz hop, grown in the area around the small town of Zatec, Bohemia, in the Czech Republic. In Germany, considerable reputations are enjoyed by the Hallertau Mittelfrüh and Tettnang aroma hops, named after areas near Munich and Lake Constance respectively.

In Britain, the delightfully named Fuggles are often used for their gentle, rounded, bitterness, but are also regarded as aroma hops. Hereford and Kent are known for their hops, the latter especially for a slightly more bitter and hugely aromatic variety called Goldings. These are at their finest in east Kent, near Faversham, allegedly in a strip of countryside a mile wide.

In North America the Cascade is the classic aroma hop, grown especially in the Yakima Valley of Washington State. There are hop-growing areas in British Columbia, Canada, too, and in similar latitudes of the southern hemisphere – in Tasmania.

THE YEAST

Among wines, it might be argued – perhaps simplistically – that there is a central division along lines of colour, between the reds and the whites. Among beers such a division concerns not colour but the type of yeast used. For centuries, all brewing employed what we now know as top-fermenting, or "ale", yeasts. In those days yeast was barely understood, except as the foam which, when scooped from the top of one brew, acted as a "starter" for the fermentation of the next. In this primitive method of brewing, the yeasts naturally rose to the top of the vessel, and were able to cross-breed with wild micro-organisms in the atmosphere. In the summer, they did so to a degree where beer spoilage made brewing impossible.

Brewers in the Bavarian Alps discovered, empirically, that beer stabilized if it was stored (in German, "lagered") in icy, mountain caves during the summer. Not only was it less vulnerable to cross-breeding; the yeast sank to the bottom of the vessel, out of harm's way. As scientists began to understand the behaviour of yeast in the 19th century, "bottom-fermenting" strains were methodically bred.

Today, all of the older brewing styles – ales, porters, stouts, German Altbier and Kölsch and all wheat beers – are (or should be) made with top-fermenting yeasts. All of the lager styles – Pilseners, Muncheners, Dortmunders, Märzen, Bock and double Bock and American malt liquors – are made with bottom-fermenting yeasts.

"Top" yeasts ferment at warm temperatures (classically 59–77°F/15–25°C), after which the beer may be matured for only a few days, or a couple of weeks, at warm temperatures. With modern means of temperature control, brewing in summer no longer poses a problem. A beer that has been "warm conditioned" will most fully express its palate if it is served at a natural cellar temperature, usually around 55°F (12°C). This is why a well-run British pub will serve ales at such a temperature. British ale can be rendered worthless by refrigeration.

"Bottom" yeasts ferment at cooler temperatures (classically 41–48°F/5–9°C), and the beer is then matured by being stored ("lagered") at around 32°F (0°C). Many mass-market beers are lagered for barely three weeks. Even in Germany, many brewers are content with four weeks, but traditionalists argue for three months. Bottom-fermenting beers taste best if they are chilled to between 45°F (7°C) and 50°F (10°C), the lighter their body, the lower the temperature and vice-versa.

In both techniques, very strong ales and lagers are matured for longer periods, sometimes for nine, or even 12 months. For whatever duration, this is a period in which the remaining yeast settles, harsh flavour compounds mellow out, and the beer gains its natural texture and carbonation (its "condition").

In top-fermenting ales that have a short period of maturation, the yeast may be settled with the aid of finings, usually isinglass. In Britain the classic ales are delivered to the pub with some working yeast still in the cask, so that they may reach the prime of condition in the cellar. This is known as cask-conditioning. Some speciality ales are bottled without filtration, or with an added dosage of yeast, as in the *méthode champenoise*. This is known as "bottle-conditioning".

Because they pre-date the true understanding of yeasts, some top-fermenting strains are hybrids. Others have picked up some "house character" from the micro-organisms resident in the brewery. Some brewers of top-fermenting specialities intention-ally use a blend of yeast, or employ different strains at different stages. Many, of course, use single-cell pure cultures, as do almost all brewers of bottom-fermenting beers. Bottom-fermenting has its origins in a more methodical, scientific, approach to brewing.

Beers made with top-fermenting yeasts are inclined to have dis-tinctly more individualistic and expressive palates, often with elements of fruitiness and acidity. Bottom-fermenting beers tend to be cleaner and rounder but the trade-off is that they may be less individualistic.

The Water

Claims about the water used in brewing were probably the most common feature of beer advertizing in the Victorian and Edwar-dian periods, and they are still to be heard.

In the 18th and 19th centuries, sources of pure water were not always easy to find. That is why towns or cities with good sources – among them, Pilsen and Munich in continental Europe; Bur-ton and Tadcaster in England – became centres of brewing.

Even today, a source of water that requires little or no treatment is an asset to a brewery. A great many breweries have their own springs or wells (this may not be the rule, but it is by no means the exception). In a good few instances, the town supply is adequate once the chlorine has been removed. Only in isolated cases is a water supply a problem. There is at least one island brewery that has to de-salinate sea water.

Even if the water does come from the brewery's own spring or well, natural salts may have to be added or removed for the production of different types of beer. As environmental concerns steadily grow, sources of pure water may once again be a marketable asset, but that time has not yet come.

"It's the water!" boast some breweries. "It's the beer!" would be a more convincing claim.

THE LANGUAGE OF THE LABEL

Abbey, Abbaye, Abdij Bier Not necessarily made in an abbey, or by monks, but imitating the Trappist style. Sometimes licensed by an abbey. See Trappist.

Ale The English-language term for a brew made with a top-fermenting yeast, which should impart to it a distinctive fruitiness. Ales are produced to a wide variety of colours, palates and strengths (see also Bitter, Brown Ale, India Pale Ale, Light Ale, Mild, Old Ale, Scotch Ale, etc). Only in some American states is the term determined by law (wrongly) to indicate a brew of more than 4 percent weight (5 by volume).

All malt Brewed only from malted grains, with no corn, rice, or other sugars.

Alt German word for "old". See Altbier.

Altbier A German term for a top-fermenting brew. Classic examples, copper in colour, mashed only from barley malt, fermented from a single-cell yeast and cold-conditioned, with an alcohol content of 4.5–4.7 by volume, are made in Düsseldorf.

Barley Wine An English term for an extra-strong ale (implied to be as potent as wine). Usually more than 6 percent by volume and classically closer to 11. Most often bottled. Both pale and dark versions can be found.

Bayrische German word for Bavarian.

"Beer" Confusingly, the Americans use the term "beer" to mean only lager. The British employ it to mean only ale. Neither is correct. Both lager and ale – as well as porter, stout, and all the Belgian and German specialities – are embraced by the general term "beer". It is all beer, so long as it is a fermented drink made from grain and seasoned with hops.

Berliner Weisse Berlin's classic "white" (cloudy), sedimented, top-fermenting wheat beer, with the quenching sourness of a lactic fermentation, the sparkle of a high carbonation, and a low alcohol content of around 3 percent by volume.

Bière de Garde French style. Often bronze or amber. Originally a strong, top-fermenting, bottle-conditioned brew intended for laying down. May have caramel flavours from long boil. Today, often bottom-fermented and filtered. 4.4–7.5 by volume.

Bitter English term for a well-hopped ale, most often on draught. Although examples vary widely, the name implies a depth of hop bitterness. There is usually some acidity in the finish, and colour varies from bronze to deep copper. Basic bitters usually have an alcohol content of around 3.75–4 percent by volume, "Best" or "Special" bitters come in at 4–4.75; the odd "Extra Special" at about 5.5.

Bo(c)k The German term for a strong beer. If unqualified, it indicates a bottom-fermenting brew from barley malt. In Germany, bock usually has more than 6.25 percent alcohol by volume, and may be golden, tawny or dark brown. Outside Germany, strengths vary, and a bock is usually dark. Bock beers are served in autumn, late winter or spring, depending upon the country. See also Maibock, Doppelbock, Weizenbock.

Brown Ale In the south of England, a dark-brown ale, sweet in palate, low in alcohol (3–3.5 by vol). In the northeast, a red-brown ale, drier, of 4.4–5. The slightly sour, brown brews of Flanders are also ales, though they tend not to use the designation.

Cask-conditioned ale Draught ale that is neither filtered nor pasteurized and has a secondary fermentation and precipitation of yeast in a vented cask in the cellar of the pub. The beer should emerge relatively clear, with a natural carbonation (albeit very light). Unworkable if the beer is chilled.

Cream Ale An American designation, implying a very pale (usually golden), mild, light-bodied ale that may actually been blended with a lager. Around 4.75 by volume.

"Dark beer" There are many, quite unrelated, styles of dark brew. If this vague term is used without qualification, it usually means a dark lager of the Munich type.

Diät Pils This has nothing to do with slimming, but was originally intended for diabetics. A German style so popular in Britain that many drinkers think there is no other kind of "Pils". Carbohydrates are diminished by a very thorough fermentation, creating a relatively high content of alcohol (about 6 percent by volume) and therefore lots of calories. In German law, the alcohol now has to be reduced back to a normal Pilsener level (5 percent by volume).

Doppelbock "Double" bock. German extra-strong bottom-fermenting beer, tawny or dark brown. Around 7.5 by volume or stronger. Southern speciality, seasonal to March and April. Names usually end in "-ator".

Dort Abbreviation used in Belgium and the Netherlands to indicate a beer in the Dortmunder Export style.

Dortmunder This indicates merely a beer brewed in Dortmund, but the city's classic style is Export (see Export).

Draught/Draft beer in a can Nitrogen has been added to imitate the creaminess of a beer drawn by pump.

Dry Beer Originally a milder adaptation of the German Diät Pils, renamed Dry Beer by the Japanese. After its great marketing success in Japan, the term Dry Beer was taken up in North America. There, the style was made milder still. American Dry Beer has a conventional alcohol and calorie content but is notable for having scarcely any taste, and no finish.

Dunkel/Dunkles German word for "dark".

Eisbock An extra-strong (Doppel) bock beer in which potency has been heightened by a process of freezing. Since water freezes before alcohol, the removal of ice (*eis*) concentrates the beer.

Export In Germany, a pale, Dortmund-style bottom-fermenting beer, bigger bodied than a Pilsner and less dry, but not as sweet as a Munich pale beer. At 5.25–5.5 by volume, stronger than either. Elsewhere: usually indicates a premium beer.

Faro Once Brussels' local style, a version of a lambic sweetened by candy sugar. 4.5–5.5 by volume.

Festbier In Germany, any beer made for a festival. Styles vary, but they tend to be above average strength, often 5.5–6 volume.

Framboise/frambozen Raspberry beer, usually based on lambic. Alcohol content varies.

Genuine Draft (and similar terms) Bottled or canned beer that, like most draughts, is unpasteurized. Unlike them, it is sterile-filtered for shelf-life.

Gueuze A blend of old and young lambic beers. Around 4.4–5.5 by volume.

Haute fermentation French for top fermentation.

Hefe- The German word for yeast, indicating that a beer is bottle-conditioned and sedimented.

Hell German word for "pale", indicating an everyday beer that is golden in colour. Ordered as a Helles (hell-es).

Ice beer (and similar terms) Otherwise conventional beers that have been frozen at some stage during fermentation or maturation, and in some cases reconstituted later. This knocks out some flavour components and perhaps concentrates others. A marketing-led technique inspired by Eisbock (see entry).

Imperial Stout See Stout.

India Pale Ale (IPA) British pale ales for the Indian Empire were made to a higher than normal strength, and given more hops, to protect them on the journey. Today, the hoppiest examples of this style are made by the new generation of American brewers. 5.0–plus, sometimes far higher.

Kellerbier German term indicating an unfiltered lager, in which there is usually a high hop content and a low carbonation. Strengths vary according to the original style.

Kloster Bier "Cloister beer". German term for a beer that is, or formerly was, produced in a monastery or convent.

Kölsch Cologne's style. Golden, top-fermenting, lagered. Softly drinkable, with a delicate fruitiness. 4.3–5.0 by volume.

Kräusen In German custom, a traditional technique of carbonation is to add a small dosage of unfermented malt sugars (in English, wort) to the conditioning tank. In a normally *kräusened* beer, the wort ferments out and the beer is conventionally fil-tered. An unfiltered beer based on this technique is called *Kräusenbier*.

Kriek Cherry beer, usually based on lambic. 5–6 by volume.

Kruidenbier Dutch-language term for spiced beer.

Lager Any beer made by bottom-fermentation. In Britain, lagers are usually golden in colour, but in continental Europe they can also be dark. In the German-speaking world and The Netherlands, the term may be used to indicate the most basic beer of the house, the *bière ordinaire*.

Lambic Spontaneously fermenting style of wheat beer unique to Belgium, notably the Senne Valley. About 4.4.

Light Ale English term describing the bottled counterpart of a basic bitter. In Scotland, "Light" indicates the lowest gravity draught beer (usually dark in colour), neither term implies a low-calorie beer.

Light Beer Or "Lite", as in Miller. In America, a beer labelled with its calorie count. It is required to be lower in calories than the brewery's "normal" product (which probably has 145–150). Light beers are usually 10–35 percent meaner. The difference is lost in two or three potato crisps or taco chips. In Canada and Australia, "Light" means lower in alcohol.

Maibock Celebratory springtime or "May" Bock, often released in April or even late March. Often pale.

Malt Liquor Not malty, and sometimes containing substantial amounts of cheaper sugars. Not a liquor, either, but usually a strongish variation on a regular American lager. Intended for a cheap "high". Some states require the term malt liquor to be applied to all beers of more than 5.0 per cent by volume.

Märzen From "March" in German. Originally a beer brewed in March and laid down in caves before the summer weather rendered brewing impossible. Stocks would be drawn upon during the summer, and finally exhausted in October. In Germany, this tradition has come to be associated with one specific style. *Märzenbier* has a malty aroma, and is a medium-strong version (classically, more than 5.5 percent alcohol by volume) of the amber-red Vienna style. It is seasonal to the *Oktoberfest*, where it is offered as a traditional speciality alongside paler beers of a similar strength. Confusingly, in Austria the term refers not to style but to gravity.

Mild English term indicating an ale that is only lightly hopped. Some milds are copper in colour, but most are dark brown. These beers were devised to be drunk in large quantities by manual workers, and have in recent years suffered from their blue-collar image. Around 3 by volume, but often relatively full in body.

Münchener/Münchner Means "Munich-style". In inter-national brewing terminology, this indicates a dark-brown lager, a style developed in Munich (although another Bavarian town, Kulmbach, also has a long tradition of dark lagers). In Munich, such a brew is clearly identified by the word *Dunkel* ("dark"), and classic examples have an alcohol content of around, 5 percent by volume. Bavarian brewers in general also impart their own distinctively malty accent to their everyday, lower-gravity (alcohol content around 3.7) pale beers. These are sometimes identified as *Münchner Hell*, to distinguish them from the same brewers' Pilsener-style product.

Nitrokeg Beer made creamy by nitrogen pressure.

Obergärig German for top-fermenting.

Oktoberfest beers See Märzen.

Old (Ale) In Australia, "Old" simply means dark ale. In Britain, it is most commonly used to indicate a medium-strong dark ale like Old Peculier, with just under 6 percent by volume. However, by no means all ales describing themselves as "old" are in this style.

Pale Ale Pale in this instance means bronze or copper-coloured, as opposed to dark brown. Pale ale is a term used by some English brewers to identify their premium bitters.

Pilsener/Pilsner/Pils Loosely, any golden-coloured, dry, bottom-fermenting beer of conventional strength might be described as such (in its various spellings and abbreviations), though this most famous designation properly belongs only to a product of "super-premium" quality. Too many brewers take it lightly, in more senses than one. In their all-round interpretation, German brewers take the style most seriously, inspired by the Urquell (original) brew from the town of Pilsen, in the Czech province of Bohemia. A classic Pilsener, has a gravity of around 12 Balling and is characterized by the hoppiness of its flowery aroma and dry finish.

Porter A London style that became extinct, though it has recently been revived. It was a lighter-bodied companion to stout, and the most accurate revivals are probably the porters made by American micro-brewers like Sierra Nevada. Around 5 percent by volume. In some countries, the porter tradition remains in roasty-tasting dark brews that are bottom-fermented, and often of a greater strength.

Rauchbier Smoked malts are used in the production of this dark, bottom-fermented speciality, principally made in and around Bamberg, Franconia. Produced at around 5 percent by volume and in Märzen and Bock versions. Serve with Bavarian smoked ham, or bagels and lox.

Saison Seasonal summer style in the French-speaking part of Belgium. A sharply refreshing, faintly sour, top-fermenting brew, sometimes dry-hopped, often bottle-conditioned, 5.5–8 by vol.

Scotch Ale The ales of Scotland generally have a malt accent. In their home country, a single brewery's products may be identfied in ascending order of gravity and strength as Light, Heavy, Export and Strong. Or by a system based on the old currency of shillings, probably once a reference to tax ratings: 60/-, 70/-, 80/-, 90/-. Alcohol content by volume might rise through 3, 4, 4.5 and 7–10. The term "Scotch ale" is used specifically to identify a very strong, and often extremely dark, malt-accented speciality from that country.

Schwarzbier "Black" or very dark beer. The most famous type is made in Köstritz, Germany (*see* page 67).

Steam Beer A name protected by the Anchor Steam Beer brewery of San Francisco. This brewery's principal product is made by a distinctive method of bottom-fermentation at high temperatures and in unusually wide, shallow vessels. This technique, producing a beer with elements of both lager and ale in its character (though also distinctive in its own right), is said to have been common in California when, in the absence of supplies of ice, early brewers tried to make bottom-fermenting beers. The very lively beer was said to "steam" when the casks were tapped.

Stout An extra-dark, almost black, top-fermenting brew, made with highly roasted malts. Sweet stout, an English style, is typified by Mackeson, which has only about 3.75 percent alcohol by volume in its domestic market but more than 5 in the Americas. Sweet stout usually contains milk sugars (lactose), and is a soothing restorative. Dry stout, the Irish style, is typified by Guinness, which comes in at around 4 percent in the British Isles, a little more in North America and as much as 8 in tropical countries. Dry stouts sometimes contain roasted unmalted barley. Imperial Stout, originally brewed as a winter warmer, for sale in the Tsarist Russian Empire, is medium dry and distinguished by its great strength: anything from 7 to more than 10.

Trappist This order of monks has five breweries in Belgium and one in The Netherlands. By law, only they are entitled to use the term Trappist to describe their products. Each of them produces strong (6–12 percent by vol), top-fermenting brews, characteristically using candy sugar in the kettle, and always bottle-conditioned.

Tripel (various spellings) Dutch-language term usually applied to the strongest beer of the house, customarily top-fermenting often pale in colour, occasionally spiced with coriander. The most famous is made in Westmalle, Belgium (*see* pages 87–8).

Trub German term for sediment.

Vienna Amber-red, or only medium-dark, lager. This was the style originally produced in Vienna. Brewers still talk of a "Vienna malt" to indicate a kilning to this amber-red colour, but the beer-style itself is no longer especially associated with the city.

Ur-/Urquell "Original"/"source of", in German. Justifiable when applied to, for example, Einbecker Ur-Bock or Pilsner Urquell, but often more loosely used.

Weisse/Weissbier, Weizenbier The German term for "white" beer, implying a pale brew made from wheat. In the north, a special renown is enjoyed by Berliner Weisse, a style in its own right (see separate entry). A different style of Weissbier is made in the south, with a more conventional alcohol content (usually a little over 5 percent by volume), a higher proportion of wheat (at least 50 percent) and a yeast (again top-fermenting) that produces a tart, fruity, spicy palate, sometimes with notes of cooking apples and cloves. Often, instead of Weissbier, the southerners prefer the term Weizen (a similar-sounding word but it means, quite simply "wheat"). If the beer is sedimented with yeast, it may be prefixed Hefe-. Southern wheat beers are also produced in dark versions (these Dunkel Weizen brews have a delicious complex of fruitiness and maltiness), and in Export and Bock strengths. Weizenbock is sometimes served as a Christmas beer.

White A term once used to describe wheat beers. Apart from those of German-speaking countries, Belgium's white beers (Witbier, Bière Blanche) are of considerable interest.

Widget Variation on "gadget". In Britain, applied especially to the capsule of nitrogen in cans or bottles of "draught" beer.

Wiesen/Wies'n Among several words that are confusingly similar to the non-German speaker, this one means "meadow". It implies a beer brewed for a carnival or festival (an Oktoberfest beer may be described as a Wies'n Märzen) or a rustic speciality (such as Küppers' unfiltered Wiess).

Witbier A Dutch/Flemish term used in Belgium and, increasingly, the United States. See White.

Zwickelbier German term for an unfiltered beer without the distinguishing features of either a Kellerbier or a Kräusenbier.

THE WORLD'S BEERS REVIEWED

THE APPRECIATION OF BEER having been contemplated, its qualities studied, the language of the label decoded, and the time for a sampling determined, where is the brew to be found? What follows is a selective review of the world's beers. It deals separately with each of the countries in which beer-brewing is an important tradition. Among them, it divides the most complex brewing nations into regions. These divisions are intended to be convenient for the traveller, but they also reflect style differences in the local beers. An overview of the local beer types is included in concise introductions to each major brewing nation or region. Each of these is followed by a **WHERE TO DRINK** section introducing some of the most interesting establishments in which beer is available, including a number of specialist shops.

Throughout, this review attempts to highlight the most interesting and distinctive beers, often from very small breweries, as well as the better-known names. The figures mentioned in the text and appearing after a beer indicate its strength (see page 6). However, they are not a measure of its quality. For example, Briljant (12; 1048; 5.2; 6.3) has a density of 12; an original gravity of 1048; a percent alcohol by weight of 5.2; and a percent alcohol by volume of 6.3. The figures always appear in that order. To avoid an endless recital of statistics, these details are given only where they might be helpful in distinguishing between two similar products, or where a beer of special interest is being discussed.

In the latter instance, there may also be a reference to Units of Bitterness (see under Hops, page 8). Units of Bitterness are only a guideline, and cannot express the complex flavours imparted by the hops, but these figures are offered for the benefit of those beer-lovers who find them helpful. Many home-brewers, and some commercial beer-makers planning new products, like to have precise readings of bitterness in well-regarded examples.

The same is true with Units of Colour. Likewise, these cannot measure the subtlety and attractiveness of colour in some beers. The system used is that agreed by the European Brewing Convention. A figure of 6–8 units, for example, might indicate a golden beer; 20–40 suggests bronze to copper; a reading in the hundreds may reflect anything from mahogany to ebony.

I have offered my own star-ratings, but merely as a guide. They assess beers according to the standards of each region:

☆ Typical of its country and style
☆☆ Above average
☆☆☆ Worth seeking out
☆☆☆☆ World Classic

An Index at the back of the book acts as a quick reference guide to breweries and their beers.

The Czech Republic

PILSEN, BUDWEIS (known today as České Budějovice) and Michelob (Michalovce) are cities in Bohemia, the medieval kingdom of Wenceslas. This province and adjoining Moravia comprise what is now the Czech Republic. The region's hop-growing and brewing traditions date back at least to the beginning of this millenium; Pilsen produced the world's first golden lager, and other cities inspired famous brand-names in the New World. Since the "Velvet Revolution", more Czech beers have come West, and more Western drinkers have visited Bohemia, especially the capital, Prague.

Bohemia still has its step-gabled breweries, set around courtyards, with imprecations to God dating to pre-Communist times in the brewhouse tiling and flagstoned corridors in the lagering cellars. But can the traditional character of its beers survive?

When Bass, of Britain, took a share in the Staropramen brewery, open fermenters were preserved and a plan for cylindro- conicals postponed. Elsewhere, though, the delicacy and complexity traditionally associated with Czech beer is being lost to methods that quickly produce larger volumes of "marketable" beers.

Where managements have changed, and beers have not been tasted since, listings are not provided here. The notes below are all based on recent tastings. Where a brewery's "principal beer" is mentioned, this will normally be a golden lager with an alcohol content of around 4.0 percent by weight and 5.0 by volume, from a gravity of 12 degrees Balling.

Where to drink in Prague

The capital has many beer taverns. The most famous, U Fleků (11 Křemenocová), in the "New Town" (the city centre), is the world's oldest brewpub, dating from 1499. This offers just one beer: a famous dark lager of 13 Balling, with a soft, spicy palate. In the "Old Town", U Zlatého Tygra (17 Husova) is a famous literary tavern selling Pilsner Urquell. For the outstanding keeping of Pilsner Urquell, some drinkers prefer U Kocoura, in the "Lesser Town" (2 Nerudova). Just off the lower end of Wenceslas Square, a turn-of-the-century shopping arcade at 20 Vodickova St has since 1993 boasted a cellar brewpub called Novomestsky Pivovar. There is said to have been a brewery on the site in 1434. The new establishment began with a creamy, malt-accented beer, served yeastily unfiltered. About 25–30 miles south of Prague, the castle of Zvikov now has a brewery, making top-fermenting brews based on the Bohemian beers of the pre-lager period. Opening hours are variable (Pivovarsky dvur Zvikov, ☎363-95660).

Budweiser Budvar

The bigger and better known of the two breweries in the city whose name it bears. *Budweiser Budvar* ☆☆☆▷☆☆☆☆ is sweetish, but with a faintly oily roundness. This brewery was established in 1895. The brewery's town-centre pub is in the former meat market, Masne Kramy, just off the main square. Masne Kramy occasionally holds pig-roasts.

Budweiser Burgerbrau

Also known as Erste ("First") Budweiser, to mark its foundation in 1795, or Samson, after its beer. The towns symbol is a fountain built in the 1720s and featuring a statue of Samson. The principal *Samson* ☆☆☆ beer is clean and soft, with a dry maltiness and delicacy of hop character. A fractionally hoppier version is sold in Britain as *Zamek*. The brewery also has a coffeeish dark lager. The town-centre outlet is the U Svejka bar at the U Samsona Hotel, also off the main square. The company also owns Regent, a brewery established by a powerful family of aristocrats in the town of Trebon, famous for its carp lakes. *Bohemia Regent* ☆☆▷☆☆☆ is well-balanced, tilting slightly to crisp, quenching, hop character. A light Vienna type is made only for the Swedish market. *Regent Dunkles* ☆☆▷☆☆☆ ("dark") has some pruney flavours. The company also has Platan, which takes its name from the plane trees of Protivin. The principal *Platan* ☆☆▷☆☆☆ has a clean punch of maltiness followed by a clear smack of hops.

Herold

Former state research brewery in the village of Breznice, about 50 miles south of Prague. Its *Hefe-Weizen* ☆☆☆ (in Czech, *Psenicne Kvasnicove*) is the first Czech wheat beer of modern times. Light, clean and notably perfumed, with distinctive dessert apple notes.

Lobcowicz

Small brewery in Vysoky Chumlec, central Bohemia. The exported *Lobkov* ☆☆ is a perfumy, dryish, malt-accented golden lager. The *Special* ☆☆▷☆☆☆ (4.4; 5.5) is hoppier and better-balanced. The tawny *Dark* ☆☆ is smooth and firm, with dryish toffee notes.

Louny

The light-bodied but malty *Tmave* ☆☆ ("dark") is among the products of this regional brewery, located in the town of Louny, NW of Prague.

Radegast

Moravian brewery, named after the spirit of hospitality. Its *Radegast Premium* ☆☆▷☆☆☆ is firm-bodied, with a very late, sharp, grassy, hop bitterness. This technologically-minded brewery is in Nosovice.

Pilsner Urquell

When fresh, *Pilsner Urquell* ☆☆☆☆ is still the world's greatest golden lager, not only because it was the first, but also for its complexity of malt and hop flavours. It is, though, reduced in character since the wooden fermenters and lagering vessels were replaced by stainless steel. The adjoining Gambrinus brewery is under the same ownership. The principal *Gambrinus* ☆☆▷ ☆☆☆ beer has a sweetish start, a slightly sticky maltiness, and an attractively hoppy bitterness in the finish. The same company owns breweries in several nearby towns. The one in

Cheb produces *Eger Urbier* ☆☆, soft, with light touches of sticky maltiness, acidic hoppiness and yeasty dryness. Another, in Domazlice, makes a very firm, smooth, dark beer called *Purkmistr* ☆☆▷☆☆☆ ("Burgomeister"). This brewery also produces a wheat beer (not tasted). In a former maltings in Pilsen, the Pivovarske Museum (Veleslavinova 6) is devoted to the history of brewing in Bohemia and Moravia. In the same street, the Parkan tavern is said to have the best Pilsner in town, sometimes unfiltered.

Starobrno

Named after its home town Brno, the principal city of Moravia. *Starobrno Export Lager* ☆☆▷☆☆☆ is appetisingly flowery, light but firm, balanced by malty sweetness. Also in Brno: hotel and brewery Pegas (4 Jakubska; fax 05422 11232) making a wheat beer, pale and dark lagers. Additionally in Moravia, the immodestly-named Excelent hotel, at Rýmařov (fax 0647 3011) has a brewhouse making a bottom-fermenting Porter.

Staropramen

The name means "Old Spring". Staropramen, founded in 1869, is in the Smichov district, close to the centre of Prague, and is the city's biggest brewery. Its principal *Staropramen* ☆☆☆ is notably soft and malty, with a full but delicate flavour. Its *Tmave* ☆☆ ("dark") is lightly toffeeish. The same company owns Holesovice, which makes malty but drier beers in the north of the city; and Branik, which produces hoppier, more aromatic, brews in the south. Both have tasty dark beers.

Velkopopovicky

To the south of Prague. This brewery produces *Kozel Premium* ☆☆, with some fruity hop flavours, and a malty *Tmave* ☆☆☆▷☆☆☆ ("dark").

Vratislavice

The flowery, dry, appetising, *Vratislav Lager* ☆☆☆▷☆☆☆ comes from this brewery, named after its home town in the north of Bohemia.

EASTERN EUROPE

THE CZECH TRADITION has also been an influence in Slovakia. The creamy, smooth, dryish, light, *Topvar* ☆☆, and the similar, firmer, drier, *Zlaty Bazant* ☆☆, are examples. So is the very dry, lively, *Hell* ☆☆ of Banská Štiavnica. *Martinksy Lager* ☆☆ is a long, malty entrant from Slovakia, but it is shame the same brewery's strong, burnt-tasting Porter is not easier to find. *Cassovar* ☆☆☆ (4.4; 5.5), with hints of raisins, toffee and coffee, is a Slovak Porter more readily available in the West.

In Poland the Piast brewery has a smooth, whiskyish, strong (4.8; 6.0) golden lager *Piast* ☆☆▷☆☆☆ and a *Strong Dark* ☆☆▷☆☆☆ (5.9; 7.4) tasting of chocolate pralines. E.B. has a treacly, whiskyish, *Red* ☆☆☆ and an aromatic, raisiny, *Porter* ☆☆☆ (22;1088;7.4;92.). Zywiec has a dryish pale lager and a very smooth and extremely coffeeish *Porter* ☆☆☆. Okocim has a similar range, but perhaps less hoppy.

Other strong Baltic Porters include a medicinal-tasting example from the *Vilnius* ☆☆▷☆☆☆ brewery, a more toffeeish one from *Utena* ☆☆▷☆☆☆ (both Lithuania); the licorice-tinged interpretation from *Aldaris* ☆☆▷☆☆☆ (Latvia); and the coffeeish *Saku* ☆☆☆ (Estonia).

Lithuania has some otherwise conventional lagers made with a proportion of peas, though the vegetable is not obvious in the flavour of the beer. This style is identified as Sirvenos. This country also has some distinctively winey-tasting "country brews" from the Birzai region, and Latvia similar products such as *Lacplesis* ☆☆☆. These are amber, malty, bottom-fermenting beers, usually made in open fermenters, demonstrating a great deal of house character. In Estonia, especially on the island of Saaremaa, farmhouse brewers sometimes make a rye and juniper beer called Kotiolu, on the lines of a Finnish Sahti.

Also in Estonia, the Russian-speaking town of Sillamae has a micro-brewery producing a deliciously malty dark lager in the Bavarian style: *Muncheni Tume Olu* ☆☆☆.

Variations on all these styles exist throughout the former Communist world. In Russia, beer had to compete with *Kvass*, fermented from rye bread, and vodka. In the Balkans, beer dominates in Croatia and hop-growing Slovenia (with its soft, malty, well-balanced "Golden Horn" beer *Lasko Zlatorog* ☆☆), giving way to wine further south.

AUSTRIA

BEING AN IMPERIAL CAPITAL, Vienna was a major brewing centre, famous for the amber-red, malty, style of lager first produced by Anton Dreher in 1841. Its principal beers today are still accented towards malty sweetness, with a faint touch of bronze in the colour, but not nearly as assertive as some Vienna-style lagers produced elsewhere.

Dreher's original Schwechat brewery, retaining flourishes of elegance, passed into one of two national groupings (the other based in Graz), which merged in 1997 under the name Brau-Union Österreich. There will no doubt be rationalisations of the range, which includes: *Hopfernperle* ☆▷☆☆, light and dry; *Steffl* ☆, light to medium in body, with a hoppier finish; a fruitier series under the *Kaiser* ☆ name; the more flowery, sherbety *Zipfer Urtyp* ☆▷☆☆; the maltier *Reininghaus-Puntigam* ☆▷☆☆ beers and the heartier Gösser selection, including the clean *Export* ☆☆ and the dark, very sweet, *Stiftsbräu* ☆▷☆☆, at 12.2 Plato but only 2.9; 3.6.

Vienna's local brewery, Ottakringer, makes the sweetish *Gold Fassl* ☆☆, with some roundness. A lager in broadly the Vienna style is produced by the Wieden brewpub, in the district of the same name (5 Waag Gasse). More of a Munich type is made by the Fischer brewpub (17 Billroth Strasse), in the suburb of Döbling, on the edge of the Vienna Woods.

Baron Henrik Bachofen von Echt has a more colourful range, all top-fermenting, in a brewpub in the wine-cellars of his Schloss, where the tram stops at Nussdorf, also close to the woods. These include the chocolatey, fruity-dry *Sir Henry's Stout* ☆☆☆ (4.8; 6); the copper, chewy *St Tomas Brau* ☆☆☆▷☆☆☆; the deep bronze, drier, complex *Doppelhopfen Hell* ☆☆☆▷☆☆☆ (30 percent wheat); and a seasonal brew made with whisky malt.

Between Linz and Salzburg, the Eggenberg brewery produces a lightly smoky "whisky malt beer", *Nessie* ☆☆☆, also a creamy but dryish *Urbock "23"* ☆☆☆ (the figure, its gravity in degrees Plato), 7.9 percent alcohol by weight, 9.9 by volume.

In Salzburg, a brewery owned by monks (but not operated by them) serves its typical Austrian beers at a Bräustübl and garden at 4 Augustiner Gasse. In Upper Austria, the monastery of Schlägl offers a more distinctive range at its Stiftskeller and garden. The Schlägl beers have a meadow-flower, honeysuckle, house character. They include a malty *Märzen* ☆☆; a fresh, sweetish *Abtei Pils* ☆☆; a soft pollen-ish golden lager of 4.3; 5.4 called *Kristall* ☆☆▷☆☆☆; the top-fermenting *Goldroggen* ☆☆☆ rye beer, with notes of apricot, passion-fruit and iron; and a pruney *Doppelmalz* ☆☆. A version of the Pils is offered with a label depicting a party, and proposing "fun"; a curious suggestion from a monastery.

Close to both the German and Swiss borders, at Dornbirn, the Mohren brewery has a light but complex, smooth, all-malt, Vienna-style lager called *Schluck* ☆☆▷☆☆☆, at 12.5; 1050; 4.1; 5.2.

SWITZERLAND

THE EARLIEST BREWERY layout in Europe dates from the 9th century, at the abbey of St Gallen, in the Swiss town of the same name. The abbey no longer makes beer, but the town still has a brewery, founded in 1895, and called Schützengarten, with its own bar-restaurant (Braustube, 35 Jakob Strasse). Its most characterful beer is its *Edel Spezial Dunkel* ☆☆ (4.0; 5.0), a deep amber brew in broadly the Vienna style, with a light chewy maltiness and a dryish finish.

Near St Gallen, the pretty town of Appenzell, known for its cheese, also has the old-estabished Locher brewery, which in 1992 pioneered the notion of special beers made at full moon. Brewer Karl Locher says these beers reflect local beliefs about the effects upon agriculture of the moon's pull – ideas which are formalised in the teachings of Rudolf Steiner. At full moon, fermentation begins more quickly, says Locher, though he is unsure of its influence upon the flavour itself. His *Vollmond* ☆☆▷☆☆☆ is a golden lager, in two strengths (3.9; 4.8 and 4.1; 5.2). Both seem smoother and drier than the brewery's regular beers. The brewery's beers tend to maltiness, as best evidenced in a toffeeish, tawny, *Dunkel* ☆☆▷☆☆☆ 4.1; 5.2).

The Full Moon beer was originally conceived for an eccentric bar called El International, in Zurich (56 Zentral Strasse; ☎462-6164) . The popularity of Vollmond has led Hürlimann to apply the full moon treatment to one of its existent beers, the earthy, nutty, chocolatey, dark lager *Hexen Bräu* ☆☆▷☆☆☆ (3.6; 4.5). The name means Witches' Brew. Hürlimann's range also includes the world's strongest regularly-produced bottom-fermenting beer, *Samichlaus* ☆☆☆☆ ("Santa Claus", in the local Swiss-German). This is brewed once a year, on December 6, the day of St Nicolas (Santa Claus). It is matured throughout the following year and released next December 6. Its starting gravity is 27.6 Plato (around 1110) and it emerges with 11.1-2 percent alcohol by weight; 13.7-14 by volume. Although it has a predictably malty nose and full body, its long maturation and high alcohol make for a surprising firmness and a brandyish finish.

Hürlimann's more conventional beers tend to clean, light and dry, with a spritzy finish. Among other major brewers, the beers of Cardinal are perhaps more flowery, those of Haldengut slightly smoky, and those of Feldschlösschen have a fruity bitterness. Even these very slight shades of difference are diminishing with brewery mergers. Haldengut and Calanda are now controlled by Heineken. The Feldschlösschen group includes Cardinal, Hürlimann, Vailaisanne and Warteck.

A Swiss brewery's range might embrace a basic lager (at more than 11.5; 1046; around 3.8; 4.75); a deluxe beer (12; 1048; 4.1; 5.12); a "special" (12.5–6; 1050; 4.3; 5.37); a dark special (13.5; 1054; 4.0; 5.0); a "festival" brew of similar strength; a "strong" beer of 16; 1064; 5.4; 6.75; and perhaps a dark strong beer of 19; 1076; 5.9; 7.3.

The odd Swiss brewery has an Altbier; *Warteck Alt* ☆☆ has a deep, tawny, colour and a hoppy finish. Others have a wheat beer; *Calanda Weizen* ☆☆ has a touch of fruit and bubblegum, with a late, lingering, hoppy finish. In Basel, the pioneering Fischer/Ueli brewpub (45 Rhein Gasse), founded in the 1970s, has a *Weizenbier* ☆☆▷☆☆☆ full of banana and plum flavours.

A member of the Hürlimann family is one of the principals of a newish national chain of brewpubs called Back und Brau. These offer a malty golden lager called *Huus* ☆▷☆☆ ("House Beer") and a toffeeish, fruity *Altbier* ☆☆ somewhat lacking in hop. In Zurich, the beers are brewed in the branch at the cinema complex in the former Steinfels detergent factory (267 Heinrich Strasse) but also fermented at the cosier student bar Taverne zur Linde (91 Universitäts Strasse). The latter seems to have the better beer. Other branches are near Berne (at the railway station in

Thun); Frauenfeld (adjoining the old brewery in the town); Langenthal (in a 400-year-old grain mill) and at Rappenswil. The Back und Brau chain offer freshly-baked quiches and baguettes, but their pride in their spent-grain bagels is open to question.

At Wädenswil, an independent Back und Brau called Wadi Wadi makes a *Weizenbier* which has encouraging reports. This brewery also makes a sweetish *Hanf Bier* using non-narcotic elements of hemp.

Another odd speciality is a beer that is intended to taste of corn (maize) – and does. It is called *Maisgold*, contains 30 percent corn (which would hardly be unusual in the United States) and is produced by the Rosegarten brewery, of Einsiedeln.

GERMANY

GERMANY'S long-held position as the nation with the most breweries was quietly ceded to the United States in 1997, but it still has around 1200. There has been huge erosion of middle-sized breweries in recent years – but between one and two hundred new small ones have opened since the late 1970s. Most of them are brewpubs, often specializing in unfiltered beers. Some, such as Johann Albrecht, are small chains.

Several of the new breweries use organically grown malting barley and hops, and some have attempted to create new speciality beers outside the classic styles.

Although now united, in history Germany has usually been a collection of separate states. The post-war division encouraged local loyalties. With Berlin in two, Germany's other great cities vied with one another, not least in their brewing traditions.

In general, the north has the driest beers; the southwest, especially the state of Baden-Württemberg, has softer brews, allegedly to suit palates weaned on wine; and the southeast (Bavaria) has sweeter, fuller-bodied products.

What is yet more interesting for the beer-lover is that each region has its own classic style. Berlin is known for its light, slightly sour, style of Weisse wheat beer, a summer quencher; Hamburg and the north in general are noted for extra-dry Pilsener-style beers; Dortmund has its confusingly named Export style, medium in both body and dryness; Düsseldorf drinks as its everyday brew a copper-coloured, top-fermenting Altbier. Cologne protects through a form of *appellation contrôlée* its pale, top-fermenting Kölschbier. Einbeck and Munich share the strong Bock beer, especially in spring, though the latter city lays claim to winter's Dopplebock. Munich is the greatest of cities for stylistic variety. It also shares a tradition of dark or Dunkel beers with Kulmbach and other Bavarian towns (though Bamberg specializes in smoked-malt Rauchbier). Munich has a special interest in amber Märzenbier and various types of Weizen wheat beers. Few of these varieties are wholly restricted to their own area or season, though they are always freshest at the appropriate time and taste best in their native place. Some brewers specialize in just one variety of beer, but more produce a range. Some brewers with regional roots have cross-bred with others to form semi-national groupings.

The biggest group includes, among others: Dortmunder Union; Küppers of Cologne; Bavaria St Pauli, of Hamburg; Einbecker; and Schultheiss, of Berlin. The second includes Dortmunder Actien Brauerei; Binding of Frankfurt; and Kindl of Berlin. Famous exporters such as Holsten and Beck's also own other breweries. The biggest-selling beer in Germany, Warsteiner, is available throughout the country, but does not have a market-share comparable with those of national brands elsewhere in the world. Happily Germany is still a land of local beers – at least for now.

Within any style, German breweries – especially the larger ones – are apt to make similar products. This is in part because clear standards are laid down by law. There is also the separate question of the *Reinheitsgebot*, the Pure Beer Law of 1516. The industry maintains that it will continue to adhere to this German law despite an EU ruling of 1987 insisting that it not be used to bar imports.

HAMBURG

Around the world, imported beer from Germany often means Holsten (from Hamburg) or Beck's (from Bremen). These two cities remain the principal ports in Germany, a largely landlocked country, and they have been exporters of beer for more than 600 years. Their great importance in the brewing industry dates back to one of the early attempts at organized trade in Europe – the 15th-century Hanseatic League.

The extra-dry speciality Pilseners produced in this part of Germany owe their character to the same circumstance. In the days when transport by water was easier than travel across land, Hamburg was twice blessed. Not only did it, as a sea-port, have Europe's greatest sales of beer, its requirement for hops was met by trade down the River Elbe from Bohemia, the classic area of cultivation. The dryness of these Pilseners echoes Hamburg's role as a great hop market. The hops were used not only for flavour but also as a natural preservative in beer that was destined for long sea journeys.

WHERE TO DRINK

Hamburg has three new-generation brewpubs, all producing unfiltered beers. Dehn's Gröninger Braukeller (in the old warehouse district, at 47 Ost-West Strasse) offers a sweetish amber lager, confusingly presented as a "Pils", and a gentle amber, Weisse). The brewery has its own butchery and four adjoining restaurants. Zum Goldenen Engel (in a 1730 building at 7 Harburger Schloss Strasse) has a Vienna-style lager. Gravensteiner Brauhaus (30 Paulinen Allee, Eimsbüttel) has a cloudy Pils and a Dunkel. This pub, near the fish market, opens only in the evening (from 6 o'clock).

Bavaria St Pauli

Names like "Bavaria" were adopted in the late 19th century by brewers who were following the south's lead in lager-brewing. The Bavaria brewery of Hamburg and the more locally named St Pauli merged in 1922. As if its name were not confusing enough, the brewery markets its products under the Astra label. The company's basic lager, *Astra Urtyp* ☆, has a pleasant, light hop aroma and palate. The premium *Astra Pilsener* ☆ has a very aromatic bouquet and palate. Astra also has a beer called *Exclusiv* ☆, in the style the Germans call *Export* (like the Dortmund variety) and a dark *Urbock* ☆ (again a confusing name, since this is a Doppelbock). In addition to that fairly standard range, there is a light-bodied but very dry Pilsener called *Grenzquell* ☆ which was for some time heavily promoted in the USA. In 1994, Bavaria St Pauli was acquired by the national group Brau und Brunnen. Their real target was probably Bavaria St Pauli's more successful subsidiary Jever (*see* page 28). Brau und Brunnen already owned the Hamburg brewery Elbschloss, which they subsequently closed, and in 1997 the group in indicated that they no longer wished to operate Bavaria St Pauli. Other brewers, and the city of Hamburg, then became involved in lengthy discussions with a view to saving it.

Elbschloss

The best beers in Hamburg were made in this brewery, by the river Elbe and close to a country house (*Schloss*) in the woods. Unfortunately, the brewery closed, and Elbschloss became a brand of Bavaria St Pauli (*see above*).

Holsten

In the days when the nobility controlled such matters as licenses to brew beer, the Duchy of Schleswig-Holstein held sway over Hamburg. The Duke of Holstein who granted the city the right to brew is remembered in the name of this company, and on its labels. Its basic local beer is the firm-bodied *Holsten-Edel* ☆. It also has a German-style *Export* ☆, with a satisfying, wholesome texture and a soft, dry *Pilsener* ☆.

Holsten is the biggest name in German beer in Britain, where one of its products has, to the uninformed drinker, become synonymous with the term "Pils". In fact, the product identified in this way is not the brewery's regular Pilsener but a version of that style originally adapted to suit the diebetic diet. There was once a reference to diet on the label, but that has now been removed.

There is some debate about the advisability of diabetics drinking even low-sugar beers, and the word diet misled drinkers into thinking this was a brew for slimmers. Yes, the malt sugars are fermented further – but this creates more alcohol, which is packed with calories. In Britain, the crisp (sometimes slightly cracker-like), pleasantly dry *Holsten Pils* ☆☆ has 4.6; 5.8. In the German market, some alcohol is removed to take the beer back to 4.0; 5.0. Holsten also has a *Maibock* ☆☆, labelled in Britain as Urbock. This strong beer has a malty dryness, with a hint of apricot. Holsten's beers are *kräusened*.

Like its main local rival, Holsten also has a super-premium product from a subsidiary brewery, located in Lüneburg, a spa town of stepped-gable houses, their styles evolving from the 14th–18th centuries. A group of them forms the old brewery and guest-house, now converted into a beautifully arranged beer museum and a restaurant serving local dishes.

The new brewery is very modern, and its very aromatic dry, hoppy beer is called *Moravia Pils* ☆☆☆. The name Moravia must have come down the Elbe at some time. The beer is notable for having a big bouquet, and it has a rather light body. In addition to Moravia, which enjoys some prestige, there are a number of minor products, some under the Bergedorf name, and associated breweries in other cities.

BREMEN AND THE NORTHWEST

Churches and monasteries dedicated to St Paul have given their name to a good few breweries in Germany, including one in Bremen, long destroyed. This does not altogether explain how one of the city's export beers came to be known as St Pauli *Girl*, and the people who might know claim they can't remember. Another noted export is Beck's, while the local brewing company is called Haake-Beck.

Bremen had the first Brewer's Guild in Germany, in 1489, and such is its beery history that it still has a large number of brewery names. Most of these names are of brewing companies that were once independent and which are still separate but linked in a complicated corporate structure. Other labels to be taken into consideration are Hemelinger (nothing to do with the once briefly popular British brand of a similar name) and Remmer. Hemelinger produces a Spezial, a somewhat perfumy but sweetish beer. Remmer produces an interestingly malty Altbier.

All of the linked enterprises in Bremen share a single complex of modern buildings, with two brewhouses, in the town centre, close to the River Weser. Outside of this group is Dressler, a company once famous for its porters, which no longer has its own brewery but survives as a beer brand name owned by Holsten.

WHERE TO DRINK

The Old Town area of Bremen, known as the Snoor, is a delight, and has some lovely taverns. The quarter also has a brewpub at 12–13 Hinter dem Schütting and Bottcher Strasse. This Schüttinger Brauerei offers a full-coloured Pils, a malty Dunkel, a darkish Maibock, a dark winter brew (*Weihnachtbier*) and local dishes.

Beck's

The single product brewed by Beck's carries no description beyond a straightforward *Beck's Bier* ☆▷☆☆. It is broadly within the Pilsener style, with a fresh aroma, a faintly flowery, firm, crisp palate and a clean, dry finish. It is light by German but heavy by international standards, and difficult to place in context. A very pale malt is used, and the hopping leans heavily towards the Hallertau aroma variety. Within the Beck's brand is a dark version, available in some markets. Beck's Bier is fermented with its own house yeast, at fairly low temperatures, and *kräusened*. The brand *St Pauli Girl* ☆▷☆☆☆ has been used on what seemed to be marginally lighter-tasting versions in some export markets.

Haake-Beck

A traditional copper brewhouse is used to produce a full range of beers for Bremen and its hinterland, and also local specialities. Both its regular *Edel-Hell* ☆ and its *Pils* ☆▷☆☆ have a floral bouquet and a light, clean palate. While its cosmopolitan cousins do not make specific claims to the style, this Pils does, and properly has a little more bitterness than either in the finish. It is *kräusened*, and – unusually – is available locally (in the Old Town, for example) in unfiltered form. This version is identified as *Kräusen Pils* ☆☆☆, and has living yeast in suspension. As if to emphasize the resultant cloudiness, it is served in cracked-pattern glasses. Even by the standards of a German Pilsener, it has a mountainous head, followed by a soft palate, with a suggestion of chewy, yeast bitterness.

Haake-Beck also produces, as a summer speciality, a Bremen interpretation of a northern wheat beer. *Bremer Weisse* ☆☆☆ is served in a bowl-shaped glass similar to those used in Berlin, and is a wonderful summer refresher. In its natural state, it has a palate reminiscent of under-ripe plums, though it is usually served sweetened with a dash of raspberry juice. It has a gravity of 7.5 Plato, producing 2.2 percent alcohol by weight (2.75 by volume). In addition to a top yeast, there is a controlled, pure-culture lactic fermentation.

Yet a third speciality, *Seefahrt Malz*, cannot strictly be rated as a beer, since it is not fermented. It is a heavily hopped malt extract, of a daunting 55 Plato, with a syrupy viscosity but a surprisingly pleasant taste. Seefahrt Malz was for a time on sale, but is now available only to eminent citizens who are invited to the House of Seafarers' annual dinner in Bremen. It is ceremonially served in silver or pewter chalices. Despite its size, the company itself has a taste for traditions. From among its towering buildings each morning emerges a line of drays drawn by Oldenburg horses to deliver beer to the people of the inner-city area.

Jever

The famously bitter *Jever Pilsener* ☆☆☆☆ is one of the few German beers to be nationally familiar in its own country. (Many names that are widely known in export markets are regional in Germany). Since the brewery was acquired by the national group Brau und Brunnen, Jever Pilsener seems to have diminished slightly in character, but its dryness still makes it a wonderful aperitif. It has a big hop bouquet, a yeasty palate, and a robust finish. The brewery has also made a smooth Jever *Export* ☆☆ and a firm-bodied *Maibock* ☆☆.

The brewery is very modern, though it does have some turn-of-the-century buildings. It is in the partially-moated town of Jever, a tourism base on Germany's Frisian coast. Friesland (an historic region straddling the borders of Germany, The Netherlands and Denmark), is also noted for intense-tasting liqueurs.

HANOVER AND LOWER SAXONY

Although this part of Germany is often associated with Korn schnapps and *Steinhäger* gin, it does also have its speciality beers. Moravia Pils and the very dry Jever (*see* pages 27 and 28) are actually brewed in the state of Lower Saxony. So is a newish speciality, called Duckstein, in character approaching something between a Belgian and an English ale. Duckstein is made in Braunschweig (Brunswick). That city also has an Altbier, as does Hanover.

More distinctively, this region is the original home of Bock beer. The Lower Saxony town of Einbeck was the biggest brewing centre in the medieval European federation of trading cities known as the Hanseatic League. The town brewed beers strong enough to survive being shipped far and wide, and its "beck" (later "bock") beers became famous. In the 1600s the Duke of Brunswick took Einbeck beer with him when he married a Bavarian noblewoman, and that is how Bock came to be so strongly associated with the southern state.

WHERE TO DRINK

There are at least a dozen brewpubs in Lower Saxony. In Brunswick, Schadt's (28 Höhe, at Am Marstall), produces a Pils with a slight wheat character. Hanover has two brewpubs. Ernst August (13 Schmieder Str; evenings only) makes a mild Pils. Roneburg (27 Königsworther Str) produces a hoppy Pils and a malty Dunkel. Statues on the facade depict emigrants to America. In Oldenburg, the brewpub Zum Henglbräu (243 Ammerländer Heer Str) makes a wide range of seasonal beers, including a hoppy Pilsener for Father's Day, a dry "East Frisian" summer wheat beer in June, and malty, tasty interpretations of a Märzen and a December Double Bock.

Einbecker Brauhaus

The town of Einbeck is worth a visit for its Late Gothic houses, their doors arched to provide access for a mobile brew-kettle, and their roofs vented to wind-dry the malt and hops. The Brodhaus tavern, on the town square, is the "tap" for the only surviving brewery, known simply as Einbecker. On the principle that the original Einbecker beers would have fermented-out on their journeys, and would have been well-hopped as a preservative measure, today's examples are made drier than those of Bavaria.

The brewery produces three styles of Bock, all with a malty aroma, a clean palate and some hoppy dryness. The *Hell* ☆☆ starts malty and finishes long; the *Dunkel* ☆☆☆ is more rounded; and the *Maibock* ☆☆☆ faintly estery, spritzy and refreshing. The latter is available from March to the end of May. All have 16.3; 1064; 5.2; 6.5.

Feldschlösschen

This sizeable brewery in Brunswick produces the top-fermenting beer *Duckstein* ☆☆▷☆☆☆, a distant revival of a local style. It is an amber, malty-fruity brew, developing to a hoppiness and a distinct tartness in the finish. Duckstein is matured over beechwood chips. The archaic spelling Brunswiek is used on the brewery's *Alt* ☆☆, which is made with a different yeast. This has a good malt character, and is very well balanced.

Gilde

The company takes its name from its origins as a civic brewery, operated by a guild. Today it produces a range of very well-made beers. Its speciality *Broyan Alt* ☆☆☆ is named after a great Hanover brewer of the 16th century. This is a top-fermenting Altbier in a similar style to those of Düsseldorf but a little stronger (12.4 Plato; 4.2 percent alcohol by weight; 5.25 by volume), slightly darker, relatively light-bodied, malt-accented, with a delicate hop character and a low bitterness. The brewery also has a regular *Gilde Pilsner* ☆▷☆☆ and a premium *Ratskeller Edel-Pils* ☆☆, both with a complex hop character and some Saaz delicacy, as well as a German-style *Edel-Export* ☆.

Herrenhauser

Smaller Hanover brewery, producing a *Pilsener* ☆☆☆▷☆☆☆ with a light, grassy, aroma; a crisp palate; and a late, appetising dryness. This beer is available with a Kosher label; the brewery opens itself to rabbinical inspection.

MÜNSTER

The university city of Münster, rich in history as the capital of Westphalia, is regarded with affection by knowledgeable beer-lovers all over Germany for the specialities produced at its Pinkus Müller brewery and restaurant. Pinkus Müller is an institution, despite its being nothing larger than a *Hausbrauerei* producing fewer than 10,000hl a year. It makes some extra-ordinary beers and has the impudence to export to the USA.

Pinkus Müller's premises in the Old Town (what people in Münster call the "cow quarter" – *Kuhviertel*) were originally nine houses. Over the years they have been integrated, with considerable rebuilding in the 1920s and some more recently. There are four dining rooms; in the main one the centrepiece is a Westphalian oven, set among Dutch tiles illustrating Bible stories. The fireplace hangs with Westphalian hams, a good indication of the style of food.

WHERE TO DRINK

Apart from Pinkus Müller, the Münster area has a tiny Heinrich Jürgens brewery (6 Hühl Str, Beckum), producing a pale Altbier. Southeast of Münster, at Oelde, the Pott-Feldmann's have a brewery with rooms (14 Bahnhof Str; ☎02522–2209). A newer entrant in the Münster area is the Klute brewpub, at Havixbeck (28 Poppenbeck), serving a mild Helles and home-baked bread.

Pinkus Müller

The brewery produces no fewer than four beers and is best known for what it describes as *Pinkus Münster Alt* ☆☆☆▷ ☆☆☆. In this instance, the term alt indicates simply an old style, without suggesting anything on the lines of the Düsseldorf classics. Pinkus Münster Alt is a very pale, top-fermenting beer made from an unusual specification of 40 percent wheat and 60 percent barley malt, to a gravity of 11.3 Plato. It has a long (six months) maturation, including a *kräusening*. The maturation takes place at natural cellar temperature, but in conventional lagering tanks in which there is a resident lactic culture. The result is a very crisp beer indeed, dry, with a faint, quenching acidity in the finish. In several respects, not least its higher gravity, relative clarity and restrained acidity, this is a different product from the Bremer or Berliner Weisse. It is wheatier than any Kölsch, yet it does not qualify as a Weizen; it is a unique speciality. In fact, the brewery does produce a *Pinkus Weizen* ☆☆▷☆☆☆, which is worthy of special attention if only for its unusual lightness, though it is characteristically low on hop bitterness, and has a fruity finish. It is a rather northern-tasting Weizen, though it has a thoroughly southern ratio of 60:40 (wheat has the majority).

There are also two bottom-fermenting beers: *Pinkus Pils* ☆▷☆☆, with a light but firm body and a hoppy dryness; and *Pinkus Spezial* ☆☆☆, a pale beer of 12.66 Plato, brewed with organically grown barley malt and hops. This clean, malty, dry beer, with a medium body, is sold in wholefood shops. Despite Pinkus Müller having all of these unusual brews, the house speciality is not a beer alone. The Müllers steep diced fresh fruit in sweetened water so that it forms its own syrup. They then add a tablespoon of the fruit and syrup to a glass of Pinkus Alt, so that its fresh flavours suffuse the beer and marry with the acidity of the wheat. The availability and contents of this confection depend upon which fruit is in season. Fruits with stones are not used, since they impart an incongruous, almondy bitterness. In summer, strawberries or peaches are favoured; in winter, oranges may be used. The fruit is steeped for a day in a pickling jar, with a kilo of sugar. When it is added to the beer, using a cylindrical glass, the result is known as an Altbier Bowl.

DORTMUND

Six or seven ranges of beers emanating from the city bear the legend "Dortmunder", much to the confusion of beer-lovers who are not familiar with Germany. The confusion has been compounded in recent years by a devastating series of mergers in this once-proud brewing city. Dortmunder Actien Brauerei, which already owned Hansa, in 1996/7 acquired and closed Kronen, which had already done the same to Thier and Stifts. This left the city's industry carved up between DAB and its traditional rival DUB (Dortmunder Union Brauerei), the latter already owning Ritter.

"Dortmunder" is an *appellation contrôlée*, since no beer brewed outside the city may, in Germany, bear the designation. In other countries, however, brewers have over the years produced beers that they have identified as being in the Dortmunder style. There was a vogue in The Netherlands and Belgium for a beer style described as "Dort".

There is, indeed, a Dortmunder style. In the days when the great brewing cities of Europe vied for ascendancy by promoting their own styles, that of Dortmund was a pale, medium-dry beer, very slightly bigger in body and higher in alcohol than its rivals from Munich or Pilsen. It was drier than a Munich pale beer, but less dry than a Pilsener.

As Dortmund's efforts were repaid with sales in other parts of Germany, and in adjoining countries, the local brewers began to refer to their characteristic beer as *Export*. That is how *Export* became a classic German style. A true Dortmunder Export beer has a gravity of 13 Plato, producing 4.4 percent alcohol by weight and 5.5 by volume, and with about 25 Units of Bitterness.

Unfortunately, the Dortmunder brewers' exposition of their classic style can be hard to find outside the city and hinterland. Although it made for a bigger local market, the industrial growth of Dortmund and the Ruhr was a mixed blessing for the city's image as a centre of fine brewing. In recent years especially, Dortmund brewers went through a phase of self-doubt: did a Dortmunder beer sound like a product for cloth-capped miners and steelworkers?

Although they have continued to make Dortmunder Export, the local brewers have in recent years neglected to promote it, preferring to concentrate on other products within their ranges, especially the Pilseners. This policy has not been a conspicuous success, nor does it deserve to be.

Dortmund should be proud of its traditional style. Dortmund-inspired Export beers are, after all, included in the portfolios of brewers all over Germany.

WHERE TO DRINK

For years, Dortmund was content to offer its beers to visitors at uninspiring bars (each representing a different brewery) set around the market square and church. Having been damaged in the war and quickly rebuilt during the recovery years of the 1950s, this area is a little lacking in colour.

In the mid-1980s, when Kronen and Thier were still independent, each separately decided to add a little romance. Both of them established brewpubs in the city-centre, each named after an early Dortmund brewer. Kronen opened Heinrich Wenker's Brauhaus on the Market Square. Wenker's is within the Zum Kronen restaurant complex.

Wenker's brewhouse stands among the drinkers in the bar area, and its speciality is an unfiltered, top-fermenting pale beer containing 15 percent wheat, called *Wenker's Urtrüb* ☆☆☆ (12 Plato). It is a fresh, clean, lightly fruity beer with some yeast "bite". Other specialities are planned.

A few minutes' walk away, right outside the old Thier brewery, is that company's offspring, Hövels Haus-Brauerei, at 5–7 Hoher Wall. There, the brewhouse is visible through a window of the restaurant.

All year round, Hövels serves a filtered brew, with a bronze colour and a malty aroma and palate, which is confusingly called *Bitterbier* ☆☆☆ (13.5). This is a smooth, tasty beer with quite a full body. Hövels has also produced some excellent speciality beers.

DAB

The middle name merely indicates a joint-stock company. Perhaps that is where the phrase "a piece of the action" originated. This very large brewing company is now part of a national grouping, with Binding, Berliner Kindl and others. In its modern brewery which is situated on the outskirts of the city of Dortmund it produces beers that generally have a light, malty, dryness.

Its *Export* ☆▷☆☆ has a slight malt accent, while remaining dry, and is on the light side for the style. The brewery's *Meister Pils* ☆ (marketed in the USA under the dismissive, lower-case name of dab beer), has a hint of malt in the nose but goes on to be dry, with some hop character in the palate and a fairly low bitterness.

There is more hop aroma, with a very clean and light palate, in the brewery's *Original Premium* ☆, marketed in the USA as Special Reserve. DAB also has an *Altbier* ☆, again with a dry maltiness and a light body. This is sold in the USA under the unflatteringly vague name of DAB Dark. In its local market, DAB has a pleasant *Maibock* ☆▷☆☆ and *Tremanator Doppelbock* ☆▷☆☆. DAB is very marketing-oriented, distributing widely in the north of Germany.

Dortmunder Hansa

In Germany, Hansa has been very active in the supermarket trade. Its *Export* ☆☆ has a good malt aroma, a soft, full body, and a dry finish. Its *Pils* ☆ is light and crisp, with some hoppy acidity.

Dortmunder Kronen

Among their home-town beers, the people of Dortmund favoured those from the Kronen brewery. Its beers were, in general, big and malty, with a clean, delicate sweetness. These characteristics were evident especially in its *Export* ☆☆☆☆, and to a lesser degree in its super-premium *Classic* ☆☆▷☆☆☆. *Pilskrone* ☆☆ has a flowery hoppiness.

The brewery also had an *Alt* ☆ with a relatively full body and a dense, rocky head. And there was a dark bock, called *Steinbock* ☆☆, with an intense crystal-malt dryness. It is to be hoped that some elements of individuality survive.

Dortmunder Ritter

These robust, matter-of-fact Dortmunder brews are popular in the industrial Ruhr Valley. The fruitiness is perhaps most evident in the *Export* ☆▷☆☆. The *Pils* ☆ has a malty start and a dry finish.

Dortmunder Thier

This brewery's dryish *Pils* ☆☆ has for the moment survived, but not its full, firm, smooth Export.

DUB

The "U" in the name refers to the union of ten or so breweries more than 100 years ago. That union sufficed until 1973, when DUB linked with Schultheiss, of Berlin. The massive "U" of the Union logo, illuminated at night, is a Dortmund landmark atop the former brewery building which, looking rather like a 1920s power station, broods over the centre of the city. The building is being re-fitted as apartments and shops, and the beer is being made at a new brewery in the east of the city. The DUB beers (all *kräusened*) have a malty sweetness and are generally mild in palate – perhaps on the bland side – and smooth. *Export* ☆☆☆ is malt-accented, and medium-bodied. *Siegel Pils* ☆ has an agreeably hoppy palate but not much finish. The super-premium *Brinckhoff's No 1* ☆, named after a founder-brewer, has a character somewhere between the two.

Dortmunder Stifts

This brewery had a strong local following in the south of the city, but its products have gradually been vanishing.

DÜSSELDORF

Where a city is lucky, or sensible, enough to have retained a distinctive style of brewing, it often reserves a special beer for particular occasions or moods. Düsseldorf takes a different view and is one of those cities (like its neighbour and rival Cologne – or Dublin) that likes to serve its speciality as its daily beer.

Düsseldorf's prized beer is much more instantly distinctive than that of its neighbour. It has a dark copper colour, is top-fermenting and is superficially similar to a British ale.

The differences in the Düsseldorf product derive not only from the typically German barley malts and hops used, but also from the use of single cell, pure culture yeasts and – perhaps most significant – a period of cold conditioning in tanks, usually for several weeks. A German would no doubt argue that the Düsseldorf beer is cleaner and smoother than a British ale. The British would argue that their ales have more individuality. As always, this is to compare apples with oranges, neither is better; they are different.

A typical Düsseldorf beer has a gravity of 12 Plato, or a fraction more. It may be made with two or three malts. Some Düsseldorf brewers favour an infusion mash, but the decoction system is also widely used. Two or three hop varieties may be employed; Düsseldorf brewers have traditionally favoured Spalt. Open fermenters are sometimes used, especially in the smaller breweries. The warmer fermentation temperatures are reflected in slightly less intense cold conditioning, at between 32°F (0°C) and 47°F (8°C), for anything from three to eight weeks. Alcohol content is typically 3.6–3.8 by weight; 4–4.7 by volume. Units of Bitterness vary from the lower 30s to the 50s; colour around 35 EBC.

After its period of cold-conditioning, Düsseldorf beer is often dispensed in local taverns from a barrel, by gravity, with no carbon dioxide pressure, blanket or otherwise. Although this method is practised in several taverns and restaurants, notably in the Old Town, it is especially associated with the city's home-brew houses. Such is the joy of this city for the beer-lover: not only does it have its own style, of some character and complexity, it has no fewer than four home-brew taverns. In these establishments, the stubby, cylindrical glasses favoured in Düsseldorf are charged as quickly as they are exhausted.

The home-brew taverns are the shrines of the Düsseldorf brewing style, and as such their beers must be regarded as German classics. The beer-loving visitor to Düsseldorf will want to visit all of them – and also to sample the beers made in the local style by the city's four other breweries, and several others in neighbouring smaller towns.

Düsseldorf's brewers may well wish that a less imitable name had emerged for their style; they call their brews nothing more memorable than Düsseldorfer Altbier. No other city has such devotion either to the production or serving of beer in this style, but brewers in several other towns have in their portfolio something which they call Altbier. In most instances, though not all, it bears a great similarity to the Düsseldorf style. "*Alt*" simply means "old", and indicates a style that was produced before the widespread introduction of bottom-fermentation in the late 1800s.

"Altbier" is the style of Düsseldorf and its brewers produce little else, except stronger brews variously called *Latzenbier* ("beer from the wood") or *Sticke* ("secret" beer) that appear very briefly in some places in winter, spring and autumn.

Of the Düsseldorf home-brew houses, three are in the Old Town (Altstadt seems especially appropriate in this instance). The fourth, Schumacher, is in the more modern part of the city centre.

Just to the west of Düsseldorf, in the town of Korschenbroich, a brewery founded in 1266, and in the Bolten family since 1764, claims to be the oldest enterprise producing Altbier. The pride in the brewery's history is well justified, though its products in those earlier centuries would undoubtedly have been quite different, and the term Altbier is relatively modern. *Bolten Ur-Alt* ☆☆☆ is a good example of the style, clean and malty in both aroma and palate, with a lightly tart balancing dryness in the finish.

At the other end of the size scale, Diebels is the biggest producer of Altbier. This fourth-generation family company has its brewery (with bar-restaurant) well to the north of Düsseldorf, in the village of Issum, near the Dutch border. *Diebels Alt* ☆☆ is smooth, with a cookie-like malt accent. The other large producers, in diminishing order, are *Schlösser* ☆▷☆☆ (syrupy maltiness); *Gatzweiler* ☆☆ (fruitiest); *Hannen* ☆▷☆☆ (spritzy, sharp); *Frankenheim* ☆☆ (light, dry, yeasty) and *Rhenania* ☆▷☆☆ (slightly thick-tasting).

WHERE TO DRINK

None of the home-brew houses should be missed. A newer entrant, in the Oberkassel area, is a Johann Albrecht brewpub (102 Niederkasseler Str) which has a hoppy Pils, a top-fermenting, malty, mild Dunkel, and local dishes.

Im Füchschen

"The Fox" is noted not only for its beer but also its food. This home-brew house, in Ratinger Strasse, produces a very good Altbier, simply called *Im Füchschen* ☆☆☆▷☆☆☆☆. It is a complex and beautifully balanced beer, its firm, fairly full body at first evincing malty notes, then yielding to lots of hop flavour from Spalt and Saaz varieties. In the end, its hop bitterness is its predominant characteristic.

The tavern's big main dining room serves hearty *Eisbein* and *Schweinshaxe* (pork dishes). It can be very busy, but is a friendly place and diners are usually happy to share tables.

Zum Schlüssel

"The Key" is not to be confused with the larger Schlösser ("Locksmith") brewery, however easy that may be. Zum Schlüssel, in Bolker Strasse, is a home-brew house. The brewery is visible from its main room. *Zum Schlüssel Altbier* ☆☆▷☆☆☆ begins with an aromatic hoppiness of palate, but its predominant characteristic is a light maltiness, with a touch of "British" acidity in the finish. It has a fairly light body and a bright clarity.

The restaurant is quite light and airy too and has something of a coffee-shop atmosphere. It was founded in 1936 (a little late for Heinrich Heine (1797–1856), who was born next door. His house is now a museum.

Ferdinand Schumacher

Despite being in a modern part of the city this home-brew house in Ost Strasse, has the polite atmosphere of times past and is a quiet place at which to relax after shopping or a day at the office. Its *Schumacher Altbier* ☆☆☆ is the lightest in palate and body, and the maltiest, very clean, with a lovely delicacy of aromatic, fruity hop character. The beer is also available at the Goldene Kessel, in Bolker Strasse.

Zum Uerige

This rambling tavern in Berger Strasse is named after a cranky proprietor. Cranky he may well have been, but it is a friendly enough place today – and produces the classic Düsseldorfer Altbier, an aromatic, tawny brew, deep in colour and flavour, with a slowly unrolling hop bitterness in its big and sustained finish. *Zum Uerige* ☆☆☆☆ beer is the most assertive, complex and characterful of the Alts. It is also the most bitter. Like all of the Düsseldorfer "house" beer, it is produced in traditional copper kettles, but this is the most beautiful brewery of them all. It also has a traditional copper cool-ship, and a Baudelot cooler, both still in use, and it is impeccably maintained and polished. The brewhouse can be seen from the most picturesque of the many bars. Every few minutes, barrels are rolled through Zum Uerige on their way to the various dispense points, while drinkers jink out of the way. Meals are not served, but Zum Uerige has its own sausage kitchen on the premises. Here, sausages of pork and liver, *Blutwurst* (blood sausage) and brawn, are produced, with spiced dripping left over to serve with malodorous Mainzer cheese that has been marinated in beer. If those flavours are not sufficiently intense, robust gastronomes are encouraged to look for the "secret" Sticke beer usually on the third Tuesday of its designated months: January and October. This is an Altbier of 14 Plato, with an extra dash of roasted malt – and it is dry-hopped in the maturation tanks. Very intense indeed. The brewery has recently added *Ueriges Weizen* ☆☆, gold to bronze; ale-y; starting fruity and spicy (cherries, ginger?) and finishing with a minerally dryness.

COLOGNE

Small brewers in the United States increasingly apply Cologne's adjectival form, Kölsch, to golden ales. Brewers in Japan do the same, often in respect of unfiltered examples. In Germany, the style is an appellation of origin, restricted to breweries in a defined area around Cologne. It is applied to a very pale, golden, brew, with a German hop character (especially in aroma), top-fermented, but lagered and filtered.

Happily, there are a baker's dozen breweries in Cologne and as many again in its hinterland. All of them produce Kölschbier, and some do nothing else. At least one has dropped other, more conventional, styles from its portfolio. Kölschbier dominates Cologne: it is possible to go into an ordinary bar in the city and be unable to find a Pilsener – even though it may be advertized outside. In the city's "home-brew" houses, of course, Kölsch is the only beer available.

Being so blessed with brewers, Cologne naturally has a great many bars and taverns, including its home-brew houses. For most of the year, it is an engrossing place in which to sample beers, except during its pre-Lenten carnival, when the drinking becomes less considered. Whether its wealth of drinking places results from, or serves to attract, the tourist is a matter for conjecture. Some people apparently go to Cologne to study its history, see its huge cathedral, or take trips down the Rhine. They should not be distracted from the city's distinctive beer by such diversions, though it is comfortably possible to enjoy both.

A classic Kölsch has a very light fruitiness in the beginning, a notably soft palate (influenced by the local water) and a very delicate finish. Although Kölschbier brewers pay a lot of attention to hop character (two or three varieties are used, often with a Hallertau accent), their aim is to achieve a light dryness in the finish and nothing too assertive.

The very subtle character of this style is no doubt influenced also by the background palate imparted by the typical Cologne yeasts. These generally create a very vigorous fermentation, followed by two, three or four weeks of cold conditioning at 32°–41°F (0°–5°C). The yeasts are relatively neutral, but may contribute a scarcely perceptible medicinal dryness. The gravity range of Kölsch beers is from just over 11 to just under 12 Plato. A typical example has 11.5 Plato and emerges at between 3.5 and 4 percent alcohol by weight. Most often, it is 4 (5 by volume). Bittering units are typically in the upper 20s.

Kölschbier is a lovely apéritif (not a bad digestif, either), often consumed as an accompaniment to snacks. On its home ground, this may mean "half a hen" (Rhineland whimsy for a wedge of cheese with a roll) or "Cologne caviare" (blood sausage). *Mettwurst* is the tartare type. "With music" means an onion garnish.

Among the home-brew beers, P J Früh's is especially clean-tasting, that of Päffgen the hoppiest and Malzmühle, appropriately, the maltiest. Each beer has its own support as a local classic, though none of the three has a clear claim to be the definitive Kölsch. Nor among the rest of the Kölschbiers does one particulary stand out, though a good claim is staked by Garde. This is a pronouncedly fruity Kölschbier, produced by an old-established private company at Dormagen-bei-Köln. Garde is one of several companies in Germany with a woman brewer.

Differences between the more widely available Kölschbiers are so subtle as to be very open to the influence of freshness (of beer or the taster). Sion is flowery and hoppy; Sester fruity and dry; Gilden fruity, with a rather heavy texture; Zunft creamy; Reissdorf light, soft and delicious; Küppers soft and sweetish; Kurfürsten and Dom sweet at the front, with a drier finish.

WHERE TO DRINK

Visitors who go to Cologne to see the Roman museum or the cathedral will find P J Früh's Cölner Hofbräu conveniently opposite, in Am Hof. Behind Früh is the Old Town, lined with bars and restaurants, especially on the Heumarkt (Haymarket). At the near end of the Heumarkt, the Päffgen Kölsch brewery family has a restaurant. At the far end is the Malzmühle home-brew café. Beside the Rhine, a pleasant ride on tram number 15 or 16 to stop at Schönhauser Strasse leads to the Küppers Kölsch brewery, where there is a restaurant serving local dishes and Wiess beer, and a very worthwhile museum of brewing (145 Altenburger Str ☎0222–373242).

The Cologne metropolitan area also embraces Bonn, where the new generation of brewpubs is represented by Brauhaus Bönnsch (4 Sternbrücke), in the city centre. This establishment has created its own specialities in a style that it describes as "Bönnsch". Its brews are cloudy-white, quenching and fruity, like a wheaty version of an unfiltered Kölsch and served in an arched elaboration of a Kölsch glass. This enterprise is linked to Sieg-Rheinische Germania brewery, in nearby Hersel, Bornheim.

P J Früh's Cölner Hofbräu

Because it is the parent of its own beer, P J Früh's is still regarded as a home-brew house. In fact, the brewery behind the restaurant became too small to cope with demand for the beer in the free trade. However, the bar and restaurant remain an institution in Cologne. The Früh brewery is now away from the city centre. *Früh Echt Kölsch* ☆☆☆ is a soft beer, delicate in both its fruitiness of entrance and its hoppy dryness of finish. It is made with only barley malt – no wheat – and hopped with the Hallertau and Tettnang varieties.

Gaffel

This brewery traces its origins right back to 1302, and is in the heart of town, just behind the railway station. It was once a brewpub, but now has a handsome "tap" at 20–22 Alter Markt, in the Old Town. *Gaffel Kölsch* ☆☆☆ is very dry, almost nutty.

Hellers

New-generation brewpub, in the premises that formerly housed a distillery making a liqueur bitters. Organically grown barley and hops are used. *Hellers Kölsch* ☆☆☆ is creamy in texture, and robust in its maltiness, hoppiness and fruitiness. There is also an unfiltered beer, called *Ur-Wiess* ☆☆☆. Hellers Brauhaus is at Roon Strasse.

There are two other new-generation brewpubs: Weiss-Bräu (24 Am Weidenbach), making a Kölsch, and a Dunkel; and hoppy Pils and Papa Joe's (14 Unter Käster, in the Old Town), producing an unfiltered, top-fermenting beer. The latter has an antique collection of mechanical novelties.

Küppers

By far the biggest producer and exporter of Kölschbier despite being a newcomer. Küppers was established 20-odd years ago in Cologne to meet the rules of appellation, so that a Kölschbier could be added to the portfolio of the large Wicküler Pils company, then brewing in Wuppertal. This move followed a court case over the appellation. Sales since, supported by hefty market-ing efforts, have clearly justified the determination behind Küppers' establishment, but tradition is harder to build. No doubt this was in mind when Küppers established its excellent restaurant and museum.

The soft and sweetish *Küppers Kölsch* ☆▷☆☆☆ is unexceptional, but the brewery wins bonus points for another gesture to tradition, its confusingly named *Wiess* beer. Although *Wiess* is the Rhineland dialect pronunciation of *Weiss* ("white"), the designation perhaps has less to do with the cloudy tone of this beer than its rustic style; Bavarians talk in the same vein about a *Wies'n* beer when they mean something that is to be served at a country fair. *Küppers Wiess* ☆☆☆ is an unfiltered version of the normal Kölsch. It still has yeast in suspension, imparting the cloudiness and an astringent, refreshing, bitter-fruit quality. The name is certainly not intended to suggest a wheat beer. Although some wheat is used for the brew, it is present only in the small proportion typical of Kölschbier.

Malzmühle

This is a home-brew café and restaurant with a pleasantly insouciant, relaxing atmosphere. At the far end of the Heumarkt in the centre of Cologne, it is all too easily missed, but shouldn't be. Its *Mühlen Kölsch* ☆☆☆▷☆☆☆☆ is mild and rounded in style, with a warm, spicy aroma and palate, reminiscent almost of marshmallow. It is a highly distinctive and delicious beer, lightly hopped with Hallertau blossoms and fermented in open vessels.

Päffgen

A beautifully kept home-brew restaurant in Friesen Strasse which has a small beer garden. Its *Päffgen Kolsch* ☆☆☆▷ ☆☆☆☆ has a soft palate with a big, hoppy bouquet. By the standards of Kölschbier, it has a very hoppy finish, too. Päffgen also has a tavern on the Heumarkt.

Sion

This was originally a home-brew, too. Its tavern, in Unter Taschenmacher, in the Old Town, offers good brisk service and a very fresh glass of its pleasantly flowery beer. *Sion Kölsch* ☆☆▷☆☆☆ is now produced under contract.

RHINELAND'S PILSENERS

Apart from those cities that are islands of their own style, the whole of the Rhine and its hinterland is dotted with well-regarded breweries. Towns without a speciality style of their own have in several cases put their best efforts behind a Pilsener, developing, as Madison Avenue might term it, a super-premium product and in several instances producing nothing else.

Several of these products were among a selection dubbed "The Premium Beers" in an article some years ago in the influential newspaper *Die Welt*. The writer, Hans Baumann, is a journalist who frequently comments on both the business and social aspects of the brewing industry. His intention was not to say that these "premium" beers were the best, but that they were labels that seemed capable of commanding a high price. His "premium" tag was gratefully seized by the breweries and he now has mixed feelings about its continued use. There are, he points out, many other good beers, not all of them as intensively marketed.

The German consumer has, however, come to believe in recent years that a brewery concentrating on one style is likely to do a better job than those with a whole portfolio of products. This is a questionable proposition. If a chef prepares the same dish every lunchtime, he is unlikely to undercook or burn it, but are his skills necessarily those of an Escoffier?

While the Pilseners of the far north are generally the driest, the same leaning is evident in Rhineland, perhaps with a softness and lightness emerging as the brewers enter wine country. Several of the most popular breweries are in the hill-and-lake region called the Sauerland. Its clean air and fresh water do much to inspire the thirst of the consumer.

WHERE TO DRINK

In Essen, home town of the Stauder brewery, one of the company's shareholders established a "house brewery" in 1984. The Borbecker Dampfbier brewery, bar and restaurant is in Heinrich Brauns Strasse. *Dampf* refers to the fact that the premises were a steam-powered brewery in the 1880s and not to the style of beer. The brew, called *Salonbier* ☆☆☆, is in the Vienna style and of Export strength. It has a clean, dry, malty palate and is available filtered or as a Zwickelbier. It's a long way from the Pilseners of the region – and a delightful contrast. Essen now has a second brewpub, Graf Beust, at 95 Kastanien Allee. This produces a golden, mild Zwickelbier and sweetish, dark Altbier.

At the opposite end of Premium Pilsener country, across the border and into Saarland, another Zwickelbier can be found, also in a "house brewery". This is the brewery guesthouse Zum Stiefel, run by the Bruch family, in the town of Saarbrücken. Another Saarland speciality, though not from a house brewery, is Bier Eiche (oak beer). This was originally produced for a festival concerning oak trees, but is now available all year round. It is a pale, top-fermenting beer of everyday gravity, with a delicate hop aroma and dryness. It is produced in Merzig, by Saarfurst, a local subsidiary of the region's Karlsberg brewery. Karlsberg, in the Saarland town of Homburg, has – of course – nothing to do with the Danish brewery of a similar name but different spelling.

Bitburger

Taking its name from its home town of Bitburg, this is a specialist "Premium" Pilsener brewery. It is a very modern place indeed, producing a Pilsener with a low original gravity by German standards: 11.3 Plato. This is thoroughly attenu-ated, to produce an alcohol content of 3.9 by weight, 4.8–9 by volume. *Bitburger Pils* ☆☆☆ is very pale, extremely light, and dry. It has a soft maltiness, a pronounced hop flavour and a very subtle, elegant, bitterness. A much-admired beer.

Herforder

Principally a Pilsener brewery though it does also produce beers in other styles. *Herforder Pils* ☆☆▷☆☆☆, is full-bodied, with a clean, mild palate. Its gravity is 12.1 and its alcohol content 3.9; 4.8–9. Herforder also produces a malty but dry *Export* ☆▷☆☆; a pale *Mai-Bock* ☆▷☆☆ and a dark *Doppelbock* ☆▷☆☆, both very malty. Herford is on the northern borders of Rhineland-Westphalia.

Irle

Another specialist Pilsener brewery. Its *Irle Edel-Pils* ☆▷☆☆ has the classic combination of a 12 Plato gravity and an alcohol content of 4; 5, it has a lovely clean palate and is very mild. The brewery is in Siegen.

König

Known as a "Premium" Pilsener brewery but also produces other styles. Its Pilsener is full-bodied, well-balanced and dry. *König Pilsener* ☆☆▷☆☆☆ has a rich aroma, a sustained, very smooth, bitterness and an assertive finish, though it has lost some of its fullness in recent years.

Königsbacher

Coblenz brewery which produces several styles. It has a number of subsidiaries, whose products include *Richmodis Kölsch* and

Düssel Alt. The enjoyable *Königsbacher Pils* ☆☆▷☆☆☆ is complex, satisfying, medium-bodied with a fresh, hoppy bouquet and a sustained bitterness in the finish.

Krombacher

Taking its name from its location in Kreutzal-Krombach, this large brewery is a specialist "Premium" Pilsener producer, proud to announce that its water comes from a rocky spring. *Krombacher Pils* ☆▷☆☆ is medium-bodied, with a definite malt accent in the nose, a clean palate, and a pleasing hop bitterness in its late finish. In the American market, the beer has been promoted as having a marked crispness, a "hop taste", and "a noticeable lack of bitterness". It is difficult to say whether the copywriter was being intentionally dishonest, or cloth-tongued.

Stauder

This is known as a "Premium" Pilsener brewery although Stauder does have other products. *Stauder Pils* ☆☆ is marketed especially to expensive hotels and restaurants. Its advertizing in Germany emphasizes cold maturation, making a play on the verb to rest. Brewers sometimes describe their beer as "resting" in maturation, and Stauder is promoted as a product to enjoy in tranquillity.

Since a long maturation also "cleans" beer, there is an implication that Stauder-drinkers are strangers to the hangover. Stauder Pils does not, however, have an unusually clean nose or palate, and there is a hint of fruitiness in its character.

Veltins

This brewery led the movement to speciality Pilsener brewing in Germany and is owed a debt of fashionability by its fellow "Premium" producers, especially its neighbours in Sauerland. It is a relatively small brewery, and its *Veltins Pilsener* ☆☆ still has something of a cult following. It is a sweetish, robust beer, with an elegant hop bitterness in the finish, and a touch of new-mown hay.

Warsteiner

Although it does have other styles this concern is known as a "Premium" Pilsener producer. It is a very up-to-date brewery, aggressively marketing and exporting its premium-priced product. *Warsteiner Pilsener* ☆▷☆☆ has a light hop bouquet, a dry, crisp, palate, and a moderately bitter finish. It is the biggest-selling beer in Germany, with a growing following in the USA.

FRANKFURT AND HESSE

In the Old Town of Frankfurt, the *Sachsenhausen*, Apfelwein, a cloudy, medium-dry alcoholic cider, is generally served. If Frankfurt has a speciality for the drinker, then this is it. There is a theory that Europe once had a cider belt, separating the wine-growing and beer-brewing areas. It is a tenuous theory, but here, the argument could, indeed, be put that Frankfurt has wine to its south and west; beer to its north and east.

In this pivotal position, Frankfurt has no beery leaning of its own, no varietal style. Nor has Hesse, the surrounding state. In so far as Germany has a centre, Frankfurt is the city that stands there. If its beers are middle-of-the-road, that is only to be expected.

What Frankfurt lacks in style, it makes up in scale. With an output in the region of 2.5 million hl, the Frankfurt brewery company of Binding is the biggest in Germany. Binding belongs to the group that also includes Dortmund's DAB and Berlin's Kindl breweries. Frankfurt's other brewing company, Henninger, is better known internationally. It has an output in the region of 1.75 million hl.

Just as it is an important state in the matter of large breweries, so Hesse has some significance for small – or, at least, independent – ones. A nationwide organization of privately owned breweries, the Bräu Ring, has its headquarters in Hesse, at Wetzlar, which is also the home of one of its members, the Euler company. Several other member-breweries are in Hesse, including Alsfeld, the Andreas Kloster brewery, Busch, Marburger and the Union-brauerei of Fulda.

WHERE TO DRINK

Frankfurt has three brewpubs. Zwölf Apostel (1 Rosenberger Str) produces a hoppy Pils and a robust Dunkel. Wäldches Bräu (Am Ginnheimer Wäldchen) makes a wide range of seasonal beers, most of them dark. Zum Mainkur (568 Hanauer Land Str, Fechenheim) produces hoppy Pils and a very malty Dunkel, and serves local dishes

In the cellar of the town hall at Wiesbaden, the Rathsbräu brewpub makes a mild Hell and Dunkel, and offers food from produce grown on its own farm. In a former ice-house which was once used to store wine, in Mainz, the Eisgrub brewpub (1 Weisslilien Gasse) offers a Pils, a Märzen and a Porter called Gambrinus.

Otto Binding, once owner of the big Frankfurt brewery, has established a somewhat smaller enterprise between Wiesbaden and Mainz, at Eltville, in wine country. He brings water by tanker from the Taunus Mountains, uses organically grown malting barley and hops, and produces an unfiltered Pilsener and a full-bodied, malty, dark beer of low alcohol content (3.2 by weight). His Kleines Eltviller Brauhaus (☎06123–2706) even serves free-range pigs' knuckles.

In the artists' and philosophers' town of Darmstadt is a shop stocking around 1,250 beers, from 250 countries. The shop is named B. Maruhn, "Der Groesste Biermarkt Der Welt", and is at 174 Pfungstaedter Strasse, in the district of Eberstadt, (☎06151–54876). The owner, Siegard Maruhn, is a jolly, enthusiastic chap, and his claim to have the world's biggest beer shop is probably safe, despite earnest competition from the USA. East of Darmstadt, Gross-Umstadt has a brewpub bearing the town's name, at 28 Zimmer Strasse. This serves an unfiltered Pilsener and a dark Export.

Binding

Germany's biggest brewing company producing a full range of beers and perhaps most noteworthy for its premium version of a German-style Export called *Export Privat* ☆☆. It has a fresh, light hoppiness in the nose; a clean, malt-accented palate; and a faintly fruity dryness in the finish. A very similar beer, but fractionally less dry, marginally fuller bodied, and slightly paler, has been brewed for the American market under the name *Steinhauser Bier* ☆☆. This has a little extra maturation, and is micro-filtered, to retain its freshness. Binding also produces *Kutscher Alt* ☆▷☆☆, a somewhat toffeeish interpretation of the style. The brewery has been very successful with Clausthaler, one of the more acceptable low-alcohol beers.

Busch

A famous name in brewing. Southwest of Frankfurt is Mainz, whence Adolphus Busch emigrated to the USA to start the world's biggest brewing company. Northwest of Frankfurt is Limburg, where a family called Busch runs a rather smaller brewery. The American Busch make 90 million hl of beer in the time it takes its German counterparts to brew 15,000hl.

The two families are not related and neither, of course, has anything to do with Bush Beer (no "c"), made in Belgium. There are, on the other hand, historical connections, though distant, between the German town of Limburg and the Belgian and Dutch provinces of the same name. As to Limburger cheese, it originated in Belgium and is still made there and in the Netherlands, but its principal centre of production is Germany. The three Limburgs also share an interest in beer. The German Limburg produces a pleasant, very mild *Golden Busch Pils* ☆▷☆☆ and a *Limburger Export* ☆☆.

Euler

The cathedral in Wetzlar gives its name to Euler's *Dom Pilsener* ☆☆, which is medium-dry. The brewery is also known for its slightly fuller-bodied *Euler Landpils* ☆☆. Other products include a deep amber, malty *Alt Wetzlar* ☆☆ (*alt* in this instance refers to tradition, not style. This is not an Altbier but a bottom-fermenting "dark" beer). Its basic *Euler Hell* ☆▷☆☆, a pale, malty beer, has an export counterpart called *Kloster Bier*. The Landpils is served unfiltered at the Wetzlarer Braustuben, adjoining the brewery.

Henninger

This may be the smaller of the two principal breweries in Frankfurt, but it is still a sizeable concern and the better known internationally. Its principal products, within a considerable range, include *Kaiser Pilsner* ☆.

STUTTGART AND BADEN–WÜRTTEMBERG

This is the place for the eclectic drinker. Here, wine and fruit brandies oblige beer to share the table, even though the state of Baden-Württemberg still contrives to have over 180 breweries.

In the Black Forest – or, at least, its greener valleys – village brewers produce tasty, sometimes slightly fruity, beers that reveal the softness of the local water. East of Stuttgart, towards the Swabian Mountains, one or two maltier beers emerge. (The term "Swabian" is widely used in Germany to indicate the culture and kitchen of an imprecise region that might be considered to stretch from Stuttgart to Augsburg.)

WHERE TO DRINK

Stuttgart has a brewpub in its pedestrianized shopping area in the city centre. The Stuttgarter Lokalbrauerei (31 Calwer Str) serves an unfiltered, Pilsener-style beer: light, clean and soft, with a fruity start and a very dry finish.

Beer-lovers will want to have a nostalgic glass at the former Sanwald Brewery *Gasthof* in Silberburg Strasse. There is also a small beer garden round the corner in Rotebühl Strasse. The old Sanwald brewery's wheat beers are now made by Dinkelacker, in Tübinger Strasse. In front of the Dinkelacker brewery is a pleasant restaurant serving the company's beers and offering Swabian dishes like *Fladlesuppe* (clear soup with strips of pancake); *Maultaschen* (Swabia's salty retort to ravioli); and *Spätzle* (egg noodles). No one ever went to Germany to lose weight and the Swabians clearly subscribe to this view.

At the end of September and for the first two weeks in October this business-like city lets its hair down for its annual fair on the Cannstatt meadows. This *Cannstatter Volksfest* is Stuttgart's counterpart to Munich's *Oktoberfest*. Beer is supplied by all three of the local breweries (three more than some cities have, though it is only half the number mustered by Munich). Special *Volksfest* beers are produced, in the Märzen style, and similar *Weihnachts* brews at Christmas.

In Heidelberg, always more swashbuckling, the old-established Café Schöneck (9 Steingasse) now houses a brewpub. Vetter's Alt-Heidelberger Brauhaus, producing a beer called 33 (denoting degrees Plato) that is one of several unratified claimants to being the world's strongest. Not far away in Weinheim, the Woinemer Hausbrauerei (23 Friedrich Str) produces an unfiltered Pilsener, a very dark Dunkel and seasonal specialities. In nearby Hemsback, the Burgbrauerei brewpub (3 Hilda Str) has a similar range.

In Karlsruhe, the Vogel brewpub (Kapellen Str) produces a very hoppy unfiltered Pils. This brewery, in a modern apartment block, works in the evenings, so that drinkers can see their beer being produced.

About half way between Heidelberg and Stuttgart, at the salt-water spa of Bad Rappenau, the Haffner brewery has its own resort hotel (33 rooms, ☎07264–8050). Its house beer is called *Kur* ("Cure") Pils.

South of Stuttgart, on the way to Lake Constance, is a brewery called Löwen (there are about 30 such, unrelated, "Lion" breweries in Germany). This Löwen brewery, at Tuttlingen, serves a Kellerpils in its restaurant. Drinkers who enjoy this excessively should be warned that there are no bedrooms.

Between Tuttlingen and Ulm, at Bingen, the Lamm brewery serves a *dunkles Hefeweizenbier* and, yet more exotic, *Bierhefebrannt*, a clear spirit distilled from beer. Closer to Ulm, at Trochtelfingen, the Albquell brewery (ten rooms, ☎07124–733) serves a Kellerbier.

Where to drink in Swabian Bavaria

South of Ulm, there are four breweries with restaurants, three with bedrooms. At Roggenburg-Biberach the Schmid brewery restaurant specializes in Dunkel and Märzen beers, but has no bedrooms. Hotel Löwenbrau (20 rooms, ☎08247–5056), at Bad Wörishofen, has a Kurpils, and is proud of its Doppelbock.

The Hirsch brewery, at Ottobeuren, has several interesting specialities including a house liqueur made by Benedictine brothers in the local monastery. The brewery's kettles are visible to guests who soak away their hangover in the indoor pool at the adjoining hotel (80 rooms, ☎08332–799/115).

Nearby at Irsee, a secularized monastery brewery produces some beers of outstanding interest, as well as having a very good kitchen. The Irseer Klosterbrauerei (26 rooms, ☎08341–432200) specializes in unfiltered beers, some matured for more than six months. A speciality called Abt's Trunk, conditioned and sold in hand-made clay flasks, has been reported to have reached a record-shattering 15 percent alcohol by weight. This sounds unlikely and the owner reckons that 12 percent by volume is more realistic. This brewery also has a *Bierbrand*.

There is also a colourful range of home-produced beers and schnapps available at the Post Brewery Hotel (22 rooms, ☎08361–30960) in the mountain resort of Nesselwang. The hotel has a small museum of beer.

Dinkelacker

This is the biggest brewery in the southwest and might just achieve this ascendancy on the basis of local sales, but exports are the decider. The brewery is best known for its *CD-Pils* ☆☆. Although this is marketed as a prestige beer, the name stands not for *corps diplomatique* but for Carl Dinkelacker, who founded the brewery in Stuttgart in 1888.

The brewery, not far from the city centre, is a blend of the traditional and the modern. Copper kettles are used, and the CD-Pils is hopped four times with half a dozen varieties (the final addition being Brewers' Gold, as the brew kettle is emptied). The CD-Pils is also fermented in the classic square type of vessel and *kräusened* during lagering; other products go into an ugly forest of unitanks.

Dinkelacker produces a range of bottom-fermenting beers that adopt a middle stance between those of its local rivals Stuttgarter Hofbräu and Schwaben Bräu. In general, Hofbräu's are the sweetest beers, Dinkel's medium, Schwaben's the driest, but these are fine distinctions since all three breweries produce typically soft southwestern beers. Dinkel has now acquired Schwaben, so those two breweries' ranges may converge.

In addition to its pale beers, Dinkelacker has a dark single bock, *Cluss Bock Dunkel* ☆☆, from its affiliate Cluss brewery in nearby Heilbronn – very malty in aroma and palate, but rather weak in finish. At its Stuttgart headquarters Dinkelacker also produces a number of specialities inherited when the local Sanwald brewery was absorbed. These include a rather thin *Stamm Alt* ☆ and two wheat beers, each made to the same specifications: the sparkling *Weizen Krone* ☆☆ and the *Sanwald Hefe Weizen* ☆☆.

Fürstenberg

The "Premium" ratings were perhaps something of a northern notion and Fürstenberg is the only southern brewery to have been dubbed in this way. It is also a house of some nobility, controlled by the aristocratic Fürstenbergs, who have been brewing for more than 500 years. The family are patrons of the arts and there is an impressive collection of German masters in the Fürstenberg Museum, at the palace of Donaueschingen, in the Black Forest. In the palace grounds, the Danube emerges from its underground source.

Donaueschingen is also the home of what is now an extremely modern brewery. A full range of styles is produced here, but the brewery is especially well known for its *Fürstenberg Pilsener* ☆☆▷☆☆☆. This beer has quite a full body, a sustained, lasting head, and a pleasantly hoppy taste in its dry finish.

Schwaben Bräu

The smallest of Stuttgart's three breweries, in the pleasant suburban township of Vaihingen. It has a large, traditional copper brewhouse and splendidly cavernous lagering cellars. The relative dryness of its beers is best exemplified by its *Meister Pils* ☆☆▷☆☆☆.

Subsidiary, Bräuchle, in Metzingen, produces a pale *Bock* ☆☆ for the whole group. The company plans a small museum of brewing, perhaps as a gesture to beer as a parent product – in the local market, it is almost as well known for its soft drinks.

Stuttgarter Hofbräu

The Hofbräu rivals, and may surpass, Dinkelacker in local sales. Its brewery is not far beyond that of Dinkelacker, on the edge of Stuttgart. It's a curiously rural fold of the city, and Hofbräu's turn-of-the-century buildings have flourishes that could be Scottish baronial. Inside, however, the brewery is uncompromisingly modern.

The name Hofbräu derives from a former royal brewery, but the present company is publicly held, with most of the stock in the hands of one person. The notion that drinkers of German wines have a soft, sweetish palate is emphatically accepted by Hofbräu, and the brewery also takes pride in its beers' not being pasteurized. Its premium product is called *Herren Pils* ☆▷☆☆.

BAVARIA: MUNICH AND THE SOUTH

Beer-lovers in other countries may be jealous of Germany in general but the focus of envy must be the state of Bavaria. No entire nation, nor even Germany's other states put together, can rival

Bavaria's tally of breweries, which still exceeds 800. Between them, they produce about 5,000 beers. About ten of these breweries are, by any standard, large (producing more than half a million hl a year). More than 500 are small (10,000hl or less) and of those, about half are tiny, (less than 2,000hl).

Almost every village has a brewery and some have two or three. The very small breweries almost always have their own inn, and often their beer is available nowhere else. There are breweries in monasteries – and convents – and in castles. The castles and baroque-rococo churches are a reminder that Bavaria was a nation of extrovert pride in the 17th and 18th centuries and when in 1919 it joined the German Republic, one of the conditions was that its Pure Beer Law be retained.

Bavaria is the home of more beer styles than any other part of Germany. Its everyday beers are not especially potent, but its specialities include the strongest beer in Germany. It grows good malting barley and virtually all of Germany's hops (and exports them all over the world), it has water in the Alps and the icy caves where the usefulness of cold maturation – lagering – first came to be understood.

The mountain and forest isolation of village Bavaria has helped its culture to survive, not only in costume, everyday dress, worship, music and dance, but also in its sense of being a beer land. Isolation was favoured by the founders of monasteries, too, in the days when they were the sanctuaries of all knowledge, including the art of brewing. If there was communication in these matters, it was across the mountains and within the forests. From the Dark Ages, the cradle of modern brewing has been slung from St Gallen in Switzerland to Munich, to Vienna, to Pilsen in Bohemia. That cradle is filled to bursting point with hearty, thirsty, Bavarians, crying *ein Prosit!* at every opportunity.

While Germany as a whole drinks 130-odd litres of beer per head each year, this figure is greatly exceeded in Bavaria where the figure is 180–90. No other state has such a defined calendar of drinking dates and styles. It may not matter much which beer you drink in the madness of the pre-Lenten *Fasching* (an answer in southern cities like Munich and northern ones like Cologne to the *Mardi Gras* of Nice and New Orleans, or the *Carnival* of Rio). However, in March and April, the appropriate beer is Doppelbock; in May, single Bock; in June, July and August Export-type beers at village festivals and Weissbier or Weizenbier in the beer gardens; at the end of September, and for the weeks that follow, Märzenbier for the Oktoberfest; by November, it is time to think of Weihnachts (Christmas) beer, which may be a variation on the festival speciality, or could be a Weizenbock.

Even the beer's accompaniments have a timetable. With the mid-morning beer, the appropriate snack is *Weisswurst*, a pair of succulent veal sausage coddled in a tureen of warm water. The veal is tempered with small proportions of beef and coarse bacon, seasoned with parsley (or chives) and sometimes onion or lemon. *Weisswurst* is so important that purists argue over its proper contents. For lunch, the beer might be accompanied by *Leberkäse*, neither liver nor cheese but a beef and pork loaf, served hot. For an early evening snack, the ubiquitous large radish of the region, which has a black skin and white flesh. The flesh is sculpted into a spiral and assaulted with salt. If the salt on the radish doesn't make you thirsty, the granules on the big, fresh, soft pretzels will do the trick.

To the foreigner, not least the beer-lover, the state of Bavaria may be synonymous with its capital city, Munich. Within Bavaria, while its claims are universally recognized, Munich and its hinterland have competition from other cities and regions where yet more breweries are to be found.

Munich boasts that it has some of the biggest and most famous breweries, and that it has nurtured more styles of beer than any other city. Within its hinterland, stretching through the regions known as Upper and Lower Bavaria, into the Alps and to the Austrian frontier, are hundreds of breweries. The city itself is fringed by small breweries making excellent beers. The Maisach and Schloss Mariabrunn breweries are just two examples. To the southwest, it is only 20 miles to the lakes and the beginning of the mountains, with more local breweries to serve the terraces and beer gardens.

South of Herrsching, on the lake called Ammersee, is the monastic brewery of Andechs, whose immensely malty beers were the extremely distant inspiration for the American Andeker brand. The brothers also have their own bitter liqueurs and fruit brandies, and there is a well-patronized Stube and terrace. Further into the Alps, near the ski resort of Garmisch-Partenkirchen, is another famous monastery brewery, Ettal, producing well-made and typically Bavarian beers but better known for its fruit brandy. Northeast of Munich near Landshut is the Klosterbrauerei Furth (now in secular hands) and also the celebrated convent brewery of Mallersdorf, just off the road to Regensburg. Another convent brewery, St Josef's, is at Ursberg, west of Augsburg, near Krumbach, on the road to Ulm.

A monastery brewery founded in 1040 at Weihenstephan, near Freising, 20 miles northeast of Munich, was to have great historical significance. Although the evidence for continuous production is hazy, the brewery survived long enough to be secularized by Napoleon and continues today under the ownership of the State of Bavaria. The Bayerische Staatsbrauerei Weihenstephan thus claims to be the oldest brewery in the world. Although there are vestiges of the monastery from the 12th century, and today's buildings are set in a restored cloister from the 17th century, the brewery is modern. It also offers some training facilities to the adjoining brewing institute.

There is only a handful of Faculties of Brewing in the world, and Weihenstephan – part of the Technical University of Munich – is the most famous. In recent years it has had difficulties, arising originally from its efforts to deal with brewers who do not work in *Reinheitsgebot* countries, but its name remains a by-word in the industry. The Weihenstephan brewery produces a full range of beers but is perhaps best known for its Kristal Export Weizenbier (very fruity, with hints of blackcurrant, and extremely dry in the finish) and its Hefeweissbier (light for the style and refreshing).

Wheat-beer brewing is especially associated with the area to the east of Munich. About 20 miles out of the city is the Erding wheat-beer brewery, perhaps the best-known of the specialist and certainly the fastest-growing. Further east, in Mühldorf, the Jägerhof house brewery of Wolfgang Unertl produces a wonderfully turbid wheat beer.

Another member of the Unertl family makes outstandingly full-flavoured, toffeeish, soft but tart, yeasty, wheat beers at Haag; the Gasthaus closes on Wednesdays. Lovers of the style should also look out for Weissbrau Schwendl, at Schalchen, and Weissbräu Graminger, near Altotting. The latter has bedrooms.

WHERE TO DRINK

Each of the principal Munich breweries has several of its own special outlets in the form of gardens, beer halls and restaurants. In Munich, the old Unions Bräu (42 Einstein Strasse) has been revived as a brewpub, offering an organically-grown, unfiltered, sweet, malty, slightly oily *Helles* ☆☆▷☆☆☆ served directly from pitched barrels. Near the old Munich airport, Flieger Bräu (2 Sonnen Strasse, Feldkirchen), in an old Schnapps distillery, offers a *Schwarzbier* ☆☆▷☆☆☆ with good espresso and dark-chocolate flavours. About 20 miles SE of Munich, near Glonn, an organic farm, butchery, bakery, brewery and restaurant offers a range of superb, lusciously malty, beers under the *Schweins Bräu* ☆☆☆ label (Herrmannsdorfer Landwerkstätten). To the west of Munich, closer to Augsburg, the *Schloss* brewery at Odelzhausen once made a double bock called Operator (nothing sinister about the name – it was dedicated to the Munich opera). As is often the case, the *Schloss* (16 bedrooms, ☎08134–602123) is more like a country house, but it has a restaurant. To the north of Munich, the brewery guest-house Goldener Hahn (☎08461–419) is at Beilngries, about half way to Nürnberg. Further north, at Lengenfeld-Velburg, the Winkler brewery guesthouse (☎09182–170) is widely known for its Kupfer Spezial beer. This much-loved brew is a dark copper colour, with gravity of 14 Plato, bottom-fermented in open vessels and matured for between 10 and 16 weeks. A remarkable feature of this family concern is that it grows and malts its own barley. Its beer is hopped with both Bavarian and Bohemian varieties. There are also brewery guest-houses to the northeast of Munich at Adlersberg (Prösslbrau, ☎09404–1822); Böbrach (Brauereigasthof Eck, ☎09923–84050); and Zenting (Kamm, ☎09907–89220).

Augustiner

The favourite brews among serious beer-drinkers in Munich are those from Augustiner. The beers are generally the maltiest among those produced by the city's major brewers and in that sense are closest to the palate traditionally associated with Munich. This is especially true of Augustiner's pale beers. The everyday *Augustiner Hell* ☆☆☆☆ qualifies as the classic pale beer of Munich, with its malty aroma and palate, soft entrance and firm, smooth finish. The brewery's interpretation of the German Export type has the brand name *Edelstoff* ☆☆☆ in Germany and, confusingly, is described as Augustiner Munich Light in the American market. "Light" refers, of course, to its colour and not to its body. This is hardly the lightest of German beers and even the slenderest of those is big by American standards. In recent years Augustiner has been emphasizing its pale beers, perhaps to the detriment of its dark styles. The basic dark beer is called *Dunkel Vollbier* ☆☆☆. There is also a *Dunkel Export* ☆☆▷☆☆☆, which has occasionally appeared in Germanic areas of the USA. The company has a number of other styles; its *Maximator Doppelbock* ☆☆☆ is marketed in the USA under the unexciting description "Munich Dark".

The maltiness of Augustiner's beers has sources close to home. No fewer than three of Munich's brewers have their own maltings and Augustiner is one. Its malt is produced in cellars that stretch like the tunnels of a mine underneath the brewery, which itself belongs to industrial archaeology. Constructed in 1885 and a magnificent example of the proud brewery edifices of the time, it is now a protected building. In the brewhouse only one in three vessels is made from copper; the other two are of stainless steel. The dark beers have the benefit of a triple decoction; the pale a double. Only aroma hops are used, in five varieties, from both Bavaria and Bohemia. Fermentation is in unusual vessels, open but with a lid that can be brought down, without pressure, to collect carbon dioxide. Fermentation is at very cold temperatures and lagering is in traditional vessels, with *kräusening*. The brewery uses wooden casks to supply beer gardens and some inns in the Munich area. The casks are pitched at the brewery, adding another traditional aroma to that of the malty air.

Augustiner has as its near neighbours Hacker-Pschorr, Spaten and Löwenbräu; all four are in the traditional "brewery quarter" behind Munich's central railway station. Paulaner and Hofbräuhaus are elsewhere in the city. In the heart of the brewery quarter, on Arnulf Strasse, is the Augustiner Keller, relatively small and much loved by the people of Munich. In the centre of the city on Neuhauser Strasse, Augustiner has its elegant, somewhat eccentric, 1890s restaurant and brewery tap, with a small Italianate garden. This building was originally constructed in 1829 to house the brewery after secularization. As its name suggests, Augustiner was originally a monastic brewery, and its original site was close to Munich's landmark cathedral, the Frauenkirche. The brewery dates at least from the 15th century, though there is some uncertainty about the claimed foundation date of 1328. It is without doubt an institution in Munich, favoured by yet a third famous outlet, the beer garden at the Hirschgarten, a public park near Nymphenburg Castle. This extremely popular picnic spot is said to accommodate as many as 8,000 drinkers, while Löwenbräu's beer garden in the huge central park in Munich holds a mere 6,000. How carefully this has been counted is open to dispute.

Ayinger

In Munich, the best-known country brewer is Ayinger. The position it enjoys in the city is evident: its beers are served in the restaurant and cabaret called the Platzl, on the square of the same name, directly opposite the Hofbräuhaus. The restaurant is owned by Ayinger and a special Platzl brew is produced – a miniature barrel of the beer is customarily set in the centre of the table, to accompany the evening's burlesque.

The Platzl beer is pleasant enough but a half-hour journey out of Munich to the village of Aying will provide just that freshness to make it taste delicious. In Aying (and in the USA) this brew is known as Jahrhundert. The name dates from the brewery's centenary in 1978. *Jahrhundert* ☆☆ is a German Export-type beer. It has some herbal hoppiness in the nose and a big, malty palate that dries in a crisp finish.

Ayinger has a full range of styles, among which several are noteworthy. *Altbairisch Dunkel* ☆☆▷☆☆☆ is a splendid example of the Bavarian dark style, with a warm, sweetly fruity aroma and coffeeish finish. *Fest-Märzen* ☆▷☆☆☆ is a little pale for the style but has a lovely malt bouquet, carrying through in the soft palate. *Maibock* ☆▷☆☆, too, is a classically malty Bavarian beer, with spicy, apricot notes. Most characterful of all is the double bock, labelled in Germany as Fortunator and in the USA as Celebrator. By whichever name, *Fortunator/Celebrator* ☆☆☆ is an outstanding example of double-bock style and a beautifully balanced beer, its richness mellowing out in a long, dryish finish. When strong brews are served at the end of winter, Germans talk about taking the "springtime beer cure". Ayinger goes further: it dubs its home village a "beer spa".

Where the Munich basin, with its crops of malting barley, gives way to the foothills of the Alps, the village of Aying provides for gentle exploration. Ayinger, with its own elderly maltings and modern brewhouse, stands on one side of the road, facing its guest-house on the other. A small beer garden, little more than a terrace, and an early baroque church complete the village square. In the square, the typical Bavarian maypole is set into a wooden tun that was once a maturation vessel in the brewery.

Ayinger also owns Höll wheat-beer brewery in Traunstein, further up the road. This imposing brewery was built in the late 19th century and has not changed markedly since. It leans sleepily into a hillside in the valley of the River Traun. Four wheat beers are produced at Traunstein. *Export Weissbier* ☆▷☆☆ is filtered and has a full, relatively sweet, fruitiness (ripe plums, perhaps?). The unfiltered *Bräu-Weisse* ☆▷☆☆ is much more tart. *Ur-Weisse* ☆☆▷☆☆☆ has a fuller, amber-red colour and bursts with fruitiness. It is also unfiltered and has the classic apples-and-cloves spiciness of a traditional wheat beer. A *Weizenbock* ☆☆☆, 17 Plato, a seasonal brew, which is pale and filtered, is available in the local market at Christmas.

Erdinger

These are the biggest-selling wheat beers in Germany. The very pretty town of Erding is located near the new Munich airport.

A building dating from 1513, at 1 Lange Zeile, is the "tap", and was once the brewery. Production switched in 1983 to a showpiece brewery on the edge of town. Local farmers are supplied by the brewery with seed and contracted to produce much of the barley and all the wheat. Among the wheat beers of Bavaria, those from Erdinger are among the cleaner, lighter and more delicate in aroma and palate. They are aimed at the popular audience rather than the traditionalist. Products include a *Kristall* ☆▷☆☆, with a touch of vanilla and dessert apple in its aroma and palate; a version described as *Mit feiner Hefe* ☆▷☆☆, with more fruitiness to it; a lightly chocolatey *Dunkel* ☆▷☆☆; and a very smooth Weizenbock, called *Pikantus* ☆☆▷☆☆☆. A marginally fuller version of the *Mit feiner Hefe* is served at Erding's autumn festival, which starts on the last Friday of August and continues for ten days.

Forschungs

This brewpub is absolutely not to be missed by any beer-lover who is in Munich during its opening months, from early March to mid October (and never on Mondays). Forschungs can seem a mirage: something between a 1930s ice-cream parlour and the control tower at a small and dubious airport. Take the suburban train to Perlach station, or a cab: the beers are strong, delicious, and available only in one-litre servings. The year-round *Pilsissimus* ☆☆☆ (13.4; 4,2; 5.2) has both malt and hops in its big aroma, with the latter shining through in its soft, dry, palate. The *Blonder Bock* ☆☆☆ begins the year at 20 (6; 7.5), then makes a modest summertime reduction to 18 (5.8; 7.0) at the end of June, beginning of July. It has a rich, fruity, maltiness, but is sweetly soft and drinkable, all the way to its big finish. An innovator established the Forschungsbrauerei in 1928, as an experimental brewery. Since World War II, it has functioned simply as a local brewery. Forschungsbrauerei is at 76 Unterhachinger Strasse, Perlach (☎089-6701169).

Klosterbrauerei Furth

This brewery, near Landshut, was only briefly owned by monks. It produces a wide range of notably sweet and creamy lagers, and a very lively *Edel Weisse* ☆☆.

Hacker-Pschorr

There is a resonance about the names of Munich's principal breweries. Not so long ago, Hacker and Pschorr were two of them. They merged, and much more recently have been taken over by Paulaner. Despite that complicated history, the brewery continues to operate, with its own range of beers. They are on the dry side and perhaps not as smooth as some Munich brews. However, by the standards of some other regions and countries, they still have a fair degree of character. Hacker-Pschorr has never been identified with any single speciality, though it has recently been concentrating on its *Pils* ☆. Its *Oktoberfest Märzen* ☆▷☆☆ and *Animator* ☆☆ double bock are both pleasant. The company's beers can be tested at Zum Pschorr-Bräu, in Neuhauser Strasse, and in summer on a terrace in the Marienplatz.

Hallertau

In the heart of the Hallertau hop-growing region, at the small town of Au. This Schloss ("castle") brewery makes a beautifully clean, very smooth, *Pils* ☆☆▷☆☆☆, with a hop character that is suitably fresh but perhaps a little reticent. There is also a very good, toffeeish, soft, amber-to-tawny, *Dunkel* ☆☆▷☆☆, among other styles. Schlossbrauerei Au/Hallertau was founded in 1590, though the present castle dates only from the mid 1800s and the brewhouse is very modern. The earlier, 1914, brewhouse, is now a bar and restaurant, decorated with advertising enamels (closed Mon, Tues).

Hofbräuhaus

Perhaps in Germany the label "HB" speaks for itself, but elsewhere the allusion is not instantly clear. It stands for "Hofbräu" ("court brew"), and is the label of brews produced for the world's most famous beer hall. Munich's Hofbräuhaus was originally the beer hall and garden of the Bavarian Royal Court Brewery. Lesser Hofbräus remain elsewhere in Germany, having passed from minor royalty into commercial hands, but the most important one still belongs to Bavaria, albeit to the state government. The garden is pleasant, though the rambling beer hall smells of stale cigarettes and the detritus of tourism. The beers are excellent, the conventional brews being malt-accented with a spritzy finish. Although the everyday beer is a fresh-tasting, malty *Export* ☆☆▷☆☆☆, the Hofbräuhaus (founded in 1589) is credited with having, originally, in its early days, introduced Bock beer to Munich. Its very malty *Maibock* ☆☆☆▷☆☆☆☆ (16.2-16.5; around1065; 6.0; 7.5) has an amber-brown colour. A similar beer called *Urbock* has replaced the more assertive winter *Delicator*. The Maibock tastes especially good accompanied by a couple of *Weisswurst*. Since its earliest days the Hofbräuhaus has also had a tradition of wheat beers. Its *Edel Weizen* ☆☆▷☆☆☆ has long been enjoyed, but *Dunkel Weizen* ☆☆▷☆☆☆ is not to be ignored: a complex beer with dense head, lavish lacework, a sweet start, toasty maltiness and a lemony tartness in the finish.

Hofbräuhaus Freising

Dating from at least the 1100s, and originally the Bishop's household brewery. It is now owned by the Count of Moy. The brewery is in a visually dramatic *Jugendstil* building. Its very fruity wheat beers include the distinctive *Huber Weisses* ☆☆☆, quite heavily sedimented, and intentionally lower in carbonation than some of its contemporaries. *Gutstetten* ☆☆▷☆☆☆ ("good place") is a dark wheat beer with a great deal of fruity complexity: tartness, apples, raisins, toffee, smoke... The town also has a newish brewpub (Erste Freisinger Gasthausbrauerei, 8 Am Lohmülbach, Lerchenfeld), offering a *Schwarzbier* ☆☆▷☆☆☆ with flavours reminiscent of mocha and Bourbon.

Hopf

Hoppy family-name, appropriate for a brewer, but not especially to a maker of wheat beers such as these. Fittingly for the style, the Hopf beers are not very hoppy. *Weisse Export* ☆☆ has a complex fruitiness (dessert apples, peaches-and-cream?). *Dunkle*

Weisse ☆☆ is spicier, with a tinge of cinnamon. *Weisser Bock* ☆☆ is more vanilla-like, and creamier. Hopf is in Miesbach, in lake country near the Tegernsee.

Kaltenberg

Although by no means the only brewery owned by an aristocrat, Kaltenberg is perhaps the best known, not least because it is in a classic Bavarian castle. The castle dates from the 13th century, but the present structure was built in the 17th century based on designs by the architect who created Neuschwanstein for "mad" King Ludwig II of Bavaria. The third King Ludwig was the last and his great-grandson, Prince Luitpold, runs the Kaltenberg brewery. In export markets Kaltenberg is known for a well-made *Diät-Pils* ☆☆, but in its local market it is noted for a malty, dark beer, with a coffeeish finish, *König Ludwig Dunkel* ☆☆▷☆☆☆, which has a gravity of 13.3 Plato.

Kaltenberg Castle is near Geltendorf, less than 30 miles west of Munich. It has a beer garden and restaurant, and in June holds a beer festival and costumed jousting between "medieval" knights (for information, ☎081931–9330). A *Dunkel Ritter Bock* ☆☆☆ 23 Plato is made during Lent ("Ritter" means "rider" or "knight"). Kaltenberg has a second brewery in a nearby town, and additionally makes a range of sherbety-tasting wheat beers.

Löwenbräu

Internationally, the best-known name among the Munich breweries is Löwenbräu. About a quarter of its output is exported and it licenses its name to be used on products in other countries. Löwenbräu's Munich-brewed beers tend toward a firm maltiness and a good hop balance. The *Helles* ☆▷☆☆, *Export* ☆ and golden *Oktoberfest* ☆☆ typify this approach. Other products include a *Pilsener* ☆☆ with a good hop attack; a *Dunkel* ☆▷☆☆ with some grainy, malt-loaf, notes; the rather gritty *Löwen Weisse* ☆; and a vanilla-tasting *Dunkelweizen* ☆▷☆☆.

The brewery owns the biggest beer hall, the 5,000-seat Mathäser, in Bayer Strasse, near the central railway station. The Mathäser has the look of a railway station itself, with its cafeteria entrance, but its 15 or so inner halls are worth exploring. There is an ornate beer-restaurant and terrace opposite the Löwenbräu brewery, and the company has one of the city's biggest beer gardens, at the landmark "Chinese Tower". This pagoda is, confusingly, in a park called the English Garden.

Paulaner

The biggest brewery in Munich is especially associated with its classic *Salvator* ☆☆☆☆ double-bock. This extra-strong, very dark beer, with deep amber highlights, has a gravity of 18.5 Plato and is made with three malts. Only Hallertau hops are used, though of both bittering and aroma varieties. The beer has a very rich start, drying out in a long finish. Its alcohol content is around 6 percent by weight, 7.5 by volume. The brewery has its origins in the early 17th century with a community of monks of St Paul, who became well known throughout the city for the strong beer they brewed, called Salvator (Saviour) to sustain themselves during Lent. Being a very strong beer, it came to be known as a "double" bock and gave rise to that style. Most other double-bock beers echo the Saviour's brew by bearing names ending in *-ator*. Double-bock beers are drunk to warm the soul as winter gives way to spring and the beer gardens think about reopening. The first new barrel of Salvator is ceremonially tapped by the Mayor of Munich or Prime Minister of Bavaria at the brewery's 3,500-seat beer hall and garden on Nockherberg three to four weeks before Easter.

The brewery was secularized in the early 19th century and has since had several owners, but it still stands on the same site, though it has grown to straddle the hill. From the modern office block, a tunnel through the hillside leads to the maltings and the brewhouse, which is still in traditional copper. The brewery uses classic fermenters and traditional lagering cellars, maturing its everyday beers (which are *kräusened*) for five or six weeks and its stronger specialities for three to eight months. Paulaner has one of Germany's first refrigeration machines, made for the brewery by Carl von Linde, and an early water turbine powered by a stream that runs down the hill. Paulaner's beers are firm-bodied and dry for Munich, often with an assertive finish. The dark *Alt-Münchner Dunkel* ☆☆▷☆☆☆ has a fine colour, a smooth, full body and a maltiness in that dry finish. The export-style *Urtyp 1634* ☆☆ has, again, a full, smooth body but a slightly tannic finish. The pale *Original Münchner Hell* ☆☆☆▷☆☆☆ is similar but milder. The brewery produces a full range of styles – with about ten principal beers – including a dry, rounded, long *Altbayerische Weissbier* ☆☆▷☆☆☆ that has helped popularize wheat beers in the USA. Paulaner also has a brewpub on Kapuziner Platz. The premises were once the Thomas brewery.

Rauchenfels Steinbier

A famous speciality produced by the addition of white-hot rocks to the brew-kettle. This technique was widely used in the days when brew-kettles were made from wood, and could not be placed over a fire. The style was revived by the inventive and entrepreneurial German brewer Gerd Borges in 1982. Originally, he brewed in Neustadt, close to the border with the former East Germany. The brewery there had lost much of its market with the division of Germany, and Rauchenfels Steinbier was seen as a speciality that might compensate in volume. Since reunification, the production of Steinbier has been moved to the Borges brewery at Altenmünster, near Augsburg. The company says it is still using the same technique, in which the kettle is brought almost to the boil by conventional methods, then finished with the hot rocks, which cause considerable caramelization of the malt sugars. The sugar-coated rocks are then allowed to cool, and placed in the maturation vessels. The brew already tinged with caramelization in the kettle begins to enjoy a secondary fermentation when it renews its contact with the rocks. The beers are made to conventional strengths, of 3.8; 4.7 *Rauchenfels Steinbier* ☆☆☆▷☆☆☆ is brewed from equal proportions of barley and wheat malt, and has a smoky, treacle-toffee palate, less dry than smooth, with a long, rounded, finish.

A version called *Rauchenfels Steinweizen* ☆☆☆, made with 60 percent wheat, is very lively, a little less hoppy, with slightly more sharpness. It is to be hoped that these beers retain their integrity and character in their new home. The brewery's other products include *Jubelbier* ☆☆▷☆☆☆, a tawny, toasty dark lager (13; 1052; 4.4; 5.5).

Schneider

This family, specialists in wheat beer, were once the brewers at the Hofbräuhaus in Munich, and more recently at premises in the street called Tal ("Dale"). The famous Schneider beer-hall in the Tal still serves the family's beers, but production is now in the Bavarian town of Kelheim, near Regensburg. The Schneiders own a brewery there that has been making wheat beer since the 1600s. There is also a "tap" at the brewery in Kelheim (closed in November). *Schneider Weisse* ☆☆☆▷☆☆☆☆ has a distinctively tan colour and a characteristic spiciness. *Aventinus* ☆☆☆☆ (18.5; 1074; 6.1; 7.7) has a huge head, an insistent sparkle, malty notes in the nose; chocolate, fruit and spices in the palate; and a lightly clove-like finish.

Spaten

One of the world's most important brewing companies, because of its influence on the beers most nations drink today. All lager beers, whether dark, amber or pale, owe much to the work of the Spaten brewery in the 19th century. The influence of the company should be far more widely recognized internationally, but perhaps its reputation has been subsumed, with those of its neighbours, into that of Munich itself.

Although it still takes great pride in earlier styles such as wheat beers (notably the dry, spicy, full-bodied and fluffy *Franziskaner Hefe-Weissbier* ☆☆▷☆☆☆ and its cleaner, sparkling *Club Weisse* ☆☆), Spaten's greatest contributions were in the development of bottom-fermenting beers; in the perfecting of the Bavarian dark style, as typified by its own *Dunkel Export* ☆☆☆▷☆☆☆☆; in the popularization of the amber type, as represented by its world classic *Ur-Märzen* ☆☆☆☆; and in the perfecting of the Munich pale variety, exemplified by its *Münchner Hell* ☆☆☆. Historically, these are classics, and are produced by blending tradition with modern technology. Spaten has its own maltings, uses traditional kettles, lauter tuns (copper in the old brewhouse, stainless steel in a new one), closed classic fermenters and horizontal lagering tanks.

Three different yeasts are used by Spaten. Pale beers of conventional gravities (including a very dry *Spaten Pils* ☆☆☆▷☆☆☆) have one yeast; the *Franziskus Heller Bock* ☆☆ another; darker brews a third. Most breweries would use only one strain for all those types, but Spaten feels that yeasts should be chosen according to their suitability to the different worts and their contribution to background palate.

The company traces its origins to a brewery of 1397, and its name (meaning "spade") is a jocular corruption of Spaeth, an early owner. The royal court brewmaster Gabriel Sedlmayr took over the company in 1807 and his son, Gabriel the Younger, became the father of modern lager-brewing. Studies carried out by Gabriel in the 1830s introduced Bavaria to more scientific methods, notably the use of the saccharometer in the control of fermentation. Sedlmayr gathered disciples who spread the reputation of Bavarian bottom-fermenting techniques, and Sedlmayr's friend and rival Anton Dreher went on to introduce the amber style of lager in Vienna in 1840–1. A year later, the Pilsen brewery produced the first pale lager. In 1873, Sedlmayr worked with von Linde on his first refrigerator, at the instigation of Dreher (Paulaner's Linde machine came later) and in 1876 he introduced the world's first steam-heated brewhouse (companies that followed liked to call themselves "steam breweries"). The present company was constituted originally from Gabriel's business and his brother Joseph's Franziskaner brewery.

Spaten is still predominantly owned by the Sedlmayr family. It is proud of its family ownership and of its traditions, and still delivers beer in Munich by horse and dray. Regrettably, the building from which they emerge looks less like a brewery than a fair-sized airport.

Stein

The origins of lagering can best be understood by a visit to this brewery, whose cellars are cut into a cliff-face that was once the border, on the river Traun, between Bavaria and Austria. There is one castle on top of the cliff, and another beneath. The Schlossbrauerei Stein has an especially juicy-tasting *Märzen* ☆☆☆ and a treacly, nutty, *Dunkel* ☆☆▷☆☆☆.

Tegernsee

This resort town on the lake of the same name has a brewery and beer-hall, Brauhaus Tegernsee, owned by one of the Dukes of Bavaria, in what was once a Benedictine monastery. The *Spezial* ☆☆▷☆☆☆ is a clean, firm, malty lager with a touch of new-mown hay. The *Doppelbock* ☆☆ has a soft, sweet, lean maltiness and a hint of roastiness. Benedictines from Tegernsee are said to have established the settlement that grew into the city of Munich.

Klosterbrauerei Weltenburg

Benedictine brewery, tracing its origins to the 11th century. Has a full range, but its speciality is its dark lager *Barock Dunkel* ☆☆▷☆☆☆, deep reddish-brown, smooth, and faintly roasty. The brewery, in Kelheim (32 Asam Str) has a beer garden and tavern, the Klosterschenke (closed Jan, Feb).

NORTHERN BAVARIA: FRANCONIA

For the beer-drinker, Munich and southern Bavaria might seem like the pearly gates, but heaven is further north. Up there Bavaria has a region that is almost a state within a state: Franconia (Franken), with Nürnberg as its largest city and Bamberg and Amberg as its most heavily breweried towns, with nine or ten apiece, subject to planned new brewpubs.

There are more small breweries in Franconia than anywhere in the world. It remains a centre of production for dark Bavarian lagers. It has more unfiltered beers than anywhere else and a greater number of eccentric specialities.

From south to north, the region stretches from Regensburg to Bayreuth, Kulmbach and Coburg, on the former border with East Germany. Due east the Bohemian Forest forms the frontier with the Czech Republic, with Ceské Budejovice (Budweis) and Pilsen nearby. To the west the small-brewery country of the Steigerwald reaches to Würzburg and wine territory.

Bamberg is the centre for a highly unusual speciality, namely the smoky Rauchbier. Kulmbach is the traditional centre for dark beers and produces some especially strong Doppelbock brews. Bayreuth has a proprietary speciality: the Maisel brewery's Dampfbier, and Schierling has its own Roggen (meaning rye) beer.

Even in towns not specifically associated with a single style, many breweries have their own minor specialities. Sometimes these are dark beers. Often they are unfiltered. While an unfiltered Kräusenbier is cause for comment elsewhere in the country, such brews are not uncommon in Franconia. As its name suggests, this type of beer is *kräusened*. Then, before the *kräusen* has worked out, the maturation vessel is tapped, revealing intentionally cloudy beer.

Another type of unfiltered beer is not *kräusened*. This is Kellerbier, which is allowed to settle in the maturation tanks before being tapped. As might be expected it has a notably low carbonation. Traditionally, this type of beer has been heavily hopped to guard against infection. An outstanding example is made by St Georgenbräu, of Buttenheim, just south of Bamberg. Another excellent Kellerbier comes from Maisel of Bamberg (there are four Maisel breweries in Bavaria, each quite separate but linked by family).

Bamberg is a town of only 70,000 people but it is a remarkable centre of brewing. On the hill that overlooks the town is the 17th-century Romanesque church of St Michael, part of a former monastery which had a brewery (the monks' brewhouse has now been converted into a Franconian Beer Museum ☎0951–53016). The town itself is a living museum, not only for its German Renaissance buildings but also for its selection of breweries. There is plenty of half-timbering and gilding about the breweries and their guest-houses, too, but their principal contribution is in terms not of architecture but of social and economic history. Two even have their own maltings so that they can do the kilning necessary to produce Rauchbier (which is made by kilning the malt over beech logs). There are also two free-standing maltings.

By no means do all of Bamberg's breweries regularly feature Rauchbier and, though the town is the centre for production, companies elsewhere have been known to produce a beer in this style. In Bamberg, the Heller brewery has Aecht Schlenkerla Rauchbier as its principal product; the family Merz's Hausbrauerei Spezial produces nothing else; Kaiserdom Rauchbier is produced in Eltmann for Bürgerbraü-Bamberg. An unfiltered, but bright, Rauchbier is made by Fischer Greuth, in Herscheid, south of Bamberg.

Among other Bamberg breweries, Fässla offers a splendid dark pre-Christmas Bock called Bambergator; Keesman emphasizes its malty but dry Herren Pils; the secular Klosterbräu has a dark beer; Mahrs has a relatively well-carbonated Kellerbier and a delicious, rich dark brew called Wunderburger Liesl. The pale beers of Bamberg all have a dry maltiness.

To the west is the Steigerwald, with woodland walks and scores of small breweries, many with their own taverns. To the east, in the country-side known as the Frankische Schweiz are more small breweries.

Some towns and villages have communal breweries where members of the public can brew their own beer. Falkenburg, Neuhaus-on-Pegnitz and Sesslach are examples. This facility is generally exercised by barley farms or tavern keepers. In the days before commercial production, a communal brewer who had a new batch ready would display a garland or a six-pointed star outside his house. The latter is a symbol of the brewer, deriving from alchemy rather than from any religious significance. In some places this practice is still followed, although it is also used by small commercial brewers. Ecclesiastical brewing was significant in the past in Franconia, but only one monastery brewery remains, the Klosterbrauerei Kreuzberg at Bischofsheim, north of Würzburg, making the malty, sherryish, copper-coloured *Echtes Klosterbier* ☆☆▷☆☆.

WHERE TO DRINK

In Bamberg, the obvious places to stay are the guest-houses of Brauerei Spezial (10 Obere König Str. ☎0951–24304), which is in the shopping area; or Brauerei Greifenklau (20 Laurenziplatz. ☎0951–95310) which has a spectacular valley view. The mandatory stop for a drink is the Schlenkerla tavern, in Dominikaner Strasse, but other brewery taps are also worth a visit; the low-ceilinged tavern of the Mahrs brewery, in Wundeburg, is a delightful "local". The Steigerwald can be explored from the Klosterbräu Hotel in Ebelsbach (☎09522–6027), specializing in a dark Märzen beer.

To the north, between Bamberg and Coburg, the Goldener Stern at Ebersdorf (24 bedrooms, ☎09562–106163) is a pub at a former brewery. Northwest of Coburg, at Gauerstadt, near Rodach, the Wacker inn (20 bedrooms, ☎09564–225) has a similar history. Northeast of Coburg, the Grosch brewery (17 bedrooms, ☎09563–4047) in Rödental, on the way to Neustadt, has an excellent dark beer. In the old brewing town of Lichtenfels, the Wichert *Gasthof* has a Kellerbier but no bedrooms. The Frankische Schweiz can be explored from the Drei Kronen brewery inn at Memmelsdorf (☎0951–944330), where an unfiltered Rauchbier is served. There are two or three more small breweries in the town.

The Schinner brewery restaurant in Richard Wagner Strasse, in Bayreuth serves an excellent Braunbier. In Nürnberg, the Altstadt brewery is an essential visit, offering beer for sale by the bottle. Their beer is also available on tap nearby. Regensburg has a number of beer-restaurants. In Arnulfsplatz, the Kneitinger brewery produces beer mainly for its own restaurant. The Spitalgarten, in Katharinenplatz, dates from the 14th century and serves local beer.

Altstadthof

Nuremberg's "Old Town Courtyard", dating from at least the 1600s, is at 19 Berg Strasse, near the Tiergärtner Tor, a gate in the city wall. The Altstadthof micro-brewery, offering its beer at small taverns alongside and its cellar, was established by Lammsbräu (*see* page 63) in 1983/4. Although Altstadthof was one of the first of the new generation in Germany, it uses antique brewing equipment. Initially, this philosophy extended to and open cooler of the classic Baudelot type, though this has now finally been retired. Wooden fermenters are still used, but oak lagering vessels are now also dormant. This revivalist style of brewery was devised by micro pioneer, the late Otto Binding, who introduced similarly classic layouts in several towns and cities elsewhere in the world. In an historic city well worth visiting, Altstadthof is a good and accessible example.

The brewery has in recent years introduced a *Schwarzbier* ☆☆☆ with an almost purple colour and intense, lingering flavours. To taste this beer is like biting into treacle toffee. It also has a very creamy, amber-red *Bock* ☆☆☆▷☆☆☆ and a flowery, hoppy *Helles* ☆☆. The beers, made from organically-grown ingredients, are unfiltered. Beneath the Altstadthof are galleries of cellars dating from the 1300s, where the Old Town's medieval brewers lagered their beer.

EKU

This brewery in Kulmbach boasts the highest ratified gravity of any bottom-fermenting beer in the world, with its *Kulminator 28* ☆☆☆▷☆☆☆☆. As its name suggests, this beer has a guaranteed gravity of 28 degrees – though analysis has revealed levels as high as 30.54. The brewery claims to mature the beer for nine months with a short period of freezing to settle protein. Since this is not done specifically for the purpose of raising alcohol content, Kulminator 28 is not labelled as an Eisbock. As the name Kulminator implies, it is a Doppelbock by style, though labelled merely as Urtyp ("original") and Hell ("pale"). It is not especially pale – the great density of malt provides an amber cast – neither is it a dark beer. The nose and palate are intensely malty, with some estery notes and a strongly alcoholic finish. It usually has an alcohol content of 9.2–9.6 (weight), 11.5–12 (volume), but this varies. Some samples have reached 11.1 (weight), 13.7 (volume).

The heavyweight title of the world is contested between Kulminator 28 and the Swiss Hürlimann brewery's Samichlaus (a Christmas beer). Samichlaus has lower gravity (27.6), a longer period of maturation (a year) and a higher alcohol content (11.2 by weight; 13.7–14 by volume). While this contest is too hard to resist, such muscle has limited application. These are beers of excellent quality but they would best be dispensed from small barrels suspended from the necks of mountain-rescue dogs.

Whether they revive or stun the recipient depends upon the constitution of the drinker. Certainly, in their fermentation, the yeast is stunned by the alcohol it produces. That explains why these beers take so long, and are so difficult, to make. Nor do they contain any of the sugars (or, sometimes, enzymes) that are used in the relatively lightweight strong beers (or "malt liquors") so frequently produced in the USA.

EKU also has a dark double-bock, simply called *Kulminator* ☆☆▷☆☆☆ (19.2; 1077; 6; 7.6); a pale, single *Edelbock* ☆☆; a somewhat conventional dark export-style beer called *Rubin* ☆☆☆; a rather full-bodied *Pils* ☆▷☆☆; and a pleasant *Weizen* ☆.

The first two initials of EKU stand for Erste ("first") Kulmbach. The "U" derives from the union of two earlier breweries that created the company in 1872. In 1996, EKU was acquired by Kulmbacher Reichelbräu.

Hofmark

This traditionalist brewery is interesting for a number of reasons: its location, east of Regensburg at Cham on the Bavarian side of the Bohemian Forest, means that its soft water emerges from the same quartz-granite bed as that of Pilsen; it was founded in 1590 and has been in one family for more than 200 years; and it still uses some traditional techniques, not least the method of fining with beechwood chips. It is also unusual in that its premium beer Das feine Hofmark is prepared in two variations: mild and bitter (designations that sound more English than German). Both are firm, smooth, beautifully balanced and complex beers. Das feine Hofmark *Würzig Mild* ☆☆ has a malt accent; *Würzig Herb* ☆☆☆▷☆☆☆ (meaning "dry" or "bitter") has a lovely hop character in both nose and finish. This brewery was a pioneer in the use of swing-top bottles.

Kaiserdom

A full range of beers is marketed under the Kaiserdom label by the Bürgerbräu brewery of Bamberg. Most tend towards the dry maltiness of the region but are unexceptional. However *Kaiserdom Rauchbier* ☆☆☆ has the distinction of being the only Bavarian smoked beer exported to the USA.

Kulmbacher Mönchshof

The dark-beer tradition of Kulmbach is best maintained by the "Monks'" brewery. Its *Kloster Schwarz-Bier* ☆☆☆▷☆☆☆☆ is a classic, with a gravity of 12.5, a full smooth body and an unrivalled dark-malt palate. The connoisseur of Bavarian dark beers might, of course, prefer the earthier character found in some of the many *Hausbrauerei* examples. Mönchshof goes back to the beginnings of monastic brewing in Kulmbach in 1349. It was secularized in 1791, becoming a family brewery, and is now part-owned by Kulmbacher Reichelbräu.

Even at the peak of Kulmbach's international repute as a brewing centre, at the turn of the century, Mönchshof was one of the smaller houses. Its range includes a very flavourful single *Klosterbock* ☆☆☆; a malty *Märzen* ☆☆; a malty export called *Maingold* ☆☆; and what is for Bavaria an unusually dry *Mönchshof Pilsener* ☆☆.

Kulmbacher Reichelbräu

If Germany can have Eiswein, it can have icy beer, too. The tradition of Eisbock has in recent years been kept alive by Kulmbacher Reichelbräu. It is a strong beer in which the alcohol content is enhanced by freezing and then removing the ice. As alcohol has a lower freezing point than water this concentrates the brew. The resultant *Eisbock Bayrisch G'frorns* ☆☆☆▷☆☆☆☆ ("Bavarian Frozen") has a gravity of 24 and an alcohol content of around 8 percent by weight, 10 by volume. A most interesting beer, smooth, dense and potent with suggestions of whisky and coffee. In 1996, after acquiring EKU (with its Kulminator 28), Reichelbräu said it would drop G'frorns. It has since indicated that it might reconsider this decision.

Lammsbräu

Organic beers from a modern, family-owned, regional brewery, established in 1628, in the pencil-making town of Neumarkt, 25-30 miles SE of Nuremberg. A wide range stretches from a fresh, malty, spicily-hopped, *Helles* ☆☆ to a malty, complex, slightly smoky "black wheat beer", *Schwarze Dunkles Weizen* ☆☆☆.

Maisel

Among the four Bavarian brewing companies called Maisel, this one in Bayreuth is by far the biggest. It has also become well known for its speciality brews, notably its highly individualistic *Maisel's Dampfbier* ☆☆☆. This is a top-fermenting beer, very fruity, with vanilla-like tones. It has a gravity of 12.2 Plato, is made with a triple decoction mash from four barley malts, hopped with Hallertaus and fermented with its own yeast in open vessels. It emerges slightly redder and paler than a Düsseldorfer Altbier, and about 4 percent alcohol by weight, 5 by volume. It is not pasteurized, even for export to the USA.

"Dampfbier" is a registered name, not intended to indicate a recognized style and Maisel earnestly disavows any intention to sound like Anchor Steam (which is different both in production process and palate). In the late 1970s, the brewery decided that "all beers were beginning to taste the same. We wanted something distinctive. We experimented, and this was the brew we liked."

The decision may also have had something to do with the move out of a magnificently castellated and steam-powered brewery of 1887 into a remorselessly modern plant next door. There is an element of nostalgia to a "steam beer" (which is how *Dampfbier* would, inescapably, translate). For the two Maisel brothers who own the brewery, nostalgia is not cheap. The entire old brewery has been mothballed, in its original working order, and is now open for tours, at 10 o'clock each morning. They can also be arranged by appointment.

Meanwhile, Maisel continues in its spotless new brewery to produce an interesting range of products, including three wheat beers. *Weizen Kristall-Klar* ☆☆☆ is, as its name suggests, a crystal-clear beer, very pale, with a champagne-like sparkle and a tannic, apple fruitiness. *Hefe-Weiss* ☆☆ is fermented out with a mixture of yeasts, *kräusened* and given a dosage at bottling. The beer has a deep bronze colour, a fresh apple-like palate and a big, fluffy body. *Weizenbock* ☆☆☆▷☆☆☆, at 17.5 Plato, has a deep tawny colour, a big body, and a sharpness that recedes into smooth vanilla and licorice tones at the finish.

Klosterbrauerei Münnerstadt

Augustine monastery brewery, founded in 1381, north of Schweinfurt. Products include a malty, textured, perfumy *Lager* ☆☆☆▷☆☆☆; a nutty *Märzen* ☆☆☆; and an aromatically malty, cakey, *Doppelbock* ☆☆☆.

Schäffbräu

This brewery is notable for its "Fire Festival" double-bock. *Schäff-Feuerfest* ☆☆☆ has a gravity of 25 Plato, and the brewery claims that it is matured for between 12 and 18 months before emerging with an alcohol content of more than 8 percent by weight; 10 by volume. It is a dark, fruity beer, with a low carbonation.

Although the brewery recommends Feuerfest as an apéritif, both its name and prune-brandy palate seem more suited to accompany deserts such as *crêpes Suzette*. So does its bottle, with wax seal and limited-edition number. The Schäffbräu brewery is located south of Nürnberg, in the Altmühltal Natural Park at Treuchtlingen.

Schierlinger Roggen

"The first rye beer for 500 years", said the advertizing, discounting the Finnish speciality Sahti. The local brewery in Schierling was a subsidiary of the aristocratic Thurn und Taxis, of Regensburg. The parent has now been acquired by Paulaner, raising a question over the future of its ranges. *Roggen* simply means rye. *Schierlinger Roggen* ☆☆☆ is a newish, top-fermenting speciality. It has a tawny, dark, colour; the dense head and fruity aroma of a wheat beer; a dry, grainy palate; and a dash of spicy, slightly bitter, rye character in the finish. A welcome innovation.

Schlenkerla Rauchbier

The most famous Bamberg Rauchbier is Schlenkerla, made for the tavern of that name by the Heller brewery. Like Scotch, Rauchbier gains its smoky palate at the malting stage. The method stems from the available means of kilning the malt. What the Scots had at hand was peat; the Franconians had beech-wood. As more modern methods of kilning evolved, a degree of tradition survived in both Scotland and Franconia, especially in the wooded countryside that surrounds the town of Bamberg.

Ricks of beech logs still burn in the tiny maltings (though it has both Saladin and drum systems) of the Heller brewery, dating from 1678. The traditional brewhouse, constructed from copper trimmed with brass, sparkles. In another room, a whirlpool makes a strange contrast with the open fermenters.

Ninety-five percent of the brewery's production is Rauchbier, usually at a Märzen gravity of just over 13.5 percent. It is made entirely from smoked malt, mashed by double decoction, hopped only once (the magic cone can hardly fight the smoke), bottom-fermented, matured for six or seven weeks without *kräusening* and not pasteurized. The resultant beer has a smoky aroma and a dryness the moment it hits the tongue, and a distinctive, full, smoky flavour that lingers in a long finish. Some people have to drink as many as five litre glasses before they begin to enjoy Rauchbier. It is, not only among beers but also among all alcoholic drinks, considered a classic. *Aecht Schlenkerla Rauchbier Märzen* ☆☆☆☆ is the definitive example, and in October, November and December there is a 19 Plato version called *Ur-Bock* ☆☆☆.

The brewery also has a Helles, but even that has a noticeable hint of smokiness about it.

Spezial
The very oldest Rauchbier producer is believed to be Bamberg's Brauerei Spezial and dates from 1536. It is an unassuming *Hausbrauerei* in a main shopping street. The Christian Merz family have their own tiny maltings and they only produce smoked beers.

Their everyday product, if it can be called that, is a Rauchbier simply named *Lager* ☆☆☆, at 12 Plato. It has a gently insistent smokiness and a treacle-toffee finish. A *Märzen* ☆☆☆▷☆☆☆☆ version of around 13.5 is even smokier in texture, bursting with flavour in the finish. There is also a November *Bock* ☆☆☆.

Tucher
One of the two large breweries that dominate the Nürnberg market is Tucher, the other being Patrizier. On their home ground, both have upset beer-lovers by swallowing smaller breweries, but Tucher's exports have brought a welcome taste of Germany to parts of the New World.

The Tucher brewery has over the years produced a dryish *Pilsener* ☆▷☆☆, a tasty malty dark beer called *Alt Franken Export Dunkel* ☆☆; a smooth double bock called *Bajuvator* ☆☆; and a somewhat mainstream *Hefe-Weizen* ☆.

Würzburger Hofbräu
Würzburg is in wine country and tried, in 1434, to banish its brewers forever. A couple of hundred years later it had acquired a Hofbräuhaus, which still produces some pleasant beers, malt-accented but well-balanced. Its *Pils* ☆▷☆☆ has a malty nose, a firm body and a hoppy finish. *Oktoberfest* ☆ is on the dark side and quite dry. There is also a *Maibock* ☆, a *Sympator* ☆ double bock and the fresh, plummy *Julius Echter Hefe-Weissbier* ☆☆. A *Schwarzbier* (not tasted) was launched recently.

BERLIN
"The champagne of beers" is a sobriquet too generously disposed. It is appropriate only to wheat brews, notably Berliner Weisse. Napoleon's troops during their Prussian campaign coined the description "the champagne of the north". Long after Napoleon was vanquished, the same "champagne" was a fitting toast in Imperial Berlin.

"Berlin white beer" has a very pale colour, an insistent sparkle, a fragrant fruitiness in the nose, a sharp, dry palate and a *frisson* of quenching, sour acidity in the finish. It is served in large bowl-shaped glasses, like beer-sized champagne saucers. To soften its acidity, it is often laced with a dash (a *Schuss*) of raspberry syrup, as though it were a *kir royal*. The green essence of the herb woodruff is also sometimes used for this purpose.

The term "white" has been used over the centuries throughout northern Europe to describe pale, sometimes cloudy, wheat beers. In the north of Germany it became the practice for such beers to contain a relatively low proportion of wheat and be characterized by a lactic fermentation. No doubt the lactic fermentation was originally accidental, but it is now a feature of the style.

There are vestiges of this type of brewing elsewhere in the north, notably in Bremen, but it is generally associated with Berlin. Because it is intended as a light, refreshing drink, Berliner Weisse is produced to a low alcohol content and with a very gentle hop rate. A typical gravity is around 7.5–8 Plato, with an alcohol content of just under 2.5 percent by weight; around 3 by volume. The beer may well have only four or five Units of Bitterness.

Between a quarter and a half of the mash comprises wheat, which has been malted. The rest is barley malt. A top-fermenting yeast is used, in a symbiosis with a lactic culture. In the production of the Schultheiss brewery's Berliner Weisse, there is also a blending with a wort that is three to six months old. The brew is then given between three and six months' maturation at warm temperatures, re-inoculated, and then allowed three to four weeks' bottle-conditioning at the brewery. Devotees of the style will keep the beer for a further one to two years in a cool, dark place (but not in a refrigerator). This ageing will bring out the extraordinary delicacy and complexity of the beer's fruitiness and fragrance.

Schultheiss Berliner Weisse ☆☆☆☆ is a beautifully complex example of the style. *Berliner Kindl Weisse* ☆☆☆, made by the biggest producer, scores points for assertiveness, but is lacking in complexity and length. Both major brewers give greater attention to their more conventional beers, which are mainstream in character.

The smaller Berliner Bürgerbräu does not have a Weissbier, but plans to develop one. Its products include a firm, smooth, malt, well-balanced *Pilsner* ☆▷☆☆; the export-style *Rotkehlchen* ☆☆ ("Robin Redbreast", after the style of glass in which it is served); the very dark, chocolatey, rummy, creamy, *Bernauer Schwarzbier* ☆☆☆; and a tawny, malty-fruity, whiskyish, *Dunkler Bock* ☆☆▷☆☆☆ (5.5; 6.8).

The Schwarzbier is named after the nearby town of Bernau, once a brewing centre noted for the style. This year-round beer is served on the second weekend in June at a pageant to mark the attack on Bernau during the wars with the Hussites of Bohemia. The attackers are said to have retreated drunk.

The range of beers is served at a lakeside tavern adjoining the brewery, in a former fishing community that is now a borough of Berlin; Bräustübl Berliner Bürgerbräu, 164 Müggel See Damm, Köpenick.

WHERE TO DRINK

Berliner Weisse is widely available, and is especially popular at the city's various lakes in summer. The Berlin Museum (14 Linden Str) has a Weissbierstube, with an interesting collection of glasses, the Kindl version of the beer, and traditional snacks. (It is currently closed for long-term renovations.) Another Weissbierstube at 51 Kinkel Strasse, in the historic centre of Spandau, also serves the Kindl version – in a range of beer cocktails, with fruits and liqueurs. "Haus der 100 Biere", at 45 Mommsen Strasse, Charlottenburg, is worth a visit. Opposite the Charlottenburg Palace, the Luisen-Bräu brewpub produces a soft, sweetish, unfiltered amber beer. On Berlin's bustling Kurfürstendamm (at no. 26), the Aschinger brewpub produces a range of lagers, including the odd seasonal Bock. In the Tegel district, a branch of Johann Albrecht (12 Karolinen Str) makes a malty beer called Kupfer ("Copper"). In the Nikolai quarter of the old East, Georgsbräu (4 Spreeufer) produces a Hell and Dunkel, and also features Korn schnapps.

THE EASTERN LANDS

There were few speciality beers in the former East Germany, though the firm-bodied, flowery, *Radeberger* ☆☆☆ and the dry, long, *Wernersgrüner* ☆☆☆ are both famous Pilseners. Radeberg is near Dresden; Wernersgrün near Zwickau, Saxony. A town north of Leipzig gives its name to *Ur-Krostitzer Pilsner* ☆☆▷☆☆☆, aromatic, firm, dry and crisp. This is not to be confused with a similar-sounding "black" beer. The smooth *Köstritzer Schwarzbier* ☆☆☆☆▷☆☆☆☆, with a flavour reminiscent of bitter chocolate, is a distinctive, very dark, lager, of conventional strength. It is made in the old spa town of Bad Köstritz, near Gera, in Thuringia.

While most of the old-established breweries in the former East are now owned by West German companies, and several others have closed, there is a new generation of brewpubs.

Between Brunswick and Magdeburg at Quedlinburg (14 Blasii Str), the Lüdde brewpub offers a Pils and a sweet, dark top-fermenting house speciality. In Thuringia, the city of Weimar has the Felsenkeller, offering a Hell, a Dunkel and seasonal specialities. In the same state, the town of Mühlhausen has the brewpub Zum Löwen (3 Korn Markt). The town is between Kassel and Erfurt.

Between Reichenbach and Auerbach, at Treuen, flavoursome Pils, Export and Bock are made at a family-owned brewery and drinks shop that survived the Communist period (Privat Brauerei Karl Blechschmidt, 33 Strasse der Jugend).

In Leipzig, Ohne Bedenken, with entrances at 5 Menckestrasse and 6 Poetenweg, is an 1899 "student tavern" and garden serving *Gose* ☆☆☆▷☆☆☆☆, a revived style in which wheat beer is spiced with coriander and salt. This remarkably drinkable brew is offered with local liqueurs and cheeses. The beer is specially made, at a brewery some miles away.

Leipzig also has the small Bauer brewery (5-7 Täubchen Weg), whose products include an outstanding *Schwarzbier* ☆☆☆, with firm, solid, licorice-toffee flavours; a taproom is planned.

The city's larger Reudnitz brewery has a rustic-style taproom at 13 Mühl Strasse, offering a soft, light-tasting *Pils* ☆☆. A seasonal *Bock* (not tasted) is also offered.

Goethe is said to have frequented the magnificent Auerbachs Keller, dating from the 1500s, beneath the 1913 arcade the Mädler Passage, in the centre of Leipzig. The beer is Krostitzer.

SCANDINAVIA

THE NORTHERNMOST LANDS of Europe evoke conflicting images: longboats full of Vikings inflaming themselves with some early brew; and modern nations using high prices and restrictive laws to curb drinking. Denmark was traditionally the least restrictive country, but the situation has eased in Sweden and Finland since they joined the European Union.

DENMARK
The first lager-brewing nation in northern Europe in 1845, when the founder of Carlsberg brought bottom-fermenting yeast to Copenhagen from Munich. Carlsberg was the brewery that "perfected" lager-brewing as a science: in 1883, its laboratory isolated the first pure-culture, single-cell yeast. Lager yeasts were subsequently classified as *carlbergensis*.

Carlsberg's lagers often have a sweetish note. Its subsidiary brand Tuborg has perhaps marginally drier brews. The company also owns Wiibroe, and has stakes in two smaller groups: one formed by Faxe, Ceres and Thor; the other by Albani and Slotsmøllen.

There are also a handful of independents. Most Danish lagers are very mild derivatives of the Pilsner style, though some Vienna types are made for Christmas, Easter or Whit. Several breweries make bottom-fermenting strong Porters or Stouts. Hvidtøl is a very sweet style, low in alcohol, brewed from barley but derived from the wheat-beers of the pre-lager era.

WHERE TO DRINK
Copenhagen has the brewpub Apollo (3 Vesterbro Gade, nr the Tivoli Gardens), making, light, tart, yeasty, unfiltered beers. A large selection of Danish beers can be found at Café Sommersko, 6 Kronprinse Kade) and at the shop Gammel Strand, on the

square of the same name (6 Naboløs). The city of Aarhus has a similar brewpub, St Clemens (10-12 Kannike Gade) and a beer shop, Chas E Vinhandel, 5 Ryse Gade. Beer bars in other cities include: Queen's Pub, 25 Vingårds Gade, Aalborg; and Biggo's Café, Grand Hotel, Jernbane Gade Odense.

Albani
Typical Danish beers, including *Giraf* ☆☆, a strong (15.4; 1063; 5.4; 6.8) golden lager – drier than its rival Carlsberg Elephant. This Odense brewery also has a malt-accented *Porter* ☆☆☆▷☆☆☆.

Carlsberg
Many versions and strengths of Carlsberg, are produced in various countries. The typical sweetness is not evident in the carbonic, astringent *Ice* ☆. It comes more to the fore in the butterscotch-tasting *Elephant* ☆☆ (16; 1064; 5.7; 7.1) and the more candyish *Special* ☆☆ (19; 1076; 7.1; 8.9). Denmark has a much more enjoyable, beautifully balanced, nutty, Vienna-style, Easter brew, *Påske Bryg 1847* ☆☆☆ (17.4; 1069; 6.2; 7.8). A similar brew is produced for Christmas. *Gamle Carlsberg/Special Dark* ☆☆ is a Munich-style lager. *Gammel Porter/Imperial Stout* ☆☆☆ (19; 1076; 6.1; 7.5) has a splendid "burnt toffee" palate.

Ceres
Celebrating the god of cereal grains. This brewery, in Aarhus, makes a *Dortmunder* ☆☆, strong (6.2; 7.7) and fruity for the style. From the group's Thor brewery, *Buur* ☆☆ (an old Danish word for "beer") is similar, perhaps sweeter. *Bering Bryg* ☆☆▷☆☆☆ is another strong lager, blended with lemon, rum and the brewery's spicy-tasting (peppery?) *Stowt* ☆☆▷☆☆☆ (rendered in a less phonetic spelling in export markets).

Faxe
In the town of Fakse. This brewery's beers are less interesting than they were. *Faxe Premium* ☆▷☆☆ is malty and dryish. Other products include a slightly syrupy *Bock* ☆☆.

FINLAND
The Finns' national epic says more about the birth of beer than the creation of the world. There is now a renaissance of beer, including the strong rye-and-juniper "Sahti". This is now produced commercially, though it is more typically brewed at home, sometimes in the sauna.

WHERE TO DRINK
Helsinki's Esplanade has "The Chapel" (in Finnish, "Kappeli"), where Sibelius once drank; now, it is a brewpub, owned by Sine-brychoff. Early brews have included a hoppy golden lager, a malty dark one and a Weizenbier (1 Etelä Esplanadi). Helsinki also has beer bars Vanha Ylioppilastalo, 3 Mannerheimte (in the former students' union building); William K, 3 Annan Katu; and Punavuoren Avhen, 12 Punavuoren Katu (the last for Belgian beer). The city of Tampere has German-style beers at a brewpub in

a former textile mill (Plevna, in the Finlayson complex, 9 Kuninkaan Katu). Turku has a somewhat eccentric brewpub in a former pharmacy (Uusi Apteeki, 1 Kasken Katu) and a beer bar nearby in The Old Bank (identified in English), 3 Aura Katu.

Hartwall
Biggest brewer in Finland, with links to Pripps, of Sweden, and Ringnes, of Norway. Produces the light, hay-ish, *Lapin Kulta* ☆ (Lapp Gold).

Koff
Second national brewer, abbreviating its brand-name from Sinebrychoff. Founded in 1819 by a Russian; now has links with Carlsberg. Pioneered Vienna-style Christmas beers with its malty *Jouluolut* ☆☆☆▷☆☆. Also known for its oily, roasty, lightly fruity, *Koff Porter* ☆☆☆▷☆☆☆☆.

Lammin
Sahti brewer, pioneer of commercial prouduction, in Lammi, about 60 miles northeast of Helsinki. Produces the minty, junipery, nutty, *Lammin Sahti* ☆☆☆▷☆☆☆☆. Has its own pub, called Sahtihaarikka, on highway 12, near Hämeenlina.

Olvi
Third national brewer, in forested country at Iisalmi, in central Finland. Beers include a toffeeish Märzen called *Vaakuna* ☆☆ ▷☆☆☆. Olvi also ferments brews at its own beer-hall in the town.

Palvasalmi Real Ale
British-style ales, sometimes available cask-conditioned. Made by sisters at Saarijärvi (tap-room: 1 Koulutie), near Jyväskylä, in central Finland. Products include a hoppy *Bitter* ☆☆☆ and *Valte* ☆☆☆, a rummy Old Ale.

PUP
In Nokia, a town that gave its name to a make of mobile phone. This lakeside micro, with its own restaurant, produces a lightly chocolatey, unfiltered lager, *Kellari* ☆☆▷☆☆☆. The acronym PUP derives from the name of the region.

NORWAY
In the matter of beer, the most expensive, and restrictive, of the main Scandinavian nations. The national brewer Ringnes has acquired many regionals. Most breweries have similar ranges, including Pilsner types, dark lagers and often a Vienna type for Christmas. The best of their beers are characteristically crisp and clean. Norway has a beer purity law similar to that of Germany.

WHERE TO DRINK
The Oslo Mikro Bryggeri (6 Bogstad Veien) is a brewpub with a linked local brewery (*see* entry). The Studenten Café (45 Karl Johansgt) is a German-accented brewpub. The oddly-named Lorry (12 Park Veien) is a corner café, lined with photographs and cartoons, offering a large selection of Scandinavian beers.

Aass

Embarrassingly named (at least to English-speakers), family-owned regional in Drammen, near Oslo. Aass actually means "summit". Beers include a deliciously nutty, Vienna-style *Jule Øl* ☆☆☆ (translates as Christmas beer) and their splendidly creamy *Bokk* ☆☆▷☆☆☆.

Akershus

Micro near Oslo. Beers include a crisp, orangey-tasting, filtered *Krystall Weissbier* ☆☆▷☆☆☆; a *Pale Ale* ☆☆☆ with a superbly hoppy, cleansing, finish; and a complex, dry, *Irish Stout* ☆☆▷☆☆☆.

Hansa

Bergen company making the hoppy *Ludwig Pils* ☆☆, and operating for visitors a traditional farmhouse brewery that makes a strong (7.2; 9.0) juniper beer in the rustic tradition of western Norway.

Mack

Seagulls' eggs are consumed in May with the grassy-malty *Mack Øl* ☆☆ from the world's most northerly brewery, in Tromsø. The English-speaker may think the stronger (5.2; 6,3) *Gull* ☆☆ more appropriate, but that name means "Gold". Other products include a chocolatey *Bayer* ☆☆▷☆☆☆ and a toasty *Bok* ☆☆▷☆☆☆.

Oslo Mikro

Pub (*see* Where to Drink) producing flavoursome ales and stouts, and small free-standing brewery making a malt-accented *Pils* ☆☆; the smooth, firm, toasty *Steamer* ☆☆▷☆☆☆, with Californian ambitions; a grainy, coffeeish, *Porter* ☆☆▷☆☆☆.

Ringnes

National brewer, with conventional range. *Ringnes Pilsener* ☆▷☆☆☆ is firm and smooth, with a pleasantly resiny hop dryness. *Ringnes Gold* ☆▷☆☆, a stronger lager (5.4; 6.8) has a cookie-like malt character, with a balancing, leafy, hoppy dryness. There is also a toffeeish *Jule Øl* ☆☆.

SWEDEN

Slightly less expensive, monopolistic, and restrictive than it once was – Sweden is seeing a minor revival of Gotlandsdrika, the junipery smoked beer of the island whose name it bears.

WHERE TO DRINK

In Stockholm, a harbourside brewpub, Gamla Stans Bryggeri (2 Tullhus, Skeppsbrokajen) produces a fresh-tasting, Saaz-accented, golden lager. Akkurat (18 Horns Gatan) is an excellent beer-pub, with cask-conditioned ales.

Ahlafors

In the village of the same name (but without the "h"), north of Gothenburg. Prize-winning homebrewer commercially producing the dry Pilsner *Ahlafors Ljusa* ☆☆.

Falcon
Major brewer, in Falkenberg. Owned by Carlsberg and Sine-brychoff. Notable for its chocolatey, vintage-dated, winter beer *Gammel Brygd* ☆☆▷☆☆☆.

Gellivare
Revived brewery, northernmost in Sweden, at Gällivere. Its *Stark* ☆☆ ("Strong") lager (4.25; 5.3) is clean and soft.

Gotlands Bryggeri
In a former church, in an historic corner of the island capital Visby. Its *Wisby Klosteröl* ☆☆☆ ("Cloister Beer") is an unfiltered, top-fermenting, beer, containing some wheat. It balances peachy fruitiness and hints of honey. Owned by Spendrup's.

Kungsholmens Kvarters
New micro, in Stockholm. Early brews included the malt-accented, complex, *Lundgrens Lager* ☆☆ and the impresively dry *Blitz Bitter* ☆☆▷☆☆☆.

Nordsjö
A husband wife run this micro on a farm at Motala, near Linköping. *Östgota Ört Öl* ☆☆☆ is a dry, lemony, herb beer. *Blåbärs* ☆☆☆ is a beautifully rounded blueberry beer.

Pripps
Biggest national brewer, owned by Ringnes. Most notable product is the creamy, licorice-tasting, fruity, dry, *Carnegie Porter* ☆☆☆▷☆☆☆. The dryish, grainy, *Extra Strong* ☆☆ (5.8; 7.2) is less candyish than some potent northern lagers.

Sofiero
Micro in the far South, at Laholm. Products include the ginger-spiced *Mårten Trotzig's Öl* ☆☆, chewy and orangey.

Spendrups
National brewer. *Spendrups Premium* ☆☆ is firm-bodied, with a malty start and a refreshingly hoppy finish. *Old Gold* ☆☆▷☆☆☆ is hoppier and very appetizing.

Vivungs
Commercial brewer of a syrupy, minty, flowery (violets?) *Gotlandsdricka* ☆☆☆, on the island at Vange.

Zeunerts
Brewery acquired and closed by Spendrup's and reopened by its staff. Products include a vanilla-ish *Export* ☆☆ (4.5; 5.6) and a caramel-ish *Alt* ☆▷☆☆☆. At Sollefteå, in the north.

THE NETHERLANDS

THE NETHERLANDS IS THE HOMELAND of international names like Heineken, Amstel, Oranjeboom and Grolsch, all known for relatively light interpretations of the Pilsener style – but in recent years the country has begun to develop a selection of more colourful beers. All of the national brewers have launched speciality products in their home market, but they have done so in response to the interest created by beers from the smaller independents, micros and brewpubs. In all, the country has 30-odd breweries.

While the Protestant north traditionally leavened abstinence with jenever gin, and trading cities like Amsterdam and Rotterdam have a history of brewing in volume for export, the Catholic provinces of North Brabant and Limburg culturally have much in common with neighbouring Belgium to the south – including its tradition of small breweries. This is especially true around the Limburg city of Maastricht. (For the visitor, geographical names can be confusing. There are also adjoining provinces called Brabant and Limburg in Belgium, and there is a city of Limburg in Germany.)

For many years, Dutch breweries were inclined to offer only an Oud Bruin (a sweetened dark lager, with low alcohol content, at about 9.0 Plato; 1036; 2–3 percent by weight; 2.5–3.5 by volume); a Pilsener (in the Netherlands, this term indicates the classic gravity of 11–12; 1044–48; around 4.0; 5.0); perhaps a "Dortmunder" (usually stronger than its German inspiration); and a seasonal Bock (15.6–17.0; 1062–68; 5.0–5.5; 6.25–7.0), sometimes spelled without the "c".

An annual festival of Bo(c)k beers, usually held in Amsterdam in October or November, is organized by the consumerist organization PINT (PO Box 3757, Amsterdam 1001 AN; fax 040–245 6018).

Many of the newer beers are more Belgian in inspiration. Several score bonus stars for assertiveness and individuality, but only a handful rate highly for consistency or keeping-quality.

WHERE TO DRINK
(Cities listed from north to south)

Alkmaar In the centre of this tourist town, famous for its cheese market, is a beer museum, with a bar, called De Boom (1 Houttil), which attempts to serve every beer in the Netherlands. Opens Tuesday–Saturday, and Sunday afternoons in summer.

Amsterdam The Dutch pioneered speciality beer bars, and run them very well. One of the best, not to be missed by any visitor, even though it is tricky to find, is In De Wildeman, 5 Nieuwe Zijds Kolk and Kolksteeg, off the shopping street Nieuwendijk, in the city centre. Interesting guest beers, and a good selection, in a former gin tasting-room. Opens at noon; closed on Sundays.

As a member of the Alliance of Beer Tappers, this establishment makes available a pocket-sized brochure listing about 30 others elsewhere in the Netherlands.

Amsterdam has several speciality beer shops. The most convenient, and highly recommended, is De Bierkoning, 125 Paleis Straat, near the royal palace. See also entries for brewpubs 't IJ and Maximiliaan.

Utrecht Jan Primus, 27 Jan van Scorel Straat, is a pioneering speciality beer bar. Opens 3.00 pm, closed Sundays. Café Belgie, 196 Oude Gracht, has 20 taps, the most in any café in the Netherlands, and offers *cuisine à la bière*.

Leiden De Wijnrank, 11 Turfmarkt, is a wine merchant with a fine beer selection.

The Hague Den Paas, 16a Dunne Bierkade, is a beer café in the old town. Opens 3.30 pm. De Wijn en Bier Boetiek, 803 Leyweg, just to the southwest of the centre, is a shop highlighting small Dutch brewers, and also offering malt whiskies.

Rotterdam Cambrinus, 4 Blaak (near metro station of same name) does some cooking with beer. Opens noon weekdays, and 2.00 pm weekends. Locus Publicus, 364 Oostzeedijk (Oostplein metro), is a well-established beer café. Opens 5.00 pm daily, 9.00 pm Sundays.

Breda De Beyerd, 26 Bosch Straat, is a pioneering beer café.

THE BREWERIES

A note on brewery names: Where breweries are named after towns, grammar may require a final "e", or a longer ending, on the company's name, but perhaps not on the beer itself, ie Grolsche is the brewery name, but the beer is called Grolsch.

Alfa

Small, old-established (1870), Limburg brewery making exclusively all-malt beers, smooth and well-balanced, with German and Czech hops. Pre-dated the speciality beer boom with its sweetish, malty, *Super-Dortmunder* ✩✩✩, the strongest example of the style (16–16.5; 1064-66; 5.5; 7.0). The brewery is at Schinnen, north of Maastricht.

Arcense Stoom ("Steam")

After a lively period as a revived independent, and very much a pioneer of speciality beers in the Netherlands, the Arcener brewery has recently had two changes of ownership and is now controlled by Interbrew, of Belgium.

There has been an Arcener Steam, reminiscent of a Kölsch, but the current emphasis seems to be on a dry, faintly salty, *Pils* ✩▷✩✩, with a touch of wheat. In a varying portfolio, the most interesting beer has been *Arcener Grand Prestige* ✩✩✩, arguably an Old Ale, but described as a barley wine. It would be sad if this strong (8.0, 10.0), rich, dark brown, smoothly fruity brew fell by the wayside. The brewery is situated at Arcen, north of Venlo in the Limburg province.

Bavaria

Family-owned, but sizable, brewery that caters primarily to the supermarket and own-label trade. The brewery is in Lieshout, North Brabant. The name probably dates from the days when the term "Bavarian" suggested lager beer. Has been known for light, sweetish, mainstream, beers but recently launched a wheat Bock (not tasted).

Brand's

Oldest brewery in the Netherlands, perhaps dating from the 1300s, known as Brand's since 1871, and still protective of its individuality, despite a takeover by Heineken in 1989. Its all-malt regular *Pils* ✩✩ has a touch of very fresh bread on the nose, a hint of grassiness in the palate, then perfumy and dry hop notes. The super-premium *Brand UP* ("Urtyp Pilsener") ✩✩▷✩✩✩

(12.5; 1050; a little over 4.0; 5.0) has become slightly more malty and less hoppy in recent years, but is still beautifully balanced and elegant, with a long finish. It has 36 Units of Bitterness. *Imperator* ☆☆☆ is a soft, clean, amber-coloured, year-round Bock (16.4; 1066; 5.2; 6.5), notable for its complexity of aromatic maltiness. *Dubbelbock* ☆☆☆ is a stronger (18.4; 1074; 6.0w; 7.5v), ruby-coloured, early winter Bock, with a great depth of aromatic, oily, buttery, fruity maltiness. *Sylvester* ☆☆☆, intended for midwinter, is a top-fermenting strong ale (18-18.5; 1072-4; 6.4; 8.0), with a deep bronze colour and a sophisticated palate, fruity, sometimes oaky; an *eau-de-vie* among beers. In spring of 1994, Brand's launched a golden-to-bronze, top-fermenting *Meibock* ☆☆☆ (17; 1068; around 5.6; 7.0), with a creamy, spicy nose; a touch of Seville orange in the palate; and a suggestion of clovey yeastiness in the finish. The brewery is in Wijlre, just to the east of Maastricht.

Breda

The old Three Horseshoes brewery (founded in 1538), in the historic north Brabant town of Breda, and the Oranjeboom ("Orange Tree") brewery, of Rotterdam, were for years both owned by Allied Breweries, of Britain. Today, only Breda operates, and it is now owned by Interbrew of Belgium. It has in recent years produced a wide range of brands, from the light *Royal Dutch Posthorn* ☆ to the firmer-bodied *Oranjeboom Pilsener* ☆. Among its newer products is *Het Elfde Gebod* ☆☆▷☆☆☆ ("The Eleventh Commandment"), a strong (5.6; 7.0) top-fermenting ale, with a full gold colour, and a creamy, malty aroma and palate, drying towards a fruity, perfumy, banana-like finish.

Budelse

Very small, old-established (1870), brewery in North Brabant, at Budel, near the Belgian border. The Kölsch-like *Parel* ☆☆▷☆☆☆ (14; 1056; 4.8; 6.0) and *Budels Alt* ☆☆▷☆☆☆ (13.5; 1054; 4.4; 5.5) are both slightly stronger than their styles would suggest. The abbey-style *Capucijn* ☆☆▷☆☆☆ (16; 1064; 5.2; 6.5) is malty, fruity, spicy and smoky, with hints of applewood. All the beers from this brewery are notably smooth.

St Christoffel

Noted for a world-class, assertively dry, Pilsener-style beer, originally called, quite simply, *Christoffel* ☆☆☆▷☆☆☆☆, now additionally described as Blond (with the sub-title Dubbel Hop). A newer beer, designated "Double Malt" (4.8; 6.0), is called *Robertus* ☆☆▷☆☆☆. This name is a personification of Robijn, the Dutch description for the reddish-brown colour of the beer. It has an aromatic malt character, with a creamy palate, and a fairly dry finish. Both beers are all-malt and are unfiltered and unpasteurized. St Christoffel is a microbrewery, established in the 1980s by Leon Brand, a member of the Limburg brewing family. The brewery is located in Roermond, a former coal-mining town, whose patron saint is Christoffel.

Dommelsche

Owned by the Belgian group Interbrew (Artois/Jupiler). Dommelsche's products include *Dominator* ☆▷☆☆☆, a strongish

(4.8; 6.0) pale lager, dry and lightly fruity. The brewery is in North Brabant, at Dommelen, not far from the Belgian border.

Drie Horne

Commercial home-brewery, founded in 1991, in Kaatsheuvel, north of Breda. Products include bronze *Trippelaer* ☆☆ (6.8; 8.5), bronze in colour, with a sweet, spicy, aromatic, faintly medicinal palate.

Drie Kruizen

"Three crosses". Micro at Westmaas, in the Rhine-Schelde delta area. Early products included a thinnish, dry *Koornbeurs Wit* ☆▷☆☆ ("Cornmarket white").

Drie Ringen

Fruity, sweetish, ales from a micro which opened in 1989 at Amersfoort, in Utrecht. Recent products include a slightly treacly, spicy, minty *Amersfoorts Wit* ☆☆, made with a German Weizen yeast; a pinkish-amber *Meibock* ☆ (5.2, 6.5), with an intense, bittersweet, marmalade taste; and a sugary-tasting *Tripel* ☆▷☆☆ (6.0, 7.5), with a hint of tropical fruits.

Grolsche

Not only the light, fluffy, *Pils (Premium Lager)* ☆☆, with a clean maltiness and a distinctive yeast character, but also a very sweet *Bok* ☆▷☆☆ in the typically Dutch dark-brown style; a much drier, amber, *Mei Bok* ☆☆ (16; 1064; a little over 4.8; 6.0); and *Grolsch Amber* ☆☆▷☆☆☆, which uses the English spelling for something similar to an Altbier with a lightly malty start and a heartily hoppy finish. In recent years, there have been seasonal beers and commemorative specials. All of the beers by Grolsche are unpasteurized.

This internationally known brewery was, surprisingly, until recent decades a small company based in the eastern towns of Enschede, in Overijssel, and Groenlo (formerly called Grolle), in Gelderland.

Gulpener

Old-established (1825), independent brewery at Gulpen, south-east of Maastricht. Locals often ask for a Pils with a "dash" (in Dutch, a *scheut*; in the Limburg dialect, a *sjoes*, pronounced almost the same as the German *Schuss*). Gulpener bottles a ready-mixed version of Pils and Oud Bruin, called *Sjoes* ☆▷☆☆, which emerges lightly malty, smooth and dryish. Other products include an aromatically malty strong *Dort* ☆☆ (15.5; 1062; 5.2; 6.5), the name abbreviated from the German city. They have also been experimenting with a perfumy version of a Belgian-style "white" beer, called *Korenwolf* ("Hamster").

In the early 1980s, Gulpener revived a regional style of the past, with its *Mestreechs Aajt* ☆☆☆. This is a faintly herbal-tasting (gentian?) sour-and-sweet summer brew, of refreshingly low strength (2.8, 3.5), claret in colour, from a blend of two beers. One of the beers has a wild yeast fermentation and is aged for at least a year in unlined wood, specifically for this, Gulpener installed tuns. This speciality is produced at a separate brewpub, called De Zwarte Ruiter (The Black Knight), at 4 Markt, Gulpen (closed Mondays). Local dishes are served as snacks.

Heineken

The most international of brewers, from a maritime country where export has always been a way of life. Half of the company's Dutch output is sent overseas, much of it to the USA, and its beers are also made by subsidiaries, associates or licensees in more than 90 breweries elsewhere. In the early 1990s, Heineken reverted to all-malt beers, abandoning the corn used by many major brewers. Despite this, *Heineken* ☆▷☆☆ itself (11.4; 1045–6; 4.0; 5.0, or fractionally less) remains lighter than most German lager beers, for example, but fuller-bodied than many international brands. The beer has a touch of grassiness; a smooth, firm body; a light hop character; and spritzy finish. A version lower in alcohol is made in the British Isles and some Nordic countries.

Heineken acquired Amstel in the 1960s, and later closed that brewery. In the Netherlands, *Amstel Bier* ☆▷☆☆ (4.0; 5.0) is fractionally fuller in colour, lighter in aroma, firmer in body, with more, slightly perfumy, hop flavours. Various overseas versions seem lighter and sharper. *Amstel 1870* ☆▷☆☆ is hoppier. *Amstel Gold* ☆ (5.6; 7.0) has some alcohol flavours. *Herfst Bock* ☆☆ (5.6, 7.0), with a toffeeish malt character, and *Heineken Tarwebok* ☆☆☆, at the same strength but containing 17 percent wheat, are seasonal specialities for October and November. Tarwebok is silky, chocolatey, fruity and complex.

The launch of a strong (1064; 16; 5.2; 6.5), and surprisingly hoppy-tasting, Vienna-style lager called *1994* ☆☆☆ in that year signalled a regular special for December–January. At a similar strength, a creamy but slightly tart top-fermenting ale called *Kylian* ☆☆▷☆☆☆ is based on the George Killian "Irish Red" made at Heineken's subsidiary brewery near Lille, France. The bottom-fermenting *Van Vollenhoven's Stout* ☆☆ (16.2; 1065; 4.8; 6.0) is creamy but lacks complexity. Heineken is headquartered in Amsterdam, and has breweries at Zoeterwoude, South Holland, and 's Hertogenbosch, North Brabant.

't IJ

Under a windmill in Amsterdam (to the east of the Central Station, at Funenkade), in what was once a public bath-house, songwriter Kaspar Peterson established this brewpub in 1984/5. The bar opens Wednesday–Sunday, 3.00–8.00 pm, but the beers can be found elsewhere. The first beers were a dryish, malty-fruity, abbey-style Double called *Natte* ☆☆ (meaning "wet") at 4.8; 6.0, and a spicy, firm, pale Triple, entitled *Zatte* ☆☆▷☆☆☆ ("drunk") at 6.4; 8.0.

These were followed by two yet-stronger counterparts, the pale *Columbus* ☆☆☆ (7.2, 9.0), with lots of malt and hop, and the dark, surprisingly dry *Struis* ☆☆☆ (8.0; 10.0), the name of which means ostrich. The brewery's symbol is an ostrich with an egg. The Dutch word for "egg" sounds like IJ, the name of the waterway on which Amsterdam harbour stands.

Jopen

Haarlem brewers producing spiced specialities. A four-grain *Bok* ☆☆▷☆☆☆ (4.4; 5.5) had lovely tangarine, anis and smoke notes; a *Hoppenbier* ☆☆☆ (5,2; 6.5) had lemon, sherbety, perfumy flavours. *Koyt* ☆☆☆ (6.8; 8.5) made with oats, was iron-ish, aromatic and arousing to the senses.

't Kuipertje
Tiny micro in Heukelum, Gelderland. Beers variable.

De Kroon
"The Crown". Very small independent, at Oirschot, North Brabant. Specialities include *Egelantier* ☆☆, a bronze, Vienna-style, lager of conventional gravity but full body (4.0; 5.0). Also has an organic Pils, and organizes a May Bock festival.

De Leeuw
"The Lion". Independent at Valkenburg, Limburg. The brewery's specialities include a soft-tasting, all-malt, super-premium Pils called *Jubileeuw* ☆☆ (4.0; 5.0). Also a sweetish *Valkenburgse Wit* ☆☆, with a hint of pineapple.

Lindeboom
"The Linden Tree". Small independent brewery in Neer, north of Roermond, Limburg. Specialities include a bronze, malty, Vienna-style lager called *Gouverneur* ☆☆▷☆☆☆ (4.0; 5.0) and a well-regarded Bock (not tasted).

Maasland
Micro established in 1989, in the North Brabant town of Oss, between s'Hertogenbosch and Nijmegen. Beers include *d'n Schele Os* ☆☆▷☆☆☆ ("the cross-eyed ox"), which contains rye, and is spiced. This Triple (6.0; 7.5) has a fruity, sherbety, perfumy, aroma; malty sweetness, and some tart, spicy, dryness in the finish. .

Maximiliaan
Named after the Austrian Emperor who gave Amsterdam the right to display the royal crown. German-accented beers from a brewpub in a former convent behind the red-light district in Amsterdam (6–8 Kloveniersburgwal).

A Kölsch-type named *Bethanien* ☆☆, after the convent, is light, clean and dry, with a touch of fruit and a very good hop bitterness. A Triple called *Casper's Max* ☆☆▷☆☆☆ (6.0; 7.5) is bronze-coloured and chewy in texture, with lots of malt and hop. *Klooster* ☆▷☆☆☆ is similar, but darker, with a toffeeish malt note. The Maximiliaan brewery also offers seasonal specials and good examples of *cuisine à la bière*. The creamy, toasty *X Porter* ☆☆☆ has been produced for the North Holland Alternative Brewers' Foundation.

Onder de Linden
Strong ales and varying specialities at a micro in Wageningen, Gelderland, in the east of The Netherlands.

Oudaen
Utrecht brewpub (99 Oudegracht). Produces a "white" beer, in cloudy and filtered forms, and seasonal specialities (not tasted).

De Ridder
Pretty brewery, dating from 1852, in the heart of old Maastricht. De Ridder means "The Knight". Acquired by Heineken in 1982, and now specializing in an unpasteurized wheat beer, *Wieckse Witte* ☆☆☆, with a slightly grainy-mealy palate and a very late

coriander finish. The brewery also has a clean-tasting strong Dortmunder called *Maltezer* ☆☆ (16; 1064; 5.2; 6.5). As its name suggests, this has a very creamy malt character.

Schaapskooi Trappist

The only abbey brewery in the Netherlands is called Schaapskooi ("Sheep's Pen"). It was established in 1885/6 to fund construction of the monastery itself, at a place called Koningshoeven ("King's Gardens"), near the city of Tilburg, North Brabant. An experimental Blond Trappist *Koningshoeven* ☆☆ (4.4; 5.5), was refreshing, with a dry maltiness. The older-established *La Trappe Dubbel* ☆☆☆▷☆☆☆ (5.2; 6.5) has a ruby colour and in recent years a drier, spicier (coriander?) flavour; very aromatic. *La Trappe Tripel* ☆☆▷☆☆☆ (6.4; 8.0) has a pale orange colour but similar flavours – perhaps livelier, gingery and fruity. The Dubbel has also appeared in much the same form under the Koningshoeven and Tilburg labels. The Tripel seems spicier in the La Trappe version; maltier under the Koningshoeven label; and hoppier and paler in its Tilburg form. *La Trappe Quadrupel* ☆☆☆, also introduced in 1992, has an orangey-red colour; a very fruity aroma; a distinctively smooth, syrupy body; and lots of flavour development, towards a big, spicy (coriander again?) finish (21–22; 1084–8; 8.5; 10.0).

Stadsbrouwerij

Husband and wife Herm and Rian Hegger, founders of the now-defunct Raaf micro, which was famous for its flavourful Witbier, now have a brewpub in the eastern city of Nijmegen at, 2 Steen Straat (beers not tasted).

Us Heit

The name, meaning "Our Father", is a reference to a Frisian viceroy and hero. The brewery was founded in a cowshed in the Friesland village of Uitwellingerga, near Sneek, by Limburger Aart van der Linde, in 1985. He began with *Buorren* ☆☆▷☆☆☆ (4.8, 6.0), a bronze-red ale, with a dry fruitiness verging on an intentional sourness. A wide range of beers, often with this house character, has been produced since.

De Zon

"The sun". Micro established in 1992/3 in Schaijk, near Oss, North Brabant. Early products included a fruity, sweet and sour Triple called *Brabants Glorie* ☆☆. Brewing intermittent.

BELGIUM

BELGIUM HAS LONG ENJOYED the world's most individualistic beers but, even in the country itself, sales of speciality brews are increasing. Elsewhere in the world, helped by the introduction of beer-oriented Belgian restaurants (in Paris, London, Montreal, New York, Philadelphia, Washington…), the appreciation of these distinctive brews is spreading fast.

Belgium's beer tradition is no Jean-come-lately. Its cidery, winey, spontaneously fermenting *lambic* family predate the pitching of yeast by brewers and its cherry *kriek*, strawberry *framboise* and spiced "white" brews pre-date the acceptance of the hop as the universal seasoning in beer. Other countries have monastery breweries but only in Belgium have the brothers have evolved their own collective style of beers. The country's five Trappist breweries, and their many secular imitators, have developed a distinct family of brews: strong, top-fermenting and bottle-matured. They often have a heavy sediment and a fruity palate, sometimes evincing hints of chocolate. Within these characteristics, however, there are clear differences between the brews, and a couple of subcategories. Some Belgian specialities are hard to categorize, although most are top-fermenting and many are bottle-matured. No country has a more diverse range even within the bottle-matured group – the Belgians are keen on this means of conditioning and sometimes refer to it as their *méthode champenoise*.

In a Belgian café, the list of beers will identify at least one member of the *lambic* family (occasionally a sweet *faro*, often a sparkling *gueuze*); perhaps a honeyish "white" beer (*witbier* or *bière blanche*) from the village or a brown (*bruin*) from the town of Oudenaarde; a local *spéciale*; and a strong, bottle-conditioned monastery (*abdij* or *abbaye*) brew. There may also be a Belgian ale, as well as local interpretations of English, Scottish and sometimes German styles. This is in an ordinary café; there will be a far greater categorization in a café that makes a feature of speciality beers, listing them by the hundred. After decades of decline when they were regarded as "old-fashioned", speciality beers began to enjoy a revival in the late 1970s. They are a joy to the visiting beer-lover, although it is necessary to know what to order. A request simply for "a beer" is likely to be met by a mass-market Pilsener.

With the revival of interest in speciality beers within Belgium, more of them have also entered export markets. They present a bewildering choice. As always, the selection of beers reflects both history and geography. The influence of the brewing customs of the surrounding nations has been accepted with shrewd selectivity by the Belgians, yet they have also contrived to be conservative and inward-looking to the point that their principal regions maintain their own traditions. The country is divided not only into its Dutch-speaking north (Flanders) and French-speaking south (Wallonia) but also has a German-speaking corner in the east and a bilingual knot around the city of Brussels. Some styles of beer are perceived as belonging not to a region but to a province, river valley, town or village.

The Belgians like to talk about beer as their reply to Burgundy. They suggest that beer is to them what wine is to France. Cheese might be an even better comparison. The beers of Belgium, like the cheeses of France, are often idiosyncratic, cranky, artisanal. Some drinkers could never learn to enjoy one of the cloudy, sour specialities of the Senne Valley any more than they could acquire a taste for a smelly cheese. In both cases, the loss would be theirs. This is drink at its most sensuous. In its native gastronomy,

Belgium is a land of beer, seafood and – after dinner – the world's finest chocolate. It is a land of German portions and French culinary skills. Beer may be served, with some ceremony at a family meal, and might well have been used in the cooking. Other countries have the odd dish prepared with beer, but Belgium has hundreds. The Belgians even eat hop shoots, as a delicacy, in the brief season of their availability, served like asparagus.

Beer is also a central theme in Belgium's history and culture. St Arnold of Oudenaarde (or was it Oudenburg?) is remembered for having successfully beseeched God, in the 11th century, to provide more beer after an abbey brewery collapsed. He is the patron saint of Belgian brewers, some of whom display his statue by their kettles. (French-speakers can, if they prefer, remember another beery miracle, that of St Arnold at Metz.) The 13th-century Duke Jan the First of Brabant, Louvain and Antwerp has passed into legend as the King of Beer: "Jan Primus" has been corrupted into "Gambrinus", by which name he is remembered not only in Belgium but also in Germany, the Czech Republic and far beyond. Jan Primus is said to have been an honorary member of the Brewers' Guild, although their present gilded premises on Brussels' Grand' Place were not built until 1701. Today, the "Brewers' House" is the only building on the Grand' Place still to be used as the headquarters of a trade guild. Today's Confederation has about a hundred members, and that represents roughly the number of breweries in Belgium. The figure has been declining for some years, although recently a number of new micro-breweries have opened. Many Belgian breweries are family owned, which can lead to problems when there is no clear succession. But however much the number of breweries fluctuates, the tally of beers increases, with new specialities constantly being launched. At any one time, there are probably more than 800 beers on the market.

FLANDERS

Flemish painters like Bruegel and the aptly named Brouwer depicted the people of their homeland as enthusiastic beer-drinkers. It has been like that for a thousand years. As Emperor of Europe, Charlemagne took an interest in brewing, and perhaps he brought the news from Aix to Ghent. The nationalistic Flemings might, however, secretly resent their famous artists' depiction of beery excess. They take pride in being hard-working, and the Early and Late Flemish schools of painting were made possible by the prosperity of Flanders at different times as an exporter of beer as well as textiles, and as a commercial centre. Flanders emerged as a principal component of the new Belgium in 1830, reasserting itself in recent years through the trading prosperity of the River Scheldt – with beer exports once again on the upswing.

As a region, Flanders stretches from the Dutch side of the Scheldt to a slice of northern France. Politically, it comprises the Belgian provinces of West and East Flanders, Antwerp and Limburg.

West Flanders, with its 15th-century canalside capital Bruges, has traditionally been known for its sour, burgundy-coloured style of beer – the classic example is Rodenbach. The province is well served by small breweries and has two of the strongest beers in Belgium, from the revivalist Dolle Brouwers and the monastery brewery of Westvleteren. East Flanders, with the proud city of Ghent as its capital, is noted for slightly less sour brown ales, produced in or near the town of Oudenaarde, which has a cluster of small breweries to the east.

The province and city of Antwerp is noted for the beautifully made De Koninck beer (a copper ale). The province also has the monastery of Westmalle, which created the Triple style of abbey beer, and in the south, the strong, golden ale called Duvel, the potent, dark Gouden Carolus and the well-liked Maes Pils.

Limburg has a less gilded capital, the pretty little town of Hasselt, known for the production of *genever* gin. It is a thinly breweried province but has the distinctive Sezoens beer from the Martens brewery; and Cristal Alken, a well-respected Pilsener beer.

WHERE TO DRINK

There are several speciality beer cafés in Antwerp. With about 500 beers, the most famous among devotees is Kulminator, 32 Vleminckveld (opens 8.00 pm Monday; noon on other weekdays; 5.00 pm on Saturday; closed Sunday). Also highly regarded is Taverne Bierland, 28 Korte Nieuw Straat, (opens noon, closed Sunday), in the Old Town. A new brewpub t'Pakhuis, on Vlaamse Kaai, offers a strong ale called Bangalijke ("scary").

After Antwerp, the largest city in Flanders is Ghent, which has a popular and well-run specialist beer café called De Hopduvel ("the hop devil"), at 10 Rokerel Straat. De Hopduvel also features the growing number of Belgian cheeses.

The beautiful tourist city of Bruges has a justifiably famous beer café called 't Brugs Beertje, at 5 Kemel Straat, an alley near Simon Stevin Plein. Open 4.00 pm; closed Wednesday. A couple of doors away is the beer-and-gin bar 't Dreupel Huisje.

Bruges also has the Halve Maan brewpub, dating from 1856. The brewery is hidden in a cobbled yard next to the *beguinage*, at 26 Walplein. The house is a creamy, hoppy, golden ale called **Straffe Hendrik** ☆☆▷☆☆☆ ("Strong Henry").

Elsewhere in Flanders, the Limburg town of Hasselt has 't Hemelrijk, in the street of the same name, at no 11. About 10km from Hasselt, a brewpub called Helchteren has opened in the stables of a castle at Houthalen and serves a tasty golden ale.

Affligem

Benedictine monastery dating from 1074, associated with early hop-growing in Flanders and England. Its beers, now made in the nearby former De Smedt brewery, include a spicy, cinnamon-tasting, *Dubbel* ☆▷☆☆ and a peppery, fruity, *Tripel* ☆☆. Affligem is near Aalst, between Brussels and Ghent.

Bavik

In Bavikhove, W Flanders. Among many styles, produces the lemony *Petrus Tripel* ☆☆▷☆☆☆ in addition to its fresh, iron tasting *Oud Bruin* ☆☆▷☆☆☆ (more of a Flemish red, like Rodenbach).

Corsendonk

Once an Augustine Priory, now a conference centre, where cap tains of industry and heads of state can drink two abbey-style beers. The site is near Turnhout, but the *Monks' Dark* ☆▷☆☆☆ ("Pater Noster" in Belgium), a raisiny Dubbel, is brewed by the Bios/Van Steenberge brewery, at Ertvelde, E Flanders. The perfumy *Monk's Pale* ☆☆ ("Agnus Dei") is made by Du Bocq, in Wallonia.

Cristal Alken

The hoppiest of the principal Belgian Pilseners is *Cristal Alken* ☆☆▷☆☆☆. This well-made Pilsener with a notably pale colour, fresh, hoppy nose; very clean, crisp palate and a smooth dryness in the finish. It is hopped principally with blossoms, including Saaz for aroma, fermented at relatively cold temperatures, lagered for a respectable period and not pasteurized. Alken and its former rival Maes are now part-owned by Kronenbourg of France.

De Dolle Brouwers

"The Mad Brewers", they call themselves. It is a typically Flemish sardonic shrug on behalf of a group of enthusiasts who rescued from closure a village brewery near Diksmuide, not far from Ostend. As a weekend project, they renovated the brewery, which dates from the mid-19th century and is a classic of its type. (Tours welcome; ☎051-502781.) They specialize in strong, top-fermenting beers, bottle-matured. The house speciality is *Oerbier* ☆☆☆, very dark and smooth, with a sweetness that is offset by licorice tones (original gravity 1100; alcohol content 6 percent by weight; 7.5 by volume). There are also several seasonal products: the brassy-coloured, honey-primed *Boskeun* ☆☆☆, an Easter beer of about 8 percent by volume; the pale, dry-hopped *Arabier* ☆☆☆ for summer, with a similar alcohol content; and *Stille Nacht* ☆☆☆, a claret-coloured Christmas brew, with hints of apple in its aroma and palate, and an alcohol content of around 9 percent. The Ostend area also has a micro-brewery called 't Steedje, producing an ale and a Triple.

De Koninck

This is a classic. This perilously drinkable, copper-coloured, top-fermenting beer fits in stylistically somewhere between an English ale (a fruity "best bitter") and a smooth Düsseldorf *Altbier*. For all its complexity of character, it pursues an unassuming occupation as the local beer of Antwerp, from the city's only brewery. The company stayed with top-fermentation when other big-city breweries were switching to Pilseners. *De Koninck* ☆☆☆ is an all-malt beer of 12 Plato, brewed by direct flame in a cast-iron kettle. It is cold-conditioned and emerges with an alcohol content of a little over 4 percent by weight and 5 by volume. De Koninck has an excellent malt character, a yeasty fruitiness and a great deal of Saaz hoppiness, especially in its big finish. Its full palate is best experienced in the draught form, which is unpasteurized. Opposite the brewery, at the Pilgrim Café (8

Boomgardstraat), drinkers sometimes add a sprinkle of yeast to the beer. In the heart of Antwerp, the beer is available at the city's oldest café, Quinten Matsijs (17 Moriaanstraat) and at Den Engel (3 Grote Markt). A newer product is the richer, stronger, *Cuvée Antwerpen* (6.0;7.5).

Duvel

This means "Devil" and is the name of the world's most beguiling beer. Duvel is much imitated in Belgium by other beers with names implying wild behaviour. With its pale, golden sparkle, *Duvel* ☆☆☆☆ looks superficially like a Pilsener. Its palate is soft and seductive. Beneath its frothy head, behind its dense lacework, this all-malt, top-fermenting beer has the power (6.7 percent alcohol by weight; 8.2 by volume) to lead anyone into temptation. The pale colour is achieved with the help of the brewery's own maltings; Styrian and Saaz hops are used; a very distinctive yeast imparts a subtle fruitiness (reminiscent of Poire Williams); the cleanness and smoothness is enhanced by both cold and warm maturation; and, in the classic, sedimented, version, the *mousse* develops from bottle-conditioning. Duvel is customarily chilled as though it were an *alcool blanc*. It is produced by the Moortgat brewery in the village of Breendonk near Mechelen/Malines. Other Moortgat products include tasty, abbey-style beers under the *Maredsous* ☆☆ label, for the monastery of that name.

Gouden Boom

The "Golden Tree" brewery is best known for its wheat beer, the soft, aromatic, fruity (apples, honey?), dryish *Brugs Tarwebier* ☆☆☆ and its complex, perfumy, malty, warming *Brugse Tripel* ☆☆☆. The brewery also makes the lighter, fruitier (peaches in brandy?), *Steenbrugge Tripel* ☆☆☆. This is brewed for the abbey of Steenbrugge, successor to that at Oudenberg, which was the home of St Arnold, patron saint of Belgian brewing. The Gouden Boom brewery has had several names in the past 100 years, and the site may have housed a tavern as early as the 1500s. Gouden Boom's museum of local brewing is open from Thursday to Sunday during summer, or by appointment (☎050-330699. Fax 050-334644).

Gouden Carolus

This is the classic strong, dark ale of Belgium. Its name derives from a gold coin from the realm of the Holy Roman Emperor Charles V, who grew up in the Flemish City of Mechelen (better known by its French name, Malines) where this beer is brewed. *Gouden Carolus* ☆☆☆, has a deep amber-brown colour, a gentle, soothing character, a hint of orangey fruitiness in the finish and, from a gravity of 19 Plato, an alcohol content of 6 percent by weight; 7.5 by volume. Recent tastings have been more rooty, licorice-like and medicinal.

Huyghe

Old-established brewery in a suburb of Ghent that switched from lagers to specialities. Products include the fruity, slightly tannic, *Brasseurs de Gand* ☆☆☆, the sweet, sherbety, abbey-style beers under the name *St Idesbald* ☆☆, and wheat-based flavoured brews, lacking in complexity, in the *Floris* ☆☆ range.

Kwak Pauwel

The odd name derives from an antique Flemish speciality. This revival, a strong (9 percent by volume), amber-red, top-fermenting brew, is notable for its spicy aroma and palate. *Kwak Pauwel* ☆☆ is a hearty, warming brew. When it first appeared in Belgium, it won attention by being served in a "yard of ale" glass, of the type allegedly handed up to coachmen when they stopped for a restorative drink.

Liefmans

This classic product is now owned by Riva, of Dentergem, in West Flanders. The mashing and brewing are carried out there, with water treated to match that of its home town of Oudenaarde, a few miles away in East Flanders. The water is low in calcium but high in sodium bicarbonate. The wort is then transferred to the old brewery in Oudenaarde, for fermentation with the house's multi-strain "top" yeast, and maturation. The basic *Oud Bruin* ☆☆▷☆☆☆ ("Old Brown") has four to six weeks' warm conditioning. The classic *Goudenband* ☆☆☆▷☆☆☆☆ ("Gold Riband") is a blend of the basic beer with a slightly stronger version that has an additional six to eight months' maturation. The two beers are centrifuged, then primed, re-yeasted and given a further three months in the bottle before leaving the brewery. On the basis that a "sipping beer" should be strong, Riva has boosted Goudenband to 6.4; 8. It is thus richer than it was, but still with considerable fruity tartness. It will continue to develop, at a natural cellar temperature, for months, and perhaps years, becoming more complex, drier and tarter. The brewery's brown ale is also used as the base for a bittersweet *Kriek* ☆☆☆, a candyish but tart *Frambozen/Framboise* ☆☆ and the very spicy *Glühkriek* ☆☆☆▷☆☆☆☆, intended to be served hot.

Maes

A flowery "Riesling" bouquet imparts distinctiveness to *Maes Pils* ☆☆. This is a light, soft, dry Pilsener-style beer. The brewery is in the village of Waarloos, north of Mechelen. The company also produces two top-fermenting beers for the abbey of Grimbergen, a Flemish village near Brussels. *Grimbergen Double* ☆☆ is a dark, fruity beer, with a chocolatey palate; it has a gravity of 15.8 Plato and an alcohol content of 5.2 percent by weight; 6.5 by volume. *Grimbergen Tripel* ☆▷☆☆ is paler, fruity, but with a more winey character; it has a gravity of 19.6 Plato and an alcohol content of 7.2 by weight; 9 by volume. (*See also* Cuvée de L'Ermitage.)

Rodenbach

The unimaginative are apt to consider Rodenbach's beers undrinkable, yet they are the classics of the "sour" style of West Flanders. They gain their sourness, and their burgundy colour, in a number of ways. The sourness derives in part from the top-fermenting yeast, a blend of three strains that has been in the house for 150 years, and from cultures resident in wooden maturation tuns. The colour, too, originates partly from the use of reddish Vienna-style malts but also probably from the caramels and tannins extracted from the oak of the tuns. These vessels, made from Slavonian oak, from Poland, are uncoated. They make a remarkable sight, each tun standing vertically from floor to ceiling. The smallest contains 15,000 litres of maturing beer; the largest 60,000 litres. There are 300 in all, filling several halls, as though this were a winery or a brandy distillery. When the maturing beer has attained its typical palate, it is stabilized by flash pasteurization so does not mature in the bottle and is not intended for laying down.

The basic *Rodenbach* ☆☆☆▷☆☆☆☆ is a blend of "young" beer (matured five to six weeks) and "vintage" brews (matured 18 months to two years). The longer-matured beer is also bottled "straight" as *Rodenbach Grand Cru* ☆☆☆☆. The basic Rodenbach has an original gravity of 11.5–11.75 Plato, emerging with 3.7 percent alcohol by weight; 4.6 volume. The Grand Cru has an original gravity of 15, but an alcohol content of only around 4.1; 5.2. The gravity is heightened by the use of non-fermented sugars and the alcohol content is diminished because some of the fermentation is lactic. There is both a sharpness and a restorative quality about these beers: perfect after a game of tennis. The Grand Cru has a slightly bigger palate and a smoother texture. Even then, some Belgians add a touch of grenadine, as though making a red *kir*. The Rodenbach brewery is in Roeselare (in French Rouliers), the centre of an agricultural area.

Several breweries in West Flanders produce beers similar to those of Rodenbach, but none with quite such a distinctive character. Perhaps the best examples are Petrus, from Bavikhove; and Ouden Tripel, from Bockor, of Bellegem.

Roman

Chocolatey, dryish, brown ales of the region, from a well-run brewery near Oudenaarde. Also makes the fruity, spicy (pineapples, vanilla, mint?) *Ename* ☆▷☆☆☆ abbey beers.

St Louis

Using casks obtained in the traditional region of production, and containing resident wild yeasts, the Van Honsebrouck brewery, of Ingelmunster, West Flanders, has for almost 30 years made beer in the lambic style under the brand-name St Louis. The widely marketed examples were sweetened and rather bland. In 1993, the brewery launched *Gueuze Fond Tradition* ☆☆▷☆☆☆, unsweetened and more traditional in style. This beer has a very refreshing acidity and a spritzy finish. Even critics of Van Honsebrouck's piratical approach are inclined to look kindly on the brewery's strong (7.2; 9) ale *Brigand* ☆☆▷☆☆☆, bronze in colour, with lots of Saaz hoppiness and some yeast bite. In 1986, the Van Honsebrouck family bought Ingelmunster Castle, and has since been using it to bottle-condition a malty, rich, port-like *Kasteel Bier* ☆☆☆ (9.6; 11), similar in style to Thomas Hardy's Ale. The castle (3 Station Straat) has its own tavern.

St Sixtus

See Westvleteren, Trappist Monastery of St Sixtus.

Sezoens

While seasonal, *saison*, beers for summer are a recognized style in the French-speaking part of Belgium, they are less evident in

Flemish tradition. *Sezoens* ☆☆☆ has the same connotation, but is the registered trademark of a distinctive and delightful product from the Martens brewery, in the Limburg village of Bocholt. It has a delightful label, too, showing a well-clad personification of winter handing the beer to a sunny "Mr Summer".

Sezoens is a pale, golden top-fermenting brew of 13.5 Plato, with 4 percent alcohol by weight; 5 by volume. It has a fresh, hoppy aroma, a firm, clean, notably dry palate, and plenty of hop character throughout, especially in the finish. The principal version of this beer is filtered, but there is also a bottle-conditioned interpretation, which emerges with a softer, fruitier, spicier character. Martens also produces an amber-red counterpart called *Sezoens Quattro* ☆☆☆. This odd name is intended to suggest The Four Seasons. The beer has a touch of coffeeish maltiness, and makes a delightful apéritif.

Devotees who track these beers down to their far-flung home village should arrange in advance to visit Brouwerij Martens Museum (32 Dorp Straat, Bocholt, B3598, ☎089-465034), which is open by appointment only. In Brussels, Sezoens is the speciality of the café De Ultieme Hallucinatie (316 Konings Straat), which is in an Art Nouveau house near the Botanical Gardens.

Sterkens

Family brewery near the Dutch border, at Meer. Makes ales, especially strong specialities in styles bottles. The earthy, hoppy, dry, *Bokrijks Kruikenbier* ☆▷☆☆ (6.0; 7.0) comes in a "gin" crock.

Stropken

The first Stropken was assertively spicy, with a hint of anise, but this subsequently yielded to a more refined Grand Cru version. *Stropken Grand Cru* ☆☆▷☆☆ is a well-made, top-fermenting beer, with an original gravity of 17.5 Plato and an alcohol content of around 5.5 percent by weight; 6.75 by volume. The name Stropken is an ironic Flemish reference to the halters that the rebellious Lords of Ghent were obliged to wear by Emperor Charles in the 16th century. Stropken, originally produced as the housebrew at the Hopduvel specialist beer café in Ghent, is now produced under contract by the Slaghmuylder brewery also in East Flanders. Slaghmuylder produces well-made abbey-style brews.

Westmalle, Trappist Monastery

The classic example of the pale, Triple style of Belgian Trappist brew is produced by the monastery of Westmalle, a village north-east of Antwerp. The monastery, established in 1821, has brewed since its early days, though it was slow in making its beer available commercially, and remains one of the most withdrawn of the Trappist monasteries. Visits are not encouraged, though appointments can be made. The smart, traditional copper brew-house is in a strikingly old 1930s building.

The brewery produces three beers. The "Single", confusingly known as *Extra*, is available only to the brothers; a shame, since this pale, top-fermenting brew is a product of some delicacy. The

Double ☆☆ is dark brown, malty, but quite dry. It has an original gravity of around 16 Plato and an alcohol content of about 5.5 by weight; just under 7 by volume. The *Triple* ☆☆☆☆ offers an unusual combination of features, being a strong, top-fermenting beer of pale, almost Pilsener, colour. Its mash is entirely of Pilsener malts from Germany and France but, in the classic procedure, candy sugar is added in the kettle. There are three hopping stages, using Styrian Goldings, a number of German varieties and Saaz. The brew is fermented with a hybrid house yeast, then has a secondary fermentation of one to three months in tanks, and is given a priming of sugar and a further dosage of yeast before being bottled. It is warm-conditioned in the bottle before being released from a gravity of around 20 Plato, it emerges with an alcohol content of around 7.2 percent by weight; 9 by volume. With its faintly citric fruitiness (and hints of thyme and rosemary), its rounded body and its alcoholic "kick", the Triple expresses very full character within six months of leaving the monastery, though bottles from 1927 are still in good condition.

Westmalle is extremely jealous of the individuality of its product, but several secular breweries produce beers in a similar style, using the designation Triple (in Flemish 'Tripel'). Some of the better examples include Vieille Villers Triple from Van Assche; Witkap from Slaghmuylder and the slightly deeper-coloured Affligem.

Westvleteren, Trappist Monastery of St Sixtus

One of Belgium's strongest beers comes from by far the smallest of the country's five monastery breweries. This is the monastery of St Sixtus, at the hamlet of Westvleteren, in a rustic corner of Flanders, near the French border and between the coast and the town best known by its French name Ypres (Ieper in Flemish). Although it overlooks a hop garden, the monastery produces beers in which malty sweetness is the predominant characteristic, with spicy and fruity tones also notable.

At no stage is the beer centrifuged or filtered, and this contributes to a fullness of flavour. The bottles are not labelled. A version with a *Green* ☆☆ crown-cork (3.6; 4,5) is gold, light and dry, with a late explosion of hop bitterness. *The Red* ☆☆ (5.0; 6.2) has a ruby colour, hints of chocolate and plum-brandy, and a sappy dryness in the finish. The *Blue* ☆☆ (6.4; 8.0) is burgundy-coloured, sweeter and fruitier, with anis notes. The *Yellow* ☆☆☆☆ (8.8; 11.0-plus) is mahogany in colour, creamy, gingery and toffeeish. The brewery sells its products only at the monastery shop (more of a serving hatch) and the café De Vrede opposite. A recorded message (057-401057) tells callers which "colour" is available. There can be long queues.

For many years, the abbey permitted a nearby secular brewery to use the name St Sixtus on a similar range of beers. The brewery is itself called St Bernard and is in Watou, near Poperinge. Its local rival Van Eecke produces a similar range of tasty yeasty, abbey-style brews, and a hoppy speciality called *Poperings Hommelbier* ☆☆▷☆☆☆.

BRUSSELS AND BRABANT

Within the extraordinarily colourful tapestry of Belgian brewing, the most vivid shades are to be found in the country's central province, Brabant, and especially around the capital city, Brussels. If the Germanic north of Europe and the Romantic south intertwine in Belgium, it is in the province of Brabant and the city of Brussels that the knot is tied. As the nearest thing Europe has to a federal capital, Brussels has some lofty French kitchens, but it also takes pride in the heartier *carbonades* of what it terms "*cuisine de bière*". On its Gallic avenues, it has some splendid Art Nouveau cafés, but the Grand' Place and the older neighbourhoods are Flemish in flavour and so is the beer.

To the east, the Flemish village of Hoegaarden is the home of the Belgian style of "white" beer. Louvain (in Flemish, Leuven) is the home of Stella Artois and the biggest brewing city in Belgium. The greatest splash of colour by far is, however, Brussels. Although it has one conventional brewery, Brussels is the local market for the *lambic* family, the most unusual beers in the world, with palate characteristics that range from a hint of pine kernels to a forkful of Brie cheese. *Lambic* is produced in the city itself and, in great variety by a cluster of specialist brewers and blenders in the Senne Valley.

The Senne is a small river that runs diagonally, often underground, from northeast to southwest through Brussels. There used to be *lambic* breweries on both sides of the city and even today *lambic* is served as a local speciality on the eastern edge of the city at Jezus-Eik. South of Brussels it is served at Hoeillaart-Overijse, where Belgium's (dessert) grapes are grown. However, it is on the western edge of Brussels that production is concentrated today spreading out into the nearby scatter of farming villages collectively known as Payottenland. Traditional *lambic*-makers brew only in the winter, and the number in production at any one time varies. So does the extent to which traditional methods are still used.

There are a couple of *lambic* breweries within the western boundary of Brussels itself and a further seven or eight active ones in the region. Also, three or four companies contract or buy brews which they then ferment, mature or blend in their own cellars. A further two or three breweries beyond the traditional area also produce beers of this type (notably St Louis and Jacobins, both from West Flanders). With a dozen or more houses producing *lambic* beers to varying degrees of authenticity, and seven or eight derivative styles, some available in more than one age, there are usually about 100 products of this type on the market, though many are obtainable only on a very limited scale and in specialist cafés.

The *lambic* family are not everybody's glass of beer, but no one with a keen interest in alcoholic drink would find them anything less than fascinating. In their "wildness" and unpredictability, these are exciting brews. At their best, they are the meeting point between beer and wine. At their worst, they offer a taste of history, as though one of those stoneware jars of beer had been lifted from the canvas of a Bruegel or Brouwer.

The basic *lambic* is a spontaneously fermenting wheat beer, made from a turbid mash of 30–40 percent wheat and the rest barley, The barley is only lightly malted; the wheat not at all. The boil can last three to six hours and the brew is hopped very heavily but with blossoms that have been aged to reduce their bitterness. The hops are used for their traditional purpose as a preservative; their bitterness is not wanted in a fruity wheat beer. In the classic method, the brew is taken upstairs to the gable of the roof, where vents are left open so that the wild yeasts of the Senne Valley may enter. The brew lies uncovered in an open vessel, and consummation takes place. The brew is allowed to be aroused in this way for only one night, ideally an autumn evening, and only the wild yeasts of the Senne Valley are said to provide the proper impregnation. After its night upstairs the brew is barrelled in hogsheads, where primary and secondary fermentations take place, further stimulated by microflora resident in the wood. For this reason, *lambic* brewers are reluctant to disturb the dust that collects among the hogsheads, which are racked in galleries with no temperature control.

Brewers outside the traditional *lambic* area who wish to make a beer of this type have been known to acquire a barrel of a Senne Valley vintage to use as a starter. In the classic method the brewer never pitches any yeast. No doubt it was originally just a question of supply, but some barrels used in the maturation of *lambic* originally contained claret, port or sherry – the last reminiscent of whisky-making in Scotland. Like the whisky-maker, the *lambic*-brewer wants his barrels to respond to the natural changes in temperature.

The primary fermentation takes only five or six days, the secondary six months. If a brew of less than six months is made available for sale, it is customarily identified as young (*jong*) or "fox" (*vos*) *lambic*. The classic maturation period, however, is "one or two summers" and occasionally three.

Terminology is imprecise, not least because of the two languages in use (and Flemish manifests itself in several dialects). *Lambic* may appear as *lambiek* and both the beer and yeast are said to derive their name from the village of Lembeek, in Payottenland. In its basic form *lambic* is hard to find, but it is served on draught in some cafés in the producing area. The young version can be intensely dry, sour, cloudy and still, like an English "scrumpy" or rustic cider. The older version will have mellowed, settled, and perhaps be *pétillant*.

A blended version of young *lambic* sweetened with dark candy sugar is known as *faro*. If this is then diluted with water, it becomes *mars*. Sometimes cafés provide sugar and a muddler. If the sugared version is bottled, it is effectively chaptalized and develops a complex of sweetness in the start, fruity sharpness in the finish. If young and old versions of the basic beer are blended in the cask to start yet further fermentation, the result, sparkling and medium-dry, is known as *gueuze-lambic*. This term is also sometimes used to describe a version that is blended and conditioned in the bottle, though such a product is properly known simply as *gueuze* and is the most widely available member of the family. The bottle-conditioning may take three to nine months, though the beer will continue to improve for one or two years after leaving the brewery and will certainly last for five. Until recent years, small *lambic* brewers did not use labels. They simply put a dab of whitewash on each bottle to show which way up it had been stored. Now labels are required by law but some of the old whitewashed bottled are still in the cellars of cafés. They are likely to contain vintage beers, made at a time when all aspects of production were more traditional.

The version of lambic in which cherries have been macerated in the cask is known as *kriek*. If raspberries are used, it is called *frambozen* or *framboise*. In recent years some very untraditional fruits have also been used. The cherry version is a very traditional summer drink in the Brussels area, and the original method is to make it with whole fruit, which ferment down to the pits. Another technique is to macerate whole fruit in juice and add the mixture to the brew. The original beer is brewed from a conventional gravity of 12–13 Plato (1048–52), though the density and alcohol content varies according to dilution, blending and maceration. A basic *lambic* has only about 3.6 percent alcohol by weight; 4.4 by volume. A *gueuze* might have 4.4; 4.5. A *kriek* can go up to 4.8;6.

Even with all of these variations at their disposal some cafés choose to offer their own blend, perhaps to offset the sourness of a young *lambic* with fruitiness of a mature one. Such a blend may be offered as the *panaché* of the house. These beers are sometimes accompanied by a hunk of brown bread with cheese, onions and radishes. A spready *fromage blanc*, made from skimmed milk, is favoured. Or a salty *Brusselsekaas* might be appropriate. The beers are served at a cool cellar temperature of around 50°F (10°C).

As if such colour were not enough, there is also a significant number of ale breweries in Brabant, especially to the northwest of Brussels.

WHERE TO DRINK

Behind the main Boulevard Anspach is the St Catherine's quarter, with bars, restaurants and a street market. At 1 Place du Jardin aux Fleurs is In 't Spinnekopke, where it is possible simply to drink, but also to dine on *cuisine à la bière*. (On Saturdays, this bar-restaurant opens only in the evening, and is closed on Sundays.)

On the streets that frame the Stock Exchange are two famous Art Nouveau bars, Cirio and Falstaff. Behind the Stock Exchange is Rue Tabora; at No 11, down an alley, is A La Bécasse, serving sweetish *lambics* from Timmermans and De Neve, and hearty local snacks. Worth a visit for its "Dutch kitchen" style. Just beyond Rue Tabora is the Grand' Place, with several terrace cafés. A short walk from Grand' Place, at 7 Rue Montagne aux Herbes

Potagères, is the 1920s café Mort Subite, serving the beer of that name. This café inspired a ballet by Maurice Béjart. For more serious beer-lovers: Le Bier Circus, 89 Rue de L'Ensignement.

A lightly fruity "White" beer is made at the brewpub Le Miroir (24 Place Reine Astrid) in the Jette district. Le Miroir is also a speciality beer café, and offers beer-friendly hot food.

Girardin Gueuze can be sampled in the region of production at In De Rare Vos (22 Markt Plaats), Schepdaal. Tiny bar at the front, dining rooms behind, and meals from mussels to horse (closed Tuesday, Wednesday; open noon other days). In the aptly named village of Beersel, the café Drie Fonteinen (3 Herman Teirlinck Plein) blends its own *Gueuze* and has a stylish kitchen. The nearby In de Drie Bronnen (31 Hoog Straat) blends its own *Kriek*. (Closed Monday, Tuesday).

In Brabant's big brewing town of Louvain/Leuven, the Domus Taverne (8 Tiense Straat) makes its own "White" beer and a honey brew. Gambrinus (13 Grote Markt) is worth a visit for its 1890s interior. Leuven's Oude Markt (old market square) is famous for its student cafés.

There are many delightful places in which to drink beer in Brussels and other Belgian cities and towns, and these are described in a regularly updated guide by the local branch of the Campaign for Real Ale (Box 5, 67 Rue des Atrebates, Brussels, Belgium B1040).

Artois

A major European brewing company that is the biggest in Belgium. The name derives from a family, not the region of northern France. *Stella Artois* ☆☆ is a Pilsener-style beer with a hint of new-mown hay in the nose. Artois, based in Leuven, also produces a Danish-style premium lager called *Loburg* ☆. Products of its subsidiaries include *Vieux Temps* ☆ and *Ginder* ☆, both Belgian-style ales, and the *Leffe* ☆☆ abbey-style ales. Stella and its erstwhile rival Jupiler now form a joint company called Interbrew, increasingly the dominant commercial force in Belgian brewing.

Belle-Vue

In so far as the phrase mass-market can be applied to *lambic* beers, it describes the relatively mainstream products of Belle-Vue, which is owned by Interbrew. These bland, sweetened, blends have always contained a proportion of the excellent traditional *lambic* from the company's older brewery, in the Brussels district of Molenbeek. This brewery, at 43 Quai du Hainaut, can now be visited (☎Brussels 410–19–35 for details). Its sample room offers an unsweetened *Gueuze*, with much more attack and dryness, called *Sélection Lambic* ☆☆▷☆☆☆. This version can also be found in some favoured cafés. Interbrew/Belle Vue also owns the De Neve brewery, in Schepdaal. It no longer brews, but continues to ferment, mature and blend, at least for the moment. The *lambics* made at Molenbeek are quite hard, with a touch of oakiness, while those from Schepdaal are fresher, crisper and more lemony-tasting.

Boon

A well-respected brewer and blender of *lambic* beers, Frank Boon (pronounced "bone") has contributed much to the revival of interest in lambic styles since he started to blend his own products some years ago at the former De Vit brewery in, appropriately, Lembeek. *Boon's Lambic* ☆☆☆☆ beers are aromatic, very lively, fruity and dry. He makes a speciality of offering a variety of ages and even of caves. His speciality blends are labelled *Mariage Parfait* ☆☆☆☆▷☆☆☆☆. Apart from cafés, the only pure blender still operating is Hanssens, of Dworp. Its fruity, rhubarby blends are well worth seeking out.

Cantillon

Tiny, working "museum brewery" producing robustly authentic lambic beers in Brussels. Well worth a visit at 56 Rue Gheude, Anderlecht (☎520-28-91). Its beers are bone-dry, but less aggressive than they once were; more lemony and refreshing. Its vintage-dated *Lambic Grand Cru* ☆☆☆☆▷☆☆☆☆ and *Framboise Rosé de Gambrinus* ☆☆☆☆ are classics. *Vigneron* ☆☆☆▷☆☆☆☆ has a hint of grape skins in its bouquet and finish.

Girardin

Growing its own wheat, and grinding some of it between stones, Girardin is indeed a traditional enterprise, though one so conservative that it does not readily accept visitors to its farm and brewery, at St Ulriks Kapelle. None of its *Gueuze* is filtered, and the version with a black label is not centrifuged, either. *Gueuze Girardin* ☆☆☆☆ is immensely complex, with suggestions of apples, sherry, wood (cedar?) and hay.

Haacht

Beyond its everyday beers (usually on the malty side), this brewery, in Boortmeerbeek, has made some effort to promote a *Gildenbier* ☆☆☆. This is an unusual, Belgian style of top-fermenting dark brown beer that is notable for its rich sweetness. It may have limited application – as a restorative perhaps – but is a part of tradition. This example has a hint of iron in the nose and licorice-toffee tones in the finish. The style was originally local to Diest, not far away on the northeast border of Brabant.

Hoegaarden "White"

Hoegaarden is a village in the far east of Brabant that is famous for cloudy "white" wheat beers. There were once 30 breweries in the area producing beers in this style. The last closed in the mid-1950s and a decade later a revivalist brewer recommenced production on a small scale. This unlikely venture has proved to be both a critical and commercial success. The brewery is called De Kluis and the beer *Hoegaarden* ☆☆☆☆▷☆☆☆☆. This brew is produced from equal proportions of raw wheat and unmalted barley. It is spiced with coriander and curaçao, both of which were more commonly used before the universal adoption of the hop as a seasoning. A top-fermenting yeast is used and there is a further dosage in the bottle, with a priming of sugar. The nature of the grist and the use of a slowly flocculating yeast in the bottle help ensure the characteristic "white" cloudiness. The beer has a conventional gravity of 12 Plato, and emerges with an alcohol content of 3.84 percent by weight; 4.8 by volume. As it ages, it gains a refractive quality known as "double shine", and its fruity sourness gives way to a honeyish sweetness.

A similar beer, aromatic and pale but stronger (18.4 Plato. 7; 8.7) and made exclusively from barley malt, is *Hoegaarden Grand Cru* ✩✩✩. As its name suggests, a beer of nobility and complexity.

Another of Hoegaarden's products is called Forbidden Fruit. *Verboden Vrucht* ✩✩▷✩✩✩ (Le Fruit Défendu) is a claret-coloured, all-malt, strong ale of 19.5 Plato (7.2; 9), which combines a spicing of coriander with a hefty helping of Challenger and Styrian aroma hops. The spicy, sweet fruitiness is very evident in the aroma, and the earthy hoppiness in the palate. A very sexy strong ale, as its label implies. In funding its growth the brewery sought partners, and is now owned by Interbrew. As production has grown the beer has lost some of its complexity. The original is now being challenged by the "White", made by founder Pierre Celis at his new brewery in Austin, Texas.

Lindemans

This classic Brabant farmhouse brewery in *lambic* country at Vlezenbeek seems an unlikely location from which to attack world markets. Nonetheless, its craftsman-made *Faro* ✩✩, *Gueuze* ✩✩, *Kriek* ✩✩▷✩✩✩ and *Framboise* ✩✩▷✩✩✩ are variously well known in the Netherlands, France and the USA. In gaining popularity, they have become much sweeter. Now a more traditional range is being launched under the rubric *Cuvée René* (the proprietor's Christian name). The first, a *Gueuze* ✩✩✩ has a magnificent freshness and a Palo Cortado sherry finish.

Mort Subite

A dice game played in the bar gave its name to the famous Café Mort Subite, in Brussels, and to the house's *lambic* beers, which are made in Kobbegem. The name may mean "Sudden Death", but *lambics* are too light to be lethal. The brewery in Kobbegem was established by the De Keersmaeker family, beer-makers since the 1700s, and they have in recent years run it as part of the Alken-Maes group. Its herbal-tasting *De Keersmaeker Faro* ✩✩✩ (actually a *lambic*) can be found in cafés in the area.

The unfiltered *Gueuze Mort Subite* ✩✩✩ is labelled to indicate re-fermentation in the bottle. The filtered version tends to be sweeter and less interesting. The De Keersmaekers also produce *lambic* (fermented and matured on the old Eylenbosch brewery, at Schepdaal) that has a nuttier character than the others.

Palm

Typically Belgian ales are produced by this medium-sized family brewery in the hamlet of Steenhuffel, to the northwest of Brussels. In Belgium a top-fermenting beer of no regional style is often identified simply as a "special" to distinguish it from a Pilsener. Hence *Spéciale Palm* ✩✩, exported to the USA under the more precise name Palm Ale. It has an original gravity of around 11.25 Plato and its yeast is a combination of three strains. Palm Ale has a bright, amber colour; a light-to-medium body; a fruity, bitter-orange aroma and a tart finish. Other products include the dry-hopped, bottle-conditioned *Aerts 1900* ☆☆☆, an outstanding example of the style.

Timmermans
These widely available *lambic* beers are made at Itterbeek in Payottenland. Timmermans produce the following: *Lambic* ☆☆▷☆☆☆, *Gueuze* ☆☆▷☆☆☆ and *Kriek* ☆☆▷☆☆☆ which are all fruity and acidic but easily drinkable.

De Troch
Very small *lambic* brewery in Wambeek, still using a coal-fired kettle. It produces an unfiltered *Gueuze* ☆☆☆, on the dark side, full-bodied, with lots of apple-like notes, but finishing light. Its more commercial fruit beers are easier to find.

Vanderlinden
A selection of Lambic beers, produced at Halle in Payottenland. Vanderlinden's *Vieux Foudre Gueuze* ☆☆▷☆☆☆ has a full colour, a dense, rocky head and a palate that is smooth and dry, with a sour-apples tartness. *Vieux Foudre Kriek* ☆☆▷☆☆☆ is lively, with lots of aroma, starting with hints of sweetness and finishing with a dry bitterness. The brewery also has a fruity *Framboise* ☆☆▷☆☆☆. Its house speciality *Duivel* ☆☆☆ is an odd combination of a *lambic* with a conventional top-fermenting beer.

Vandervelden
Piney-tasting *Oud Beersel* ☆☆☆ lambics from a museum-style brewery and café in Beersel (232 Laarheid Straat).

FRENCH-SPEAKING BELGIUM

Perhaps it is the softness of the language: summer beers called *saisons*, winter-warmers like Cuvée de l'Ermitage and Chimay Grande Réserve, apéritifs like Abbaye d'Orval. Or maybe the rolling, wooded countryside, occasionally hiding a brewery in its folds. The French-speaking south seems a restful, contemplative place in which to drink. Just as there are fewer people in the south, so the breweries and beer styles are thinner on the ground, but they are rich in character.

When, as sometimes happens, a beer menu in Belgium lists "Wallonian specialities", it is referring to *saisons* and monastery beers from four provinces. Among these, the province of Hainaut has the most breweries, including the celebrated one at the abbey of Chimay. The province of Namur, named after its pleasant and historically interesting capital city, has the Rochefort monastery brewery. The province of Liège has the famous Jupiler brewery, producing the biggest-selling Pilsener in Belgium.

WHERE TO DRINK

The best base for an exploration of Wallonia is the handsome and historic town of Namur, on the River Meuse. This has an outstanding beer-bar, L'Eblouissant, 27 Rue de l'Armée Grouchy. Opens noon (Mon–Fri) and 7.00 (Sats). Closed Sundays except for folk music performances, often Irish. There is also a beer shop, La Table de Wallonie (6 Rue de la Halle).

Other recommended cafés in French-speaking Belgium include: in Charleroi, Beau Lieu (3 Rue du Commerce); in Liège, La Vaudrée, 149 Rue St Gilles; in Mons, L'Alambic (25 Place du Marché aux Herbes) and La Podo (43 Rue de la Coupe).

Bush Beer

This distinctive and extra-strong brew takes its name from that of the family Dubuisson (*buisson* means "bush") by whom it is made, in the village of Pipaix in the province of Hainaut. The family renamed the beer Scaldis for the American market, to avoid conflict with the US brewers Busch. Scaldis was the Latin name for the River Scheldt.

Under either name, *Bush Beer/Scaldis* ☆☆☆ might be more accurately described as an ale. It has a copper colour, a gravity of 24.5 Plato (1098) and an alcohol content of 9.6;12. Produced with a top-fermenting yeast and filtered but not pasteurized, it emerges with a chewy, malty, perhaps nutty palate and with a hoppy dryness in the finish. A Christmas version is dry-hopped.

Chimay Trappist Monastery

The best-known and biggest monastery brewery in Belgium. Its products are, in the monastic tradition, top-fermenting strong ales, conditioned in the bottle. Within this tradition, the Chimay beers have a house character that is fruity, both in the intense aroma and the palate. Beyond that, each has its own features. Each is distinguished by its own colour of crown cork (*capsule*). The basic beer, *Chimay Red* ☆☆☆, has a gravity of 6.2 Belgian degrees, 15.5 Plato, 1063, with 5.5 percent alcohol by weight; 7 by volume. It has a full, copper colour, a notably soft palate and a hint of blackcurrant. The quite different *Chimay White* ☆☆☆ has a gravity of 7 Belgian degrees; 17.35 Plato (1071) and an alcohol content of 6.3; 8. It has a firm, dry body, slender for its gravity, with plenty of hop character in the finish and a quenching hint of acidity. This noble beer is very highly regarded by the brewery, but it does not have the most typically Chimay character. A return to type is represented by the *Chimay Blue* ☆☆☆☆, which has a gravity of 8; 19.62 (1081) and an alcohol content of 7.1; 9. This has, again, that characteristically Chimay depth of aromatic fruitiness – a Zinfandel, or even a port, among beers. Chimay Blue is vintage-dated on the crown cork. If it is kept in a dark, cool place (ideally 65°F/19°C, but definitely not refrigerated), it will become markedly smoother after a year and sometimes continues to improve for two or three, drying slightly as it progresses. After five years, it could lose a little character, but some samples have flourished for a quarter of a century. A version of Chimay Blue in a corked 75cl bottle is called *Grande Réserve*. The larger bottle size and different method of sealing seem to mature the beer in a softer manner. With different surface areas and air space, a slightly larger yeast presence and the very slight porosity of cork this is not fanciful. In its efforts to keep its yeast clean and pure, Chimay seems to have slightly lost complexity in recent years, but its beers are still classics.

The full name of the abbey is Notre Dame de Scourmont, after the hill on which it stands near the hamlet of Forges, close to the small town of Chimay in the province of Hainaut. The monastery was founded in 1850, during the post-Napoleonic restoration of abbey life. The monks began to brew not long after, in 1861–62. They were the first monks in Belgium to sell their brew commercially, they introduced the designation "Trappist Beer" and in the period after World War II perfected the style.

La Chouffe

Visitors to the Ardennes love calling in at this farmhouse site for a beer and a meal at La Chouffe microbrewery and pub. It is at Achouffe, in a valley near Houffalize, just north of Bastogne. The chief beers, both with a clean, soft, lightly malty fruitiness, are the pale *La Chouffe* ☆☆▷☆☆☆ (6.4; 8) and the darker, more wine-like, *McChouffe* ☆☆, which is of Scottish inspiration.

Cuvée de l'Ermitage

Hermitages were the first homes of monks in the western world and there were many in the forests of Hainaut in the early Middle Ages, but no one is certain which of two sites gave their name to this brew. It is certainly worthy of being enjoyed in a reflective moment, though not necessarily to the ascetic taste. *Cuvée de l'Ermitage* ☆☆☆ is a very dark and strong all-malt brew of 18.7 Plato, with an alcohol content of 6 percent by weight; 7.5 by volume. It is produced from three malts and heavily hopped with an interesting combination of Kent Goldings and Hallertaus (both for bitterness) and North-ern Brewer and Saaz (both for aroma). It has a distinctively creamy bouquet, a smooth start with hints of sweetness, then a surprising dryness in the finish – almost the sappiness of an Armagnac. Cuvée is the local speciality of the old Union brewery at Jumet, on the edge of Charleroi. The brewery produces a range of top-fermenting beers of its parent, Maes.

Jupiler

The biggest-selling Pilsener beer in Belgium takes its name from Jupille, near Liège, where it is produced by a brewery that for many years rejoiced in the odd name Piedboeuf. In recent years, the company itself has become known as Jupiler. Although it has lost some of its hoppiness, *Jupiler* ☆ remains dry and soft and is a pleasant enough mass-market beer.

Orval Trappist Monastery

There is a purity of conception about both the brewery and the monastery of Orval. The brewery provides its own distinctive interpretation of the monastic style and offers just one beer: *Orval* ☆☆☆☆. This brew gains its unusual orangey colour from the use of three malts produced to its own specification, plus white candy sugar in the kettle; its aromatic, apéritif bitterness derives from the use of Hallertau and (more especially) Styrian Goldings, not only in the kettle but also in dry-hopping; its characterful acidity and spicy sage notes come from its own single-cell yeast in its primary and bottle fermentations and a blend of several bottom cultures, including *Brettanomyces*, in its secondary. As to which of these procedures is most important in imparting the *goût d'Orval*, there may be some debate. The triple fermentation process is certainly important, but the dry-hopping is also a critical factor. The beer has an original gravity of 13.5–14 Plato (1055+) and emerges with an alcohol content of more than 5.0 percent by weight, around 6.2 by volume. Its secondary fermentation lasts for five to seven weeks, at a relatively warm temperature of around 60°F (15°C). Its bottle-conditioning, regarded by the brewery as a third fermentation, lasts for two months, again at warm temperatures. The beer should be kept in a dark place, ideally at a natural cellar temperature. If it was bought in a shop, give the beer a few days to recover its equilibrium and pour gently. It should improve for about a year and, although its character may then diminish, it could keep for five years.

This is a short period in the life of an abbey that was founded in 1070 by Benedictines from Calabria, rebuilt in the 12th century by early Cistercians from Champagne and sacked in several conflicts along the way, in the 17th century leaving most of the ruins that stand today. From the 18th century, there are records of brewing having taken place in the restored abbey, which was then sacked in the French Revolution. The present monastery, with its dramatic, dream-like purity of line, subsumes Romanesque-Burgundian influences in a design of the late 1920s and 1930s. The monastery makes its beer, crusty brown bread and two cheeses, of the Port Salut and (in a somewhat distant interpretation) Cheddar types, and sells them to tourists in its gift shop.

Meanwhile, in its corner of the province of Luxembourg, not far from the small town of Florenville, the "valley of gold" dreams. Legend says that Countess Mathilda of Tuscany lost a gold ring in the lake in the valley. When a fish recovered the ring for her, the countess was so grateful that she gave the land to God for the foundation of the monastery. The fish with the golden ring is now the emblem of Orval and its beer.

No other beer can be said to match the character of Orval but there are secular products in a broadly similar style. One example from this part of Belgium is the beer of the microbrewery at Montignies sur Roc. And from Flanders, there is Augustijn, produced by the Van Steenbergen brewery.

Rochefort Trappist Monastery

Perhaps the least known of the Trappist breweries, but one that has gained in reputation in recent years. The monastery's name is Notre Dame de Saint-Rémy, and it is at Rochefort, east of Namur. The beers are identified by their gravity in Belgian degrees. *Rochefort 6* ☆☆▷☆☆☆ (6; 7.5) has a russet colour and a slightly herbal palate. *Rochefort 8* ☆☆☆ (7.3; 9.3) is tawnier and fruitier, with a suggestion of figs. *Rochefort 10* ☆☆☆▷☆☆☆☆ (9; 11.3) is dark brown, rich, with depths of fruity and chocolatey flavours.

Saison 1900

Its date recalling the brewery's height of production. During the digging of huge quarries nearby, this is a splendidly quenching beer. *Saison 1900* ☆☆☆ is full-bodied, well-hopped, and very evidently spiced with ginger. It is produced by the brewery Lefèbvre, at Quenast, just across the border from Hainaut into

Brabant.Other beers from this brewery include *Barbãr Honey* ☆☆▷☆☆☆, which lives up to its name; the greyish, grapefruity, *Blanche de Bruxelles* ☆▷☆☆☆; the perfumy *Abbaye de Floreffe Double* ☆☆☆ (with anise) and complex *Triple* ☆☆.

Saison Dupont

Farmhouse brewery specializing in variations on the Saison theme, at Tourpes, near Leuze, in the province of Hainaut. Its principal product, *Saison Dupont* ☆☆☆ has a big, rocky, creamy head; a sharp, refreshing attack; and a long, notably hoppy, dry finish.

Saison de Pipaix/Brasserie à Vapeur

Steam-powered brewery, operated at weekends by school-teacher Jean-Louis Dits and his wife Vinciane Corbisier, at Pipaix, also near Leuze. *Saison de Pipaix* ☆☆☆▷☆☆☆☆, which has a very fresh, orangey, character, contains six "botanicals", including anise, black pepper and a medicinal lichen. Such experiments have extended even to the use of ash leaves, as prescribed by the Benedictine Abbess Hildegarde (1098–1179).

Saison Régal

From a relatively rustic brewery at Purnode, in the Namur province. *Saison Régal* ☆☆ is firm, well attenuated, with a teasing balance between aromatic hoppiness and fruitiness.

Saison de Silly

Farmhouse brewery at the village of Silly, in Hainaut. Its *Saison de Silly* ☆☆☆ is notable for being aged in the traditional way, in metal tanks for about a year. This imparts a distinctive wineyness and tartness. Unfortunately, this example is not bottle-conditioned.

FRANCE

BEING TRUE LOVERS OF FOOD and drink, the French enjoy not only wine but also beer. They have two brewing regions: the North, especially French Flanders, around the city of Lille, specializes in *bières de garde*, similar in style to some Belgian ales; and the East, centred on Strasbourg, makes a lighter interpretation of German lagers. Breweries in both regions have in recent years begun to produce malty *bières de mars* – seasonal March beers – which are something of a new fashion.

The national brewers are Kronenbourg/Kanterbrau (with the same parent), along with Mützig, 33 and Pelforth (owned by Heineken), but there are also 20-odd smaller companies, ranging from sizable independents to the tiny Brasserie Bobtail, which makes yeasty Anglo-Belgian specialities at St Séverin, in the Périgord. There are additionally about 15 brewpubs. A pioneer was Les Brasseurs, making Belgian-accented beers on the railway station square in Lille; one of the more recent is the Frog and Rosbif, producing English ales at 116 Rue St Denis, Paris.

Annoeullin

Family brewery at the town of the same name, between Lille and Lens. Produces *Pastor Ale* ☆☆▷☆☆☆, despite its name a spicy, fruity bière de garde; and *L'Angélus* ☆☆☆, a perfumy wheat beer.

Bailleux/Au Baron

Brewpub on the Belgian border at Gussignies, north of Bavay. Its *Saison Médard* ☆☆▷☆☆☆, beautifully balanced and long, might better be described as a *bière de garde*.

Castelain

Sweetish *bières de garde* under the name Ch'ti (local patois for a Northerner), from a brewery at Bénifontaine, near Lens. *Ch'ti Brune* ☆☆▷☆☆☆, with port-like notes, is the best balanced. The fruitier *Saint Patron* ☆☆☆ (6; 7.5) is bottled *sur lie* (on a yeast sediment).

La Choulette

Farmhouse brewery making *bières de garde* at Hordain, south of Valenciennes. *Sans Culottes* ☆☆☆▷☆☆☆☆ has a yeasty note like that of champagne. The darker *La Choulette* ☆☆☆ is softer. *Brassin Robespierre* ☆☆☆ is golden, smooth and strong.

De Clerck

Flemish-sounding brewery in Peronne, Picardy, producing the dryish, fruity, *bière de garde Pot Flamand* ☆☆▷☆☆☆.

Duyck

This family brews France's best-known *bière de garde, Jenlain* ☆☆☆, at the hamlet of the same name, near Valenciennes. The beer is notably spicy, with suggestions of vanilla and anise.

Fischer/Pêcheur

Sizable lager brewery near Strasbourg; also owns Adelshoffen. Very commercially inclined. Products include *Adlescott* ☆☆▷☆☆☆, a lightly smoky *bière au malt whisky*, and a peatier version called *Adelscott Noir* ☆☆☆.

Gayant

The strong, golden *Bière du Démon* ☆☆▷☆☆☆ (9.6; 12) and the malty *St Landelin* ☆☆ are produced by this brewery at Douai.

Meteor

Independent lager brewery at Hochfelden, 20 miles from Strasbourg. Lagers include a copper-coloured Vienna-style: *Mortimer* ☆☆▷☆☆☆ (6.4; 8), smooth and malty but well balanced.

Pelforth

Once called the Pelican brewery (the suffix was added to imply *fort*, meaning strong). Produces the aromatically malty dark lager *Pelforth Brune* ☆☆▷☆☆☆ (5.2; 6.5); a roastier *Porter* ☆☆; the top-fermenting French version of *George Killian* ☆☆☆ (5.2; 6.5) "Irish Red Ale" and the woody, sappy "whisky beer" *Amberley* ☆☆▷☆☆☆. The brewery, near Lille, is owned by Heineken.

St Sylvestre

Classically artisanal brewery at St Sylvestre, between Steenvoorde and Hazebrouck, near the Belgian border. Its *Trois Monts* ☆☆☆☆ is a top-fermenting *bière de garde* with a slightly sour, winey, character. *Bière des Templiers* ☆☆☆▷☆☆☆☆, served *sur lie*, is fruity, creamy and sappy. Both have around 6.0 percent alcohol by weight; 8.5 by volume.

Schutzenberger

Independent lager brewery in Strasbourg. Products include a faintly hazy, yeasty, golden lager, *Bière Sur Lie* ☆☆▷▷☆☆☆; a pleasantly hoppy strong golden lager called *Jubilator* ☆☆ (5.6; 7) and a smooth, fruity-malty, yet-stronger, Vienna-style lager called *Cuivrée/Copper* ☆☆☆ (6.4; 8).

Septante Cinq

Liqueur-ish *bière de garde* made by the 1896 Grande Brasserie Moderne, at Roubaix. The name *Septante Cinq* ☆☆▷▷☆☆☆ is an allusion to the alcohol content of 7.5 by volume.

Theillier

Husband-and-wife brewery in house dating back to 1670 at Bavay. Making a rich, sweet, malty, *bière de garde*: *la Bavaisienne* ☆☆☆.

THE GRAND DUCHY OF LUXEMBOURG

ALTHOUGH IT SHARES its name with a province of Belgium, and has economic ties with that country, the Grand Duchy of Luxembourg is a sovereign state. In its styles of beer, the Grand Duchy leans towards another immediate neighbour, Germany, though Luxembourg's beers are generally less assertive in flavour.

The country even claims that its Purity Law is similar to Germany's, though Luxembourg's permits adjuncts. One of the fishier additions was minced pike, added to warm beer in the 1700s to cure fevers.

Luxembourg, which is only about 60 miles from end to end, accommodates five breweries (and once had 36). Luxembourg City has Réunies/Mousel et Clausen. A second large brewery, Bofferding, is to the west, in Bascharage. A third, the biggest exporter, is Diekirch, to the north, in the town of the same name. The remaining two are much smaller: in the north-west, Simon, of Wiltz; in the south-west, Battin/Gambrinus, of Esch-sur-Alzette.

Bofferding

The curiously-named *Lager Pils* ☆☆ (3.9; 4.8) has a flowery aroma, lemony palate and crisp finish. *Hausbéier* ☆☆ (4.0; 5.0), in a swingtop bottle, has a gold to bronze colour and a smoother malt accent. *Fréijoers* (not tasted) is an unfiltered Pils for spring (May 21-June 21). The brewery also has a *Christmas Beer* (the name is rendered in English), a dark lager at 4.4; 5.5.

Diekirch

This brewery's Pilsner, *Diekirch Premium* ☆☆ (3.9; 4.8) has a broad, earthy, appetising, hop bitterness. *Exclusive* ☆☆ (4.2; 5.1) has some perfumy hop dryness. The bronze to amber *Grande*

Réserve ☆☆▷☆☆☆ (5.5; 6.9) has an almost slippery smoothness and finishes with a nutty dryness. This has something of the character of a Maibock. The brewery also has a dark lager, *Brune* (not tasted).

Réunies/Mousel et Clausen

Similar sweetish beers at 3.9; 4.8 are produced under the *Henri Funck Lager* ☆ and *Mansfeld* ☆ names. If there is any difference, perhaps Mansfeld is slightly fuller, and drier in the finish. At the same strength, *Letzenbuerger Gold Premium Pils* ☆▷☆☆ has a smoother malty sweetness and a tarter hop finish. *Altmunster* ☆▷☆☆ (4.4; 5.5) has no umlaut but plenty of malty creaminess. *Mousel Luxembourg Black Lager* ☆▷☆☆ (3.9; 4.8) is actually amber in colour, and very sweet. The range, and an unfiltered (*Gezwickete* ☆☆) version of the Pils, can be tasted at a gasthaus, Mousel's Kantine, at the brewery (Rue Emile Mousel, Clausen, Luxembourg City). This interpretation has some sticky maltiness and a good, lingering, hoppy finish.

THE BRITISH ISLES

SOPHISTICATED VISITORS are often astonished to see how many British and Irish drinkers seem to enjoy indifferent, locally brewed, versions of uninteresting international lagers. These two countries have, in British ales such as Bitter, and Irish stouts, brews that are increasingly world-renowned. In fairness, almost half the beer consumed in Britain is ale, and the Irish are at least as loyal to stout. In no other countries do speciality styles enjoy such a market share.

Even to the British, ale can be an acquired, adult, taste. The writer Graham Greene, whose own family had a renowned brewery, recalls in *A Sort of Life* that he "hated" his first pint but that when he tried a second, he "enjoyed the taste with a pleasure that has never failed me since". The delights afforded by the classic draught ales of Britain might be compared to the pleasures offered by the red wines of Bordeaux. Both have a subtlety of colour; a fresh fruitiness; dashes of sweetness and counter-strokes of dryness; and sometimes a hint of oak.

The dry stouts of Ireland have the qualities ascribed by Hugh Johnson in his *World Atlas of Wine* to true Amontillado sherries: "Dry and almost stingingly powerful of flavour, with a dark, fat, rich tang."

The British term "real ale" implies a secondary fermentation or maturation on yeast, either in the bottle or, more frequently, in the cask in the cellar of the pub. Bottle-conditioning or cask-conditioning require fairly cool cellar temperatures typically in the lower to mid-50s°F; 11–13°C. Cask-conditioned ales are to British brewing what château- or domaine-bottled wines are to Bordeaux or Burgundy.

Cask-conditioning requires cellar skills, and this type of beer is constantly under threat. An easier alternative is filtered and pasteurised keg beer, and in recent years this processed form has been "enhanced" by the use of nitrogen in the dispense system. "Nitro-keg" produces a cosmetic creaminess.

THE BREWERS

Britain's biggest brewing company was formed in 1995/6, when Scottish and Newcastle acquired Courage. S and N was originally formed from McEwan's and Younger's in Scotland, and Newcastle Breweries, in England. It also operates Theakston's, but since the merger has closed Home, of Nottingham. Courage also owns John Smith's, but has closed Webster's.

The merged Scottish Courage overtook Bass, which also owns Tennent's, of Scotland, among other breweries. Bass has sought to regain leadership by biddng for Carlsberg-Tetley, a Danish-British joint venture, which also embraces Ind Coope. The other national brewer is Whitbread, which also owns Boddington's, of Manchester. Guinness has breweries in both Britain and its native Ireland, making its famous stout, ales such as Kilkenny, and Harp lager. These companies have between them about 20 free-standing breweries; some also own chains of brewpubs.

The once-famous ale producer Ruddles, of Rutland, is owned by Grolsch, of The Netherlands; and Cain's, of Liverpool, by the Danish brewers Faxe and Ceres. There are around 50 old-established independents, some owning more than one brewery; more than 100 micros, and a slightly greater number of brew-pubs. Altogether Britain has well over 300 breweries.

WHERE TO DRINK IN BRITAIN

Britain has more than 60,000 pubs, and more than half of those serve cask-conditioned ale. Standards of cellaring and service vary greatly. The 5,000 pubs chosen each year for *The Good Beer Guide* are nominated by members of the consumerist Campaign for Real Ale, CAMRA (230 Hatfield Road, St Albans, AL1 4LW ☎01727 867201). The guide, which is also available from bookstore chains, additionally identifies which pubs offer accommodation.

Most visitors to Britain arrive in the capital, where out-of-town beers can be expensive and badly kept. In fairness, cask beers prefer not to travel too far. A much more satisfying experience may well be obtained if the drinker does the travelling, whether for a long weekend or for a browse of two or three weeks around the British Isles. Starting in London, the review below takes an anti-clockwise tour of the British Isles.

LONDON AND THE SOUTH

Perhaps because the most renowned hop-growing county, Kent, is in the southeast, many of the Bitters brewed in this part of the country have traditionally been on the dry side. Kent is especially noted for Goldings hops, which impart an aromatic, resiny, dryness. This hoppy dryness is best tasted if the beer is served with an especially light carbonation, though this southern practice is diminishing in face of competition from the maltier, nuttier, northern ales, which are customarily presented with a creamy head.

WHERE TO DRINK IN LONDON

The capital is lucky enough to have two world-class local breweries, Fuller's and Young's, and they have some of the best pubs. In Central London, The Guinea, in Bruton Place, a mews hidden off the northeast corner of Berkeley Square, is a delightful Young's house, dating from the 1400s; equally elusive and worthwhile is The Star, 6 Belgrave Mews West, for Fuller's ales. In the museum country of Kensington/ Chelsea, The Anglesea, on Onslow Gardens, offers ales from five brewers. Further west at Parson's Green (close to its Tube station), The White Horse has the classic mild Highgate Dark, London's best-kept Draught Bass (sometimes dry-hopped on the premises), guest taps, and it hosts beer events.

Among the most central brewpubs is The Orange, 37–9 Pimlico Road; noted for its *Porter* ☆☆. In the heart of London, the restaurant Alfred's (closed Sun) offers seasonal "New British" cuisine with a selection of the country's bottled beers (245 Shaftesbury Ave, Bloomsbury end; ☎0171-240-2566). Nearby in Covent Garden (50 Earlham St, London WC2H 9HP ☎0171-813-2233), Belgo Centraal is a fashionable brasserie with its own beer-shop, featuring in both instances the fare of Flanders and Wallonia. The older Belgo Nord is on the edge of inner London at 72 Chalk Farm Rd, NW1 (☎0171-267-0718). For all three of these establishments, reservations are recommended.

Shop: The Beer Shop, 14 Pitfield St, near Old St Tube station has a wide selection of German, Belgian and British brews, including some made on the premises. Pitfield's *Liquorice Porter* ☆☆☆ is especially flavoursome.

DAYS OUT/WEEKENDS

Along the Thames Valley, every brewery offers good, country ales. Go via the regatta town of Henley (Brakspear's at many pubs; try The Anchor, Friday St); Abingdon (Morland's at The Brewery Tap, Ock St), to Oxford (Morrell's fruity *Varsity* ☆☆, at lots of pubs; try The Old Tom, 101 St Aldates). Venture further north to Banbury, for Hook Norton's dry, hoppy, ales at Ye Olde Rein Deer, Parson's St.

South to the sea, via Horsham (King and Barnes at The Stout House, 29 Carfax) or lovely Lewes (*Harvey's*, at the Lewes Arms, off the High St), to Brighton (to taste the revived classic *Dark Star* ☆☆☆, a beautifully rounded Old Ale, at the Evening Star, a cosy brewpub at 55 Surrey St, near the railway station; the hoppy, slightly salty *Kemptown* ☆☆, in the arty neighbourhood of the same name, at the Hand in Hand brewpub, 33 Upper James St; or

Bad Habit ☆☆, a dark Mild, at the Font and Firkin in a former church in The Lanes).

East, via Kent hop country around Faversham, where the local Shepherd Neame ales are well presented at The Crown and Anchor and many others at The Elephant, both on The Mall.

On to Canterbury, where The Tales (opposite the Marlow Theatre) offers very dry ales from the Goacher's micro-brewery, of Maidstone, as well as Belgian specialities. Return via Chiddingstone for a fruity pint of Larkins at The Rock.

Brakspear

Rhymes with Shakespeare. Contemporary playwright John Mortimer deems it his favourite brewery. Its gently drinkable, dryish, beers have become even better in recent years. The typically hoppy accent (East Kent Goldings, Hereford Fuggles) is most evident in the "ordinary" *Bitter* ☆☆☆☆, which has 38 EBU (9 Plato; 1035; 2.7; 3.4). The *Special Bitter* ☆☆☆ with 48 EBU but a higher gravity (1043) is beautifully balanced. Pretty brewery, at Henley-on-Thames.

Freedom

Rare instance of a lager-led British micro. Freedom opened in 1995, liberating itself from convention with a *Premium Pilsner* ☆☆☆. At its best, this beer has a fresh, soft, rounded maltiness; a smoothness; and a late, flowery, dry, hoppiness; but it can be variable. The brewery is in a mews opposite the White Horse pub, Parson's Green, London. Its beers are served there.

Fuller's

London brewery (see it on the road from Heathrow airport) that consistently wins awards. The flowery, light, *Chiswick Bitter* ☆☆☆ is a refreshing delight at 2.8; 3.5. *London Pride* ☆☆▷☆☆☆ (3.3, 4.1) seems to have lost some of its fruit, but is still a very complex brew. *Extra Special Bitter* ☆☆☆☆ (4.4, 5.5) is hugely so. *Golden Pride* ☆☆☆ is a honeyish, but quite dry, pale barley wine (22; 1088; 7.4; 9.2). Among recent specialities, a big, rounded, coffeeish *London Porter* ☆☆▷☆☆☆ is an especially welcome addition.

Gale's

The corked, bottle-conditioned *Prize Old Ale* ☆☆☆▷☆☆☆☆ (23.5; 1094; 7.2; 9.0) has such a dry fruitiness, and alcoholic warmth, as to be reminiscent of a Calvados. This fruitiness, and lots of sappy, aromatic, bitterness, characterize the range. The handsome brewery is on the edge of Portsmouth.

Guinness, London

This British branch brewery struck out on its own in 1996 with *Harwood's Porter* ☆☆☆ (4.0; 4.8), named after the reputed pioneer of the style in the 1720s. Guinness' interpretation is light, dry and drinkable with a hint of hop-sack aroma.

Harvey

A beautiful Victorian-Gothic brewery. Its seasonal (February/ March) bottle-conditioned, *Porter* ☆☆☆▷☆☆☆☆ has yeasty flavours that seriously challenge Dublin Guinness. In summer, there is a dry-hopped *Thomas Paine Ale* ☆☆▷☆☆☆ (named after the 18th-Century political philosopher, who lived in Lewes, the brewery's home town, near Brighton). The fruity *Elizabethan* ☆☆☆▷ ☆☆☆☆, brewed during the winter months, is magnificent (22.5; 1090; 6.7; 8.3).

King and Barnes
Bottle-conditioned beers have become a speciality, winning an international reputation for this small local brewery in Horsham, Sussex. *Festive* ☆☆☆, with a herbal, licorice-like, hop aroma, good malt background and sweet apple fruit character, is perhaps the flagship brew. Seasonals have notably included a spicy, dusty, *Brown Malt Ale* ☆☆☆▷☆☆☆☆; a big, oily, *Rye Beer* ☆☆☆; and a hop-varietal *Challenger Ale* ☆☆☆▷☆☆☆☆, lemony and dry.

Morland's
Georgian landscape painter George Morland (1763–1804) was a member of the family. The beers tend to be malt-accented, with a touch of yeasty dryness, as typified in *Old Speckled Hen* ☆☆ (12.5; 1050; 4.1; 5.2). Morland's home is in Abingdon, Oxfordshire, an old malting and brewing town, but this beer is named after a famous MG car made there.

Shepherd Neame
A wine-grower as well as being a long-established brewery (founded 1698, though there was probably an abbey brewery 500 years earlier), in the heart of East Kent hop country. Local hops are featured, but not with sufficient emphasis. The "ordinary" bitter, *Masterbrew* ☆☆☆▷ ☆☆☆☆, is well balanced, with good hop flavours and bitterness. The bottle-conditioned *Spitfire* ☆☆☆ is dry-hopped with East Kent Goldings. *Bishop's Finger* ☆☆ ▷☆☆☆☆ is maltier (12.5; 1050; 4.1; 5.2). A *Porter* ☆☆☆, containing liquorice root, has the bouquet of a well-sherried malt whisky.

Whitbread
Founded in London, and historically known for porters and stouts. Whitbread's *Mackeson Stout* ☆☆☆, originally from Hythe, Kent, now emerges from the north, at Samles-bury, Lancashire, an odd home for a beer that tastes like sweetened espresso. This brewery also now produces the fruity (apricot, anise?) *Gold Label* ☆☆☆, which pioneered pale barley wines.

Young's
A live ram is the mascot; geese guard the brewery; and there are two dozen dray-horses… all in an inner London neighbourhood, where the River Wandle meets the Thames. Recent research has put back the date of this brewery to 1581, which would make it Britain's oldest. Its *Bitter* ☆☆☆▷☆☆☆☆ is famously dry, but not as assertive as it once was. The *Special* ☆☆☆ is very well balanced. *Ramrod* ☆☆☆▷☆☆☆☆ is more malt-accented. *Winter Warmer* ☆☆☆ is dark, luscious, fruity, but surprisingly dry (13.5; 1055; 4.0; 5.0). Young's Export Special *London Ale* ☆☆☆▷☆☆☆☆ has lost some of its aroma but is still a robustly hoppy beer (16; 1062–4; 5.l; 6.4). *Old Nick* ☆☆☆▷☆☆☆☆ (21; 1084; 5.7; 7.2) is a classic dark barley wine, with some liqueur-ish fruitiness (a hint of banana?). The creamy *Double Chocolate Stout* ☆☆☆ meets the promise of its name, in both aroma and palate.

EASTERN ENGLAND

From London, it is only 30 or 40 miles to the rustic countryside of East Anglia, the region that grows the biggest share of England's malting barley. This is also a region that historically enjoyed much Flemish influence; is it fanciful still to find that in the yeasty fruitiness of some local beers?

In Essex, the first stop, north of Chelmsford, might be The Compasses, at Littley Green, for Ridley's full-flavoured, hoppy ales. This area also has appetisingly hoppy brews from the micro Crouch Vale.

Across the county line in Suffolk, the micro Mauldon's, of Sudbury, makes malty brews including the spicy-tasting stout *Black Adder* ☆☆▷☆☆☆. The county's several other micros include, in nearby Clare, Nethergate, known for its iron-tinged *Old Growler* ☆☆▷☆☆☆ and *Umbel Ale* ☆☆☆, with almost the sensation of biting on coriander seeds. In Ipswich, Tolly Cobbold has a medicinally hoppy *IPA* ☆☆. No visitor should miss the timewarp resort of Southwold, to taste Adnams' on its home ground.

In Norfolk, the micro Woodforde has a brewery tap called The Fur and Feather, at Salhouse, near Norwich. The city itself has the Finnesko and Firkin brewpub, Dereham Rd.

Return via Cambridge for the brewpub Ancient Druids (Napier St), which also has Charles Wells' slightly sulphury *Bombardier* ☆☆. The Cambridge Blue, in Gwydir St, has Nethergate ales.

Adnams

Noted wine merchants as well as brewers. It seemed like a Scotch whisky allusion, too, when British beer-writer Roger Protz observed that he found a salty, tangy, "seaweedy" character in the complex ales of this harbourside brewery. The outstanding Bitter is *Adnams' Extra* ☆☆☆ (a similar beer is bottled and canned as *Suffolk Strong*), with a dry, flowery, piney, resiny aroma of finest Fuggles hops. The full-bodied pale ale *Broadside* ☆☆☆ blends hoppy, dryness and hessian notes with oily, treacly, maltiness. A draught version has 12.5; 1049; 3.6; 4.7; a stronger, bottled counterpart 17; 1069; 5.2; 6.3. The aromatic, toffeeish, barley wine *Tally-Ho* ☆☆☆ is available on draught at Christmas.

Elgood

A Georgian mill and granary in the Cambridgeshire town of Wisbech became a brewery in 1795, and opened a visitor-centre for its bi-centenary. Products include the contract-brewed *Norvig Original Viking Ale* ☆☆☆, a yeasty, fruity, spicy, toffeeish speciality created by brewing scientist Keith Thomas. The yeast used in secondary fermentation was obtained from farmhouse brewers in western Norway. Another unusual yeast, recovered from an 1825 shipwreck, is used in the slightly sooty-tasting *Flag Porter* ☆☆☆.

Greene King

Graham Greene, in celebration of his 80th birthday, mashed a special "edition" of the family brewery's *St Edmund Ale* ☆☆▷☆☆☆, a malty but crisp barley wine (15; 1060; 5.2; 6.5).

This independent, but large and commercially aggressive, brewery is in the town of Bury St Edmund's, Suffolk. Its most interesting beer is *Strong Suffolk* ☆☆☆▷☆☆☆☆, a dark blend, a proportion of which is aged in unlined oak for between one and five years – a technique better known across the water in Flanders (14.5; 1058; 4.8; 6.0). The result is oaky, winey and iron-like. Greene King's products are in general on the fruity, dry side. *Abbot Ale* ☆☆▷☆☆☆☆ (12.5; 1049; 4.0; 5.0) has lost some spicy interest but gained in hop aroma. The brewery is near the ruins of an abbey that grew up on the site of St Edmund's murder.

McMullen

The Irish family McMullen came to the malting and brewing town of Hertford in 1827, and in 1832 launched a beer called *AK* ☆☆☆. The origin of the name is the constant subject of speculation, but the beer is a classic pale Mild, full of flavours: dry maltiness, leafy hoppiness, and refreshing acidity (9.0; 1033; 3.0; 3.7). Other products include well-regarded limited editions under the rubric Special Reserve the fresh-tasting, crisp, fruity, bottled, *Castle Pale Ale* ☆☆▷☆☆☆; and the smooth, fruity, *Strong Hart* ☆☆ (5.6;7,0).

Ridleys

Bishop Ridley was martyred at the stake in 1505. A descendant lives in the family's 18th Century grain mill and owns the 1842 brewery, at Hartford End, in a rustic fold of Essex. Products include the well-rounded *ESX Best* ☆☆; the perfumy, jammy, *Rumpus* ☆☆; and the toffeeish but dry *Old Bob* ☆☆☆.

Woodforde

On a farm at Woodbastwick, near Norwich. Outstanding micro, whose products include *Mardler's Mild* ☆☆☆▷☆☆☆, which is toffeeish but smooth and firm, finishing with a touch of apple-like tartness; *Wherry Best Bitter* ☆☆☆▷☆☆☆, with lime-like hop aromas and flavours; the pale, dry, aromatic, *Baldric* ☆☆☆▷☆☆☆; an Old Ale called *Norfolk Nog* ☆☆ which starts malty but finishes with a touch of sharpness; and the brandyish, peppery, complex *Headcracker* ☆☆ barley wine.

YORKSHIRE

England's biggest county considers itself a nation in its own right, and steadfastly protects its customs. Its brewing tradition of using double-deck "Yorkshire Square" fermenters leaves it with a family of yeasts that are as headstrong as Yorkshiremen. Perhaps that is why the character of its creamy, yeasty, nutty ales has been so well sustained. Traditionally, this creaminess and nuttiness is enhanced by the serving of the beer through a tight tap to create a dense head.

In the old steel city of Sheffield, the Frog and Parrot brewpub (Division St) produces from malt extract a potent (31; 1125; 13.5; 16.9), but still soft and smooth, winter ale called *Roger and Out* ☆☆☆▷☆☆☆☆.

There are also sweetish, fruity ales from the Fat Cat/Kelham Island brewpub (23 Alma Street), which has links with the Old Toad, in Rochester, New York. Ward's, a sturdy Victorian brewery owned by Vaux, produces distinctively malty ales, including a *Mild* ☆☆▷☆☆☆ which has a dash of dark candy sugar. Nearby Barnsley has the South Yorkshire Brewing Company, whose *Black Heart Stout* ☆☆ is full of chocolate-toffee notes.

Leeds, the commercial capital, is famous for Tetley's and handy for Timothy Taylor's. Nearby Dewsbury has the famous West Riding beer pub on its railway station. Nearby brewing towns include Batley (with hoppy ales and eccentric specialities from the Blackmoor micro); Wakefield (with a wide selection of full-flavoured, hoppy-flowery, ales from the micro Clark's); and Huddersfield (with robust, fruity, ales at the Sair Inn, a revived brewpub, at Lane Top, Linthwaite). There are several other micros, including the new Rudgate, which makes the firm, dry and hoppy *Battleaxe* ☆☆ at Tockwith, between Harrogate and York. In Harrogate, the Rooster micro is noted for hoppy ales, sometimes varietal.

The Viking and Roman city of York is a better base from which to explore rural brewing towns like Tadcaster and Masham. The first is known for pale ales, thanks to water with a dash of calcium sulphate. The second may owe its brewing tradition to the abbeys of the Yorkshire Dales. In York, an 1850s pub called The Maltings (Tanner's Moat, Lendal Bridge) is noted for cask ales. Micros to the east include Old Mill, making dry, hoppy, almost herbal, ales at Snaith; Hull Brewery, noted for its well-rounded *Mild* ☆☆; and Malton, in the town of the same name, whose products include the coffeeish *Pickwick Porter* ☆☆.

Black Sheep

Paul Theakston left the family brewery some years after it lost its independence, and in 1992 started this tiny rival in the same town, Masham (population 2,000), near Ripon. Black Sheep is in the buildings, dating from the mid-1800s, of a brewery taken over by Theakston's in 1919. In its revived form, the brewery uses stone (slate) "Yorkshire Square" fermenters. The yeasty dryness typical in traditional Yorkshire ales is notably evident in the *Special Bitter* ☆☆☆. There is a maltier, mint-toffee depth in the stronger *Riggwelter* ☆☆▷☆☆☆ (4.6;5.7)

John Smith

Magnificent Victorian brewery, with small museum, in Tadcaster, near York. No longer uses "Yorkshire Squares", but there is still some local character in John Smith's *Bitter* ☆▷☆☆ and the sweeter *Magnet* ☆▷☆☆. The brewery is owned by Scottish Courage, and produces the famous *Imperial Russian Stout* ☆☆☆☆, with flavours reminiscent of fruit cake, burnt currants, dark sherry, chocolate and coffee (24–27; 1098–1107; 7.6–8.5; 9.5–10.5). For decades, this was the only brew to use the name "Imperial Stout".

Samuel Smith

The two Smith breweries are next door. This branch of the family remains robustly independent, and still has "Yorkshire Squares" (slate), not to mention wooden casks. All the products are malt-accented and very well rounded. *Old Brewery Bitter* ☆☆▷☆☆☆ is a lighter counterpart to the bottled *Pale Ale* ☆☆☆. Another bottled beer, *Nut Brown* ☆☆☆, is the maltiest, nuttiest, example of the style. The firm, well-balanced, dryish, *Porter* ☆☆☆ was once marketed as a stout. The silky *Oatmeal Stout* ☆☆☆☆, launched in the 1980s, was the first revival of this style. All of these beers are around 12.5; 1050; 4.0; 5.0. The powerful, estery, *Imperial Stout* ☆☆☆▷☆☆☆☆, launched in the 1980s, helped create new interest in this style (18; 1072; 5.6; 7.0). *Winter Welcome* ☆☆☆ (13.5; 1054; 4.8; 6.0) a wonderfully winey strong ale, is also a relatively new brew.

Tetley
The classically creamy, nutty Yorkshire ale is Tetley *Bitter* ☆☆▷☆☆☆. Other products include a distinctively rummy *Mild* ☆☆▷☆☆☆. The brewery, in Leeds, ferments in Yorkshire Squares, made from stainless steel.

Theakston
Tiny brewery famous for its *Old Peculier* ☆☆☆. This soft and fruity dark brew with its intentionally archaic spelling, is a classic Old Ale (14–15; 1057; 4.2; 5.6).

Theakston products also include a yeastily dry *Best Bitter* ☆☆ and the stronger *XB* ☆☆. The family lost financial control of the brewery in the 1980s, but it is still in operation. Theakston ales are also produced in the parent company's brewery in Newcastle.

Timothy Taylor
In Brontë country at Keighley. Revered for its *Landlord* ☆☆☆, one of England's finest bitters, with a superb interplay of juicy maltiness; hard, Dales water; and a flowery, almost heathery, hop character.

THE NORTHEAST

Big Lamp
Named after a street-lamp outside the original brewery, which was established in 1982. This Newcastle micro's products include a very hoppy *Premium Bitter* ☆☆; the spicier fruitier *Prince Bishop* ☆☆▷☆☆☆; and the chocolatey *Old Genie* ☆☆ (1070; 17.5; 5.9; 7.4).

Border
Northernmost brewery in England, in Berwick. Opened in 1992, on the site of a 17th-century brewery. Beers include *Old Kiln Ale* ☆☆, very fruity, tart and more hoppy than at first.

Butterknowle
In a schoolhouse at Bishop Auckland, County Durham. This micro's smooth, delicious, brews include *Banner Bitter* ☆☆☆ hop-accented, but with beautifully-combined flavours; the flowery, nutty, malty, *Conciliation Ale* ☆☆▷☆☆☆; and *Old Ebenezer* ☆☆☆, with a suggestion of toasted walnuts.

Camerons
Old-established brewery in Hartlepool. Known especially for its complex, nutty, firm, smooth, full-flavoured bitter called *Strong-arm* ☆☆▷☆☆☆. Now owned by Wolverhampton and Dudley.

Durham Brewery
Newish (built in 1994) micro in Bowburn, County Durham. Products include the refreshing, clean, appetising, hoppy, dry, golden Bitter *Magus* ☆☆▷☆☆☆.

Federation
A definitive northern brewery, in that it is owned by working men's clubs. Enjoys minor celebrity for having its beer served in the House of Commons but deserves to be more widely known. Its malty-buttery brews, some under the name Buchanan, include *High Level Brown Ale* ☆☆▷ ☆☆☆. The company once operated a former Buchanan's brewery in Newcastle. The brewery is in Gateshead, across the river.

Hadrian
Named after the Roman Emperor who built the wall between England and Scotland. This Newcastle micro is renowned for its wide range of refreshing, hoppy, ales. *Gladiator* ☆☆▷☆☆☆, delicate despite its name, is a good example. *Legion Ale* ☆☆▷☆☆☆ blends toffeeish malt with fruity, American, Cascade hops. Beers available at the Cooperage pub on the quayside.

Hexhamshire
Farmhouse brewery in Hexham, a country town near Hadrian's Wall. Beers available at the Dipton Mill Inn (on the road of the same name). Brews include the malty, grainy, *Whapweasel* ☆☆.

Hodges
Newish (1994) micro in Crook, County Durham. Products include the malty, whiskyish, *Hodges Original* ☆☆.

Mordue
Two brothers who live in a former brewery in Wallsend founded this micro in 1995. Beers include *Workie Ticket* ☆☆, dryish, nutty, malty but well-balanced; and the lemony-tasting *Geordie Pride* ☆☆☆, made with American Liberty hops.

Newcastle
Famous for the first northern-style *Brown Ale* ☆☆☆ which has been made since the 1920s. With the amber-brown colour and nutty maltiness comes a distinctive (though subtle) winey note.

Vaux
Rhymes with "forks". Large independent brewery in Sunderland. Beers include a notably smooth brown ale, *Double Maxim* ☆☆▷☆☆☆; a flowery honey beer, *Waggledance* ☆☆▷☆☆☆; and a toasty, spicy, Christmas ale called *St Nicholas* ☆☆▷☆☆☆.

SCOTLAND
A colder country that specializes in rich, sweetish, malty, warming ales, often tawny or dark in colour and sometimes strong. These are often identified, in ascending order of strength as Light, Heavy, Export and Wee Heavy (the last, an ale so strong that it can be

offered only in a small serving). Or 60/-, 70/-, 80/, 90/-, etc. (The symbols refer to shillings, an old unit of currency.) Scotland was a great brewing nation until the takeovers and mergers of the 1960s, and in recent years Edinburgh has become a lively city in which to drink good beer.

Among British giants, Bass owns Tennent's mainly known for its lager in Glasgow. In the old brewing town of Alloa, Carlsberg-Tetley produces various lagers and *Archibald Arrol's 80/-* ☆☆, malty, dryish and faintly medicinal. This company also owns Edinburgh's Rose Street brewpub, which makes malty ales from extract. At the other end of the country, *Wild Cat* ☆☆▷☆☆☆ is a dryish, malty, tasty ale from the Tomintoul microbrewery, in the mountain village of the same name, in the scenic world-renowned Speyside whisky territory.

WHERE TO DRINK

Edinburgh: The Guildford, 1 West Register St; Frazer's Bar, 14 George st; The Cumberland, on the street of the same name, in the Georgian "New Town"; The Bow Bar, Victoria St; Bennet's, next to the King's Theatre. The Bank is a bar and hotel at 1–3 South Bridge (☎0131–556–9043). T.G.Willis, at 135 George St, is a food hall with an upstairs bar that serves breakfast from 7.00 and beer from 8.00 am.

Glasgow: Blackfriars, 35 Bell St; Brewery Tap, 1055 Sauchiehall St; Tennents Bar, 191 Byres Rd.

Aberdeen: Carriages, 101 Crown St.

Belhaven

With monastic beginnings in the harbour village of Dunbar, between Edinburgh and the border, Belhaven has always had romance. It has also had classic Scottish ales. The *70/-* ☆☆▷▷☆☆☆ typifies their complexity and depth. *Sandy Hunter's* ☆☆☆, named after a great Belhaven brewer, has a delightfully light touch of malt. *St Andrew's* ☆☆▷☆☆☆ is remarkably soft, with a suggestion of pineapple fruitiness. The *90/-* ☆☆☆ is a classic strong Scotch Ale (17.5; 1070; 5.9; 7.3). A similar brew is bottled as "Wee Heavy".

Borve House

Eccentric micro/brewpub at Ruthven, near Huntly, north-west of Aberdeen. Products to date have included the fairly sweet *Cairm Porter* ☆☆▷☆☆☆ made with licorice, and the dis-tinctly smoky *Borve Extra Strong* ☆☆☆ which has some of its primary fermentation and all of its secondary in casks which have been used firstly to mature bourbon and then Scotch (21; 1085; 8.0; 10.0).

Broughton

Novelist John Buchan was born at Broughton, near Biggar (between Glasgow and the border). Hence the local micro-brewery's *Greenmantle Ale* ☆☆ which has an interesting balance of malt and hop. *Special Bitter* ☆☆ is a dry-hopped version of this. *Merlin's Ale* ☆☆ is golden and dry. *The Ghillie* ☆☆ is more aromatic. *Black Douglas* ☆☆ is a treacly dark ale. *Old Jock* ☆☆

is dark, malty and very tasty, despite a name that could have distinctly sweaty undertones. *Scottish Oatmeal Stout* ☆☆▷ ☆☆☆ is a lightly silky interpretation.

Caledonian

With its open kettles fired by direct flame, Caledonian is the crucible of Edinburgh's brewing traditions. Managing director Russell Sharp once worked for Chivas, and his ales are the maltiest in Scotland. The lightly malty *Caledonian 70/-* ☆☆▷☆☆☆ evokes memories of the Heavy from the long-gone Bernard's brewery. Another deceased brewery is honoured by the name Deuchar's, on the hoppy *IPA* ☆☆▷☆☆☆. The *80/-* ☆☆☆ is beautifully balanced. *Double Amber* ☆☆☆▷☆☆☆☆ is full of Golden Promise maltiness, and reminiscent of the ales from Campbell, Hope and King. *Merman* ☆☆☆ is a dark malty ale for winter. *Edinburgh Strong Ale* ☆☆☆, which has been reduced slightly in strength (16; 1065; 5.2; 6.5), is the basis for MacAndrew's in the USA. Caledonian holds an annual festival in early June (☎0131–337–1286).

Harviestoun

Farmhouse micro-brewery at Dollar, near Stirling. A wide range of interesting ales includes the nutty-fruity *70/-* ☆☆.

McEwan/Younger

The sweetish *McEwan's 80/-* ☆▷☆☆, a cask-conditioned ale, and a similar canned product called *Export* have some following in Scotland. The darker *Younger's No 3* ☆▷☆☆ has recently become hard to find. All of these beers have gravities of just above 10.5; 1042; 3.3; 4.4. In the Americas, *McEwan's Scotch Ale* ☆☆☆ packs a much more obvious punch (22; 1088; 6.4; 8.0). A similar beer is marketed in Belgium as *Gordon's* and in France as *Douglas*.

Maclay

New ownership has given fresh life to this Victorian brewery in Alloa. The bronze-coloured *70/-* ☆☆▷☆☆☆ has a clean, sweet maltiness; the darker *80/- Export* ☆☆ has a perfumed maltiness. The *Scotch Ale* ☆☆▷☆☆☆ has a grainy note of fresh soda bread (4.0; 5.0). *Old Alloa Ale* ☆☆☆ is full-bodied, with flavours reminiscent of candy sugar (17.5; 1070; 5.2; 6.5). *Oat Malt Stout* ☆☆☆ is made with that version of the grain, rather than the rolled form. It has a touch of sweetness, suggestions of dark chocolate and a long finish. Maclay's has also contract-brewed the gingery, perfumy, oily, dry *Leann Fraoch* ☆☆☆ (Scottish gaelic for heather ale); and also *Grozet* ☆☆☆, an astonishingly refreshing, wheat-based beer with gooseberries and bog myrtle.

Orkney

In a former schoolhouse, in the windswept hamlet of Quoyloo, on the largest of the Orkney Islands. Beers include the chocolatey *Dark Island* ☆☆☆ (11.3; 1045; 3.7; 4.6) and the sweeter, winier *Skullsplitter* ☆☆☆ (20; 1080; 6.8; 8.5).

Traquair

A manor house (or castle?) in which Bonnie Prince Charlie once took refuge, near Peebles in the Borders. Like any other large residence, it originally had its own brewery, enterprisingly put back into operation by the Laird (lord of the manor) in 1965. When he died in 1990, his daughter Catherine, then only in her mid-twenties, took over, supervising the running of the place, and has since expanded the brewhouse.

Uncoated wooden fermenters are used, and *Traquair House Ale* ☆☆☆☆ has a touch of oaky earthiness to balance its dark-malt nuttiness (18.5–21; 1074–82; a little over 5.6; 7.0). *Jacobite* ☆☆☆ is a slightly stronger, sweeter, spiced brew, and there is a *Bear Ale* ☆☆▷☆☆☆ of a more conventional strength (12.5; 1050; 4.0; 5.0). The house can be visited and holds an annual beer festival at the end of May (☎01896–830323).

THE NORTHWEST

The Lake District, Lancashire, and the Manchester–Liverpool area are dotted with breweries. The beers of the northwest tend to be dry, though there is no obvious reason for this particular accent.

The Northern Lakes have fruity-tasting ales (including an occasional bramble brew) from the micro Yates, of Westnewton, and spritzy ones from the Old Crown brewpub at Hesket Newmarket.

No visitor to the Southern Lakes should miss The Mason's Arms, Strawberry Bank, Cartmel Fell, near Windermere. This pub has a huge selection of brews, and makes its own, including a *Damson Beer* ☆☆☆ which is deliciously full of fruit and flavour.

WHERE TO DRINK

Manchester: Britain's first American-style brewpub/restaurant is Mash and Air, in the Canal St nightlife area. Early brews have included a lightly gritty, spritzy *IPA* ☆☆▷☆☆☆ (4.2; 5.3) and a smooth medicinal, *Scotch Ale* ☆☆▷☆☆☆ (4.8; 6.0). German, Belgian and British beers are offered with the foods of the United Kingdom at the Market Restaurant, Edge St.

Liverpool: The Ship and Mitre, 133 Dale St, for *St Arnold's* ☆☆☆, a Belgian-style ale, both toffeeish and tart, and the spicier *Redemption* ☆☆☆ from the city's Passageway brewery. Also sometimes available at the Cain's brewery tap.

Boddington

Manchester brewery known for its distinctively pale *Bitter* ☆. This has lost much of its assertive dryness over the years, especially since the brewery (now owned by Whitbread) began to emphasize the creamy head.

Cain's

A Victorian landmark in Liverpool. After decades under the name of Higson's, the brewery in 1991 re-established the name of its founder, Robert Cain, a swashbuckling immigrant from Cork in Ireland. Its *Traditional Bitter* ☆☆▷☆☆☆ is packed with flavour: soft maltiness; spicy, hoppy dryness and a fresh, honeydew fruitiness. *Formidable Ale* ☆☆ is hoppier, drier with an almost gingery flavour.

Coach House

Victims of the closure of Greenall Whitley brewery, in Warrington, on the Mersey, established this award-winning micro. Products include the malty, whiskyish *Posthorn* ☆☆ strong bitter and the medicinal *Blunderbus* ☆☆ strong porter.

Holt

Unpretentious to the point of being taciturn, but this brewery is famous among beer-lovers in Manchester. Extremely distinctive notes of black malt, high hop rates and the dry fruitiness of the house's hybrid yeast in a roasty, dry *Mild* ☆☆☆ and an intense, austere *Bitter* ☆☆☆. The brewery tap is The beer is available in the city-centre at the Old Monkey, 90-92 Portland St.

Hyde

Country-style brewery in the urban heart of Manchester. Not to be overlooked. Its *Bitter* ☆☆▷☆☆☆, with a malty texture, a clean fruitiness, and a long, hoppy finish, is a particular delight. The beers can be found at The Jolly Angler, Ducie St, behind Piccadilly Station.

Jennings

Rural independent brewery at Cockermouth in Cumbria. Its lively *Cocker Hoop* ☆☆☆ has a confident hit of refreshing happiness.

Lees

Dry, malty ales from a respected brewery among the cotton towns on the edge of Manchester. Noteworthy for its strong *Harvest Ale* ☆☆☆▷☆☆☆☆, made each year from the new season's malt (Maris Otter, Yorkshire) and hops (Goldings, East Kent), and released in late November, with a vintage date. This pale brew has a warm, fruity (lemony?) aroma; a smooth palate; and a lot of hoppy dryness in the finish (30; 1120; 9.2; 11.5).

Mitchell's

Family-run brewery in the old country town of Lancaster. Newish and notable is *Lancaster Bomber* ☆☆▷☆☆☆, with a good balance of maltiness and Styrian hops.

Moorhouse's

Noted for its *Pendle Witches Brew* ☆☆, named after a local hill that has associations with devil-worship. This robust ale counterpoints sweet maltiness and herbal-tasting dryness. The brewery is in the old cotton town of Burnley, Lancashire, and originally made a hop-flavoured soft drink.

Robinson's

Sizable independent brewery in Greater Manchester whose products include a bronze-coloured *Best Mild* ☆☆▷☆☆☆ which is a very good example of the style. A *Bitter* ☆☆ is pale and dryish. *Frederics* ☆▷☆☆☆ is fruity and golden and the powerful *Old Tom* ☆☆☆ has a warming dash of alcohol (20; 1080; 6.8; 8.5).

Thwaite's

A brewery noted for its complex *Best Mild* ☆☆☆ and *Craftsman Premium* ☆☆▷☆☆☆ among a range of nutty-tasting ales. Thwaite's is situated in the old brewing town of Blackburn in Lancashire.

BURTON AND THE MIDLANDS

The brewing capital of Britain is Burton-on-Trent, a small town between the West Midlands city of Birmingham and the East Midlands cities of Derby and Nottingham.

Benedictine monks apparently brewed in Burton as early as the 1200s. The water of the Trent Valley has a calcium sulphate content that favours pale, firm-bodied beers, helps to highlight the hop character, and makes for good keeping qualities. Hops, notably Fuggles (known for their soft, aromatic, bitterness), are grown nearby in Hereford and Worcester.

Via the rivers Trent and Humber, the town became a major exporter of beer to continental Europe and the British Empire, especially of Pale Ale to India.

Burton has the principal Bass brewery, plus a tiny micro in its famous museum (☎01283-511000). The micro produces short runs of special brews, often very characterful. The same is true of the Samuel Allsopp small brewery, at Ind Coope, also in Burton. The main Ind Coope brewery has produced many cask ales but its future, along with that of its parent company Carlsberg Tetley, is uncertain. The town also has Marston's (a large independent) and Burton Bridge (a micro with a pub).

Shropshire and the "Black Country" of the West Midlands have a tradition of sweetish ales, and have managed to retain several very old brewpubs, though some have faltered in recent years. The revived Beacon Hotel brewery, 129 Bilston St, Sedgley, Dudley, is a fine example of a Black Country brewpub, with its rich, smooth, complex *Sarah Hughes Ruby Mild* ☆☆▷☆☆☆. In nearby Brierley Hill, Batham's is a classic small Black Country brewery, producing a *Bitter* ☆☆▷☆☆☆ that subtly balances maltiness of palate with light hoppiness of finish. The brewery tap is The Vine (locally known as The Bull and Bladder), Delph Rd, Brierley Hill. Its local rival in Dudley is Holden's, with a characteristically malty range. The Enville Brewery, on the Earls of Stamford estate, near Stourbridge, is a promising newcomer. Its soft, smooth, flowery *Enville Ale* ☆☆☆ is primed with honey from the estate.

Derby has classic imports and hoppy house-brews at The Brunswick, near the railway station.

The biggest city of the East Midlands, Nottingham, also on the Trent, has sweetish ales from the independent Hardy and Hanson. In Nottinghamshire, the Mansfield brewery has ales with something of an across-the-county line Yorkshire taste. Leicester has Everards, with malty but dryish ales. In Rutland, Ruddles produces a hoppy *Best Bitter* ☆▷☆☆ and the malty

County ☆. At Stamford, Lincolnshire, the revived Melbourn brewery has been maturing some credibly Belgian-tasting fruit beers in a *lambic* vein.

Banks's
A cult following attends the malty, tasty, medium-dark Mild that is the principal product of this sizeable independent brewery in the West Midlands. The beer is known simply as *Banks's* ☆☆☆.

Bass
Internationally, the best-known British brewer, with a wide range of products. In Britain, the cask-conditioned ale known as *Draught Bass* ☆☆▷☆☆☆ is an established classic, though is less complex in its fruity dryness than in the days of "Burton Union" fermentation and dry hopping. Its big brother, *Worthington White Shield* ☆☆☆▷☆☆☆ is a long-famous bottle-conditioned ale. It is less clovey than it was, but still a fine pale ale. Such a brew is a sophisticated taste, and a company the size of Bass deserves praise for persevering with this speciality.

Bateman
Renowned for a successful battle to remain independent in the mid-80s. Classic country brewery in vegetable-growing country at Wainfleet, near Skegness, Lincolnshire. Its "Good, Honest Ales" are all smooth, firm, malty and beautifully balanced, sometimes with a spicy hint of anise and lots of flavour development. The premium Bitter *XXXB* ☆☆☆ is rightly celebrated.

Burton Bridge
Micro with adjoining pub, at 24 Bridge St. Wide selection includes a dry and coffeeish *Porter* ☆☆☆ that is available bottle-conditioned. The newer Tickle Brain ☆☆☆ is a peppery abbey-style ale.

Highgate
Newly independent brewery, formerly owned by Bass. Renowned for *Highgate Dark* ☆☆☆▷☆☆☆, a classic mild, with a smooth complex of maltiness and fruitiness and a touch of iron. *Highgate Old* ☆☆☆ (1053; 14.5; 4.1; 5.1) is a fuller-flavoured winter brew. Saddler's Best Bitter (not tasted) is a new product.

Ind Coope
Burton brewery of Carlsberg-Tetley. Noted for its cask-conditioned *Burton Ale* ☆☆☆, with a great depth of flavour and a big hop character. A similar beer, filtered and pasteurized, is marketed in the USA under the Double Diamond name.

Marston
This brewery heroically, and expensively, extended its Burton Union fermentation system (see Bass) to ensure the clean, dry, gently fruity (Cox's Orange Pippin?), nutty character of its *Pedigree* ☆☆☆☆, which is described as a Bitter, but is surely the classic Burton Pale Ale. The creamy, fruity, *Owd Roger* ☆☆▷☆☆☆ (20; 1080; 6.1 7.6) tops a range that also includes some adventurous special editions under the title Head Brewer's Choice.

Titanic
Micro in Stoke-on-Trent, birthplace of the vessel's captain. Beers have wry names like *Lifeboat* ☆☆▷☆☆☆ (sweetish aromatic Bitter).

WALES

The Welsh had a recognized national style of beer in the 8th century, according to Brian Glover in his book *Prince of Ales*. His interpretation of records from that time is that Welsh ale, laced with honey, cinnamon, cloves and ginger, was sweeter, spicier and thicker than English brews. Today, Wales has no distinct style, but its ales do still lean towards a slightly sticky sweetness. Traditional, farmhouse, brewing has survived longest in the mountainous north and rural west of Wales, areas where there are now a number of relatively recently established micros. The north has Dyffryn Clwyd at Denbigh and Plassey at Eyton. The northwest has Cambrian, at Dolgellau. Mid Wales has Red Lion, at Llanidloes. West Wales has the Pembroke and Watkin micros, the latter at Llandeilo and and the Tynllidiart Arms brewpub in Capel Bangor. The handful of older-established breweries all grew up with the coal and steel industries on the more cosmopolitan south coast. That stretch also has the micro Bullmastiff in Cardiff, and the Joiner's Arms brewpub in Bishopston, Swansea.

Brain's

Cardiff brewing company established by Joseph and Samuel Brain in 1882. Known for its slogan, "It's Brain's you want". Its *S.A.* ☆☆☆ ("Special Ale") is smooth, malty, dryish and delicious, arguably the Welsh classic. Brain's *Dark* ☆☆▷☆☆☆, a relatively full-bodied Mild, is also recommended.

Crown Buckley

Malty-fruity ales, notably *Reverend James Bitter* ☆☆. Reverend James was a Methodist minister who married into the Buckley family. The brewery, now owned by Brain's, is at Llanelli, a steel and Rugby Union town west of Swansea, and not far from Laugharne, the setting for Dylan Thomas's "Under Milk Wood".

Felinfoel

Also in Llanelli, whose local industry pioneered the canning of beer for Felinfoel. Noted for its nutty *Double Dragon* ☆☆▷ ☆☆☆, marketed in the USA as Welsh Ale.

THE WEST COUNTRY

The most westerly brewery in Britain is also one of the strangest. It is The Bird in Hand brewpub, in Paradise Park, at Hayle, Cornwall. Paradise Park is a garden in which rare birds are bred. It supports itself by attracting visitors – and by selling them a choice of three hearty ales in its pub.

With monastic origins in the 1400s, The Blue Anchor, at Helston, on the Lizard in Cornwall, is Britain's oldest brewpub and is noted for its range of strong ales under the name *Spingo*. The St Austell brewery, in the same town, has the well-balanced, but hop-accented *Tinners' Ale* ☆☆, honouring Cornwall's mining industry.

One of Devon's most highly regarded breweries is Blackawton, a micro founded in 1977 and producing sweetish ales, but this county is rich in younger breweries. Across the county line in

Somerset, the village of Wiveliscombe even has two breweries: Cotleigh (founded in 1979), producing hoppy ales; and Golden Hill (1980), making the more malty (but well-balanced) Exmoor Ales. Somerset also has, in West Lydnford, the Cottage Brewery, noted for its creamy, fruity, **Norman's Conquest** ☆☆▷☆☆☆ strong ale (1066; 16.5; 5.6; 7.0). The historically interesting cities of Bath and Bristol are dotted with good pubs. Bristol has a wonderfully refreshing, cleansing, dry **Bitter** ☆☆ from the Butcombe microbrewery and a range of soft, malt-accented ales from Smiles.

Across the county line in Gloucestershire, Freeminer at Sling, in the Forest of Dean, produces clean, well-balanced ales, including a ginger speciality brewed during the summer months; Uley makes hoppy ales in Dursley. The handsome and historic Cotswold town of Stow-on-the-Wold is the location of Britain's prettiest brewery, Donnington, which makes malt-accented ales of great subtlety.

A more southerly exploration would sample the brews of Dorset: lightly hoppy ales from the partly thatched Palmer's, of Bridport; the magnificently tasty, hoppy **Tanglefoot** ☆☆▷☆☆☆, from Hall & Woodhouse, of Blandford.

In Wiltshire, Salisbury has the old-established Gibbs Mew (noted for **Bishop's Tipple** ☆☆▷☆☆☆, an intense, dry, dark, strong ale: 16.5; 1066; 5.2; 6.5) and the micro Hop Back (with its flowery, resiny, **Summer Lightning** ☆☆▷☆☆☆ and the lemony **Thunderstorm** ☆☆▷☆☆☆ wheat beer). Nearby at Netheravon, the micro Bunce's makes a hoppy but well-balanced **Best Bitter** ☆☆, the more aromatic **Pigswill** ☆▷☆☆; the winey **Old Smoky** ☆☆ and an apple-tinged **Wheat Beer** ☆☆☆. Devizes has Wadworth, and Swindon accommodates both the old-established Arkell's (noted for its complex, assertive, **Kingsdown** ☆☆) and the micro Archer's, which makes clean, fruity ales.

Ash Vine
The very aromatic, smooth, fruity, licorice-tasting **Hop & Glory** ☆☆ a bronze-coloured ale, is winning plaudits for this micro in Trudoxhill, Frome, Somerset.

Courage
The cask-conditioned ales under the Courage name are produced at the company's brewery in Bristol. The best-known is the full-bodied, hoppy, long **Directors' Bitter** ☆☆. The fruity **Bulldog Pale Ale** ☆☆, now reduced in strength to 4.0; 5.0, is made under contract by Usher's.

Ringwood
The godfather of new, small breweries in many parts of the world is Peter Austin, who in 1977/8 established the pioneering micro Ringwood in the Hampshire town of that name, in the New Forest. As a consultant, he has since helped many others in four continents to do the same. Ringwood's ales have a firm body, a dry maltiness, lots of hop character, and a syrupy fruitiness. The brewery is noted for its pale **Old Thumper** ☆☆☆ (15; 1060; 4.8; 6.0).

Thomas Hardy/Eldridge Pope

The famous, vintage-dated *Thomas Hardy's Ale* ☆☆☆☆ is produced by this handsome brewery in Dorchester. The Victorian poet and novelist Thomas Hardy lived in the town, and set most of his work in the area. He knew the owners of the brewery, and wrote lyrically of the local beer. This strong (30-plus; 1125; a little over 9.6; 12.0), ale was originally produced for a festival to commemorate Hardy, and is now made in regular, dated batches. New "vintages" are very sweet and sticky, but it is bottle-conditioned and becomes drier with age, gaining sherryish notes. Other products include the dryish, malty-fruity *Thomas Hardy Country Bitter* ☆☆▷☆☆☆ and the soft, fresh, fruity *Royal Oak* ☆☆▷☆☆☆.

Ushers

Thankfully now restored to lively independence after a dark period of ownership by the unlamented Watney's. Products include the beautifully balanced *Founder's Ale* ☆☆▷☆☆☆; a very hoppy, pale (almost American in style) *IPA* ☆☆☆; a smooth, nutty, old ale called *Particular* ☆☆☆; the toffeeish, slightly smoky, *Dark Horse Porter* ☆☆▷☆☆☆; and *Mann's Brown Ale* ☆☆☆, a classic, albeit in the light tasting, sweetish Southern style.

Wadworth

Towering 1890s brewery, with earlier origins, located in the country town of Devizes in Wiltshire. Its famous *6X* ☆☆ drinks bigger than its gravity (10; 1040; 3.4; 4.3) would suggest, with a rich, Cognac-like fruitiness and a fresh touch of hoppy acidity. *Farmer's Glory* ☆☆▷☆☆☆ (11.5; 1046; 3.6; 4.5), darker and earthier in style, is replaced in the winter months with the more malty *Old Timer* ☆☆▷☆☆☆ (14; 1055; 4.6; 5.8). Green hops, straight from the harvest, are used to make a brief seasonal brew in mid-September called *Malt and Hops* ☆☆☆ (11; 1043; 3.6; 4.5) which is full of the cleansing floweriness of Herefordshire Fuggles.

IRELAND

THE LAND OF DRY STOUT. While the best known examples are produced by Guinness of Dublin, the style is also upheld by Murphy and Beamish – both of Cork, second city of the Republic. A newer Irish stout comes from the Biddy Early micro in Inagh, County Clare.

A brewpub called The Porter House opened in Parliament St, Dublin in 1996. Its products include a *Plain Porter*, a Stout named after the long-gone brewery Wrassler's (said to have been favoured by Michael Collins), an *Oyster Stout*, a *Red Ale* and a strong brew called *An Brainblásta* (an explosive rendition of the Irish Gaelic for a "tasty drop"). A Porter and an Irish Red are promised by the new Celtic Brew micro, near Dublin, in

Enfield, County Meath. This brewery began with a golden ale. The New Dublin micro opened in 1996/7 with a more English style of ale. In the north, a cask-conditioned reddish brew called Mountain Ale is made by the Whitewater micro at Kilkeel, Newry, County Down.

Beamish

Beamish Genuine Stout ☆☆▷☆☆☆ is creamy, chocolatey and delicious – least dry of the style (9.75; 1039; 3.4; 4.2). The brewery has recently test-marketed an Irish Red. The site of production, at the south end of town, may have had a brewery since the 1600s. Messrs Beamish and Crawford, who established the present company in 1792 to make porter, were Scottish-Irish Protestant landowners. The brewery is now owned by Scottish Courage.

Caffrey's

Thomas Caffrey was a past owner of this 1800s brewery, now owned by Bass, in Belfast. *Caffrey's* ☆▷☆☆☆ is a smooth, nutty, fruity, light-tasting ale served under nitrogen pressure.

Guinness

Richard Guinness was an estate manager for a clergyman, and made beer for his boss's table. The rector left £100 to Richard's son Arthur, who in 1759 bought a disused brewery near an abbey in Dublin. Over the years, Guinness's various Stouts have lost much of their fruity, earthy intensity, but they are still the driest and most complex of the style. The bottle-conditioned *Guinness Extra Stout* ☆☆☆☆ sold in Ireland best expresses the character (9.75; 1039; 3.4; 4.2). *Draught Guinness* ☆☆☆ in Britain, Ireland and the USA has a similar specification but less complexity, and a nitrogen-induced foam. The same is true of "draught" Guinness in a can. The bottled Guinness in the USA is stronger (4.8; 6.0) and versions in some parts of continental Europe and the Tropics yet more potent (6.0; 7.5). Tropical countries who are served from Dublin get an especially complex, winey, blend that is a classic in itself.

Other Guinness products include several typically Irish, reddish, buttery ales and a tasty barley wine, under the *Smithwick's/Kilkenny* ☆☆☆ name, from a subsidiary brewery in that handsome town; similar ales at Cherry's in Waterford; and the slightly darker, drier *Macardle's* ☆☆ ales, made in Dundalk. There are also several versions of *Harp* ☆▷☆☆, a lager of no especially Irish character, produced in various breweries.

Hilden

Lonely cask ale brewery at the Georgian Hilden House, Lisburn, County Antrim. *Hilden Ale* ☆☆☆, splendidly hoppy.

Murphy

Murphy's *Irish Stout* ☆☆▷☆☆☆ is a distinctively toasty-tasting, malty interpretation of the style. Murphy's has a lightly malty *Irish Red* ☆ in the British market and a slightly more characterful *Amber* ☆ in the US. The brewery, at the north end of the town, originally took its water from a well consecrated to Our Lady. The brewery dates from the 1850s, and was founded by a family who also made whiskey. It is now owned by Heineken.

Southern Europe

THE FASTEST-GROWING consumption of beer in Europe is in Italy, where the bright young things of prosperous northern cities like Milan regard wine as a drink for their parents. Brewers in other European countries have poured their most sophisticated beers into the Italian market, and now local companies are responding with their own specialities.

One of the more interesting Italian breweries (with its "moustachioed man" trademark) is Moretti, headquartered in Udine, to the north of Venice. In winter, the restaurant adjoining its offices serves a yeastily unfiltered version (ordered as *integrale*, meaning "whole") of the basic *Moretti* ☆☆ beer, which in its normal form is a clean and lightly spritzy Pilsener. Moretti is also very proud of its export-style *Sans Souci* ☆☆ (15 Plato; 1060; 4.5; 5.6), which has a flowery hop aroma and a smooth, malty finish. The brewery also has a higher-gravity (16; 1064; 5; 6.25), all-malt version of a Münchener dark, called *Bruna* ☆☆▷☆☆☆. Its most specialized beer, however, is the deep red *La Rossa* ☆☆☆ (18; 1072; 6; 7.5), that is also all-malt, as evidenced by its rich aroma and palate. Sad to say, Moretti is no longer family owned. A controlling share is now held by Heineken.

The smallest brewery in Italy is Menabrea. The largest is Peroni, producer of *Nastro Azzuro* ☆▷☆☆, and the very similar *Raffo* ☆▷☆☆, both well-balanced Pilseners in the light Italian style.

A beer in the style of a "red ale", *McFarland* ☆☆▷☆☆☆ (13.5; 1054; 4.4; 5.5) is made by Dreher (now owned by Heineken). The most exotic speciality, a deeper copper-red in colour, is *Splügen Fumée* ☆☆☆, made with medium-smoked Franconian malts, by Poretti (in which Carlsberg has a share).

Off the coast of Italy, the French island of Corsica has a strongish (4.8; 6.0) beer called *Pietra* ☆☆▷☆☆☆ flavoured with chestnuts. This brew is creamy, dryish and nutty. Whether chestnuts specifically can be identified in the flavour is open to question.

Elsewhere in Southern Europe, Spain has some pleasantly dry Pilseners and a good few stronger lagers in broadly the Dortmunder Export and Bock styles. Some Portuguese breweries include in their ranges a dark lager. This is sometimes blended with Madeira wine and chocolate to make a cocktail called a goat's foot (*Pé-de-Cabra*).

On the island of Malta, the top-fermenting specialities of the *Farsons* ☆☆☆ brewery are all worthy of attention: a genuine *Milk Stout* (1045); a darkish Mild ale, *Blue Label* (1039); a very pale, dry ale called *Hop Leaf* (1040); and a darker, fuller-bodied ale, *Brewer's Choice* (1050). Greece has relaxed its Beer Purity Law, which dated from its royal family's historic links with Germany.

CANADA

IN SOME COUNTRIES, beers from Canada have enjoyed a fashionability based on images of mountains, forests, wildlife and lakes. To drape all this behind names like Labatt and Molson, mass-market brewing companies based in big cities, is to stretch a point. Nor has the Canadian identity of either been sharpened by their international relationships with other brewing companies.

As elsewhere, many of the most interesting beers are produced by micros and brewpubs. Many micros have tasting rooms or shops.

WHERE TO DRINK

In Montreal, l'Ile Noire (342 Ontario St E) tries to feature all of Quebec's micros. Fûtenbulle (342 Ontario Wt E) also has a wide selection of local beers. Near Montreal is the tiny brewpub/micro Mon Village at St Lazare (2760 Côte St Charles). Quebec City has the brewpub L'Inox (37 Rue St André).

In Toronto C'est What (67 Front St) ferments its own specials, the Bow and Arrow (1954 Yonge and Davisville) is a speciality beer pub and Allen's (143 Danforth Ave) has a sophisticated range. Also in Ontario, in the whisky- and beer-making town of Waterloo, the Huether Hotel (59 King St N) had a brewery in the late 19th century and has once more. Its Lion Brewery offers a tasty lager, and ales in Canadian and British styles. Near Waterloo, Heidelberg has an eponymous brewpub (2 King St).

Regina Saskatchewan has several brewpubs, including the Barley Mill (6807 Rochdale Bvd), Bonzzini's (4634 Albert St S), the Bushwakker (2206 Dewdney Ave), and Brewsters (see entry). Saskatoon has Cheers (2105 8th St E); Clark's Crossing (3030 Diefenbaker Drive); and The Fox & Hounds (7 Assiniboine Drive). In Alberta, Calgary has a Brewsters, and Buzzard's (140 10th Ave SW) has a good selection by Prairie standards. In the west, Fogg n' Suds is a small chain of speciality beer-bars.

Al Frisco's

Trendy cafe, making its own beers, in the premises that previously housed Toronto's pioneering Amsterdam brewpub (John St and Richmond W). Brews include a light-tasting *Continental Lager* ☆☆ with a good, perfumy hop note; a toffeeish, grainy, *Red Ale* ☆▷☆☆ and a toasty-yeasty *Wheat Beer* ☆▷☆☆.

Algonquin

Marketing-oriented micro on the site of a famous old brewery (1870–1971) in Formosa, Ontario. A wide range includes *Country Lager* ☆▷☆☆, sweetish and flavourful, with a faintly astringent finish; and a pleasant but mild *Special Reserve Ale* ☆☆, with a fuller colour and a fruity, tart palate.

Aux 4 Temps

The "Four Seasons" micro, of St Hyacinthe, near Montreal, began in 1996 with a lightly clovey, orangey, German-style what beer called *Stouque* ☆☆☆ ("Stook").

Beauce

A family of Belgian origin established this micro at St-Odilon, in the Beauce maple-tapping region near Quebec City. Belgian-accented ales and a full-flavoured maple beer, *l'Erable* ☆☆▷☆☆☆.

Big Rock

Micro the foothills of the Rockies, at Calgary Alberta and growing at a remarkable rate. Its well-made brews, unpasteurized but tightly filtered, have included the perfumy, malty, dry *XO Lager* ☆▷☆☆; the hoppy *Royal Coachman Dry Ale* ☆☆; a dry, malty, smooth, golden *Pale Ale* ☆▷☆☆; the slightly hoppier *Albino Rhino* ☆☆; a straw-coloured Bitter called *Classical Ale* ☆☆▷ ☆☆☆, malty in the palate and nicely hoppy in the finish; an amber-red, malty-fruity *Traditional Ale* ☆☆▷☆☆☆, with a dryish finish; a smooth, sweetish, light-tasting brown ale called *Warthog* ☆☆; the malty-buttery *McNally's Extra* ☆☆☆ (5.6; 7.0), a classic Irish-style ale; the confusingly named, bronze *Springbok Ale* ☆☆ (4; 5), with a flowery aroma, a light start and a dry finish; a coffeeish, creamy *Porter* ☆☆; the stronger (4.8; 6), richer *Cold Cock* ☆☆▷☆☆☆ winter porter; *Magpie Rye Ale* ☆☆▷☆☆☆, minty, spicy, smooth and dry and a mahogany ale contradicting itself as *Black Amber* ☆☆▷☆☆☆ (5.6; 7.0) with rooty, anis-like flavours.

Boréale

Punning brand-name of Les Brasseurs du Nord, a micro at St Jérôme, just N of Montreal. Brewer Laura Urtnowski produces a spritzy, dry, slightly tannic *Blonde* ☆▷☆☆; a malt-accented *Rousse* ☆☆, now with more hop balance than it originally had; a creamy, coffeeish, Sambuca-like *Noire* ☆☆▷☆☆☆; and a smooth, malty candy in *Forte* ☆☆ (6.4; 8.0).

Bowen Island

Island near Vancouver with own micro producing slightly grainy, malt-accented ales. *Special Bitter* ☆☆ has a good hop balance.

Brasal

Brasserie Allemande in full, though the founders are Austrians. Well-equipped micro, emphasizing the German Beer Purity Law, is in Montreal. Products include a light lager, *Legère* ☆; the smooth, dry *Hopps Bräu* ☆☆▷☆☆☆, in broadly the Pilsener style; the malty, "juicy", *Ambré Special* ☆☆ (4.9; 6.1) and a dark, malty-fruity *Bock* ☆☆☆ (6.25; 7.8).

Brewsters

Small chain, with two brewpubs in Calgary and three in Saskatchewan, at Regina and Moose Jaw. Products include several undistinguished lagers; the light but smooth *Wild West Wheat* ☆▷☆☆; a hoppy, herbal-tasting *Bitter* ☆☆; a buttery *Brown Ale* ☆☆; a spicy, maple-tasting *Barley Wine* ☆☆; and a dryish, coffeeish *Stout* ☆▷☆☆.

Brick

Pioneering, now sizable, micro. Founded by Jim Brickman in the brewing and distilling town of Waterloo, Ontario. Principal products are the very light, fresh-tasting *Red Baron* ☆▷☆☆; and the all-malt *Brick Premium Lager* ☆☆, sweetish, firm-bodied, with some dryness in the finish. Seasonal specials have included a tawny, malty-roasty *Brick Bock* ☆☆▷☆☆☆ (5.2; 6.5).

La Cervoise
This brewpub (4457 Bvd St Laurent) is on the main thoroughfare that divides Montreal. Products include *Futée* ☆, a grainy golden ale; *La Main* ☆▷☆☆, a sweetish, amber-red ale; and *Dubliner* ☆☆, a coffeeish stout. Production has been from extract, but small batches are also made from full grain.

Le Cheval Blanc
This Formica-clad tavern (809 Ontario St E, Montreal) has now sired a micro. An extensive range includes a very dry wheat beer, *Death Valley* ☆▷☆☆; a darker, better balanced counterpart, *Bière Rousse* ☆☆; a subtle, complex, maple brew *Tord Vis!* ☆☆▷☆☆☆; a smooth, malty, Scotch Ale, called *Loch Ness* ☆☆☆ (4.8; 6.0), with a good, clean finish; and the stronger (5.6; 7.0), darker, more toffeeish, pruny, roasty, *Titanic* ☆☆▷☆☆☆.

Coonners
Pioneering micro that has undergone changes not only of ownership but also of location. It is now at the former Sculler brewery, in St Catherine's, Ontario. Products have included a fruity-hoppy *Pale Ale* ☆☆; a more malty *Bitter* ☆☆ and a roasty, dry but smooth *Imperial Stout* ☆☆▷☆☆☆.

Creemore Springs
Spring water is taken two miles by tanker to the brewery, in the town of Creemore, 80-odd miles NW of Toronto. Creemore was a railhead for an agricultural region, and now has second homes for Toronto weekenders. The brewery is in an 1890s hardware store. The only product, *Creemore Springs Premium Lager* ☆☆☆, has a dense head; a light, Saaz-accented, hoppiness in the aroma; a firm, malty body; a soft, hoppy palate; and an elegant, light but lingering, hoppy finish. It is not pasteurized.

Denison's
Wheat beers and lagers from a Toronto brewpub with its own restaurant complex (75 Victoria St). Products have included a very sweet, fruity *Weizen* ☆☆☆; an unfiltered *Lager* ☆☆; a firmer, Export-style, golden *Spezial* ☆☆; the chocolatey *Royal Dunkel* ☆☆▷☆☆☆; and a malty-fruity *Märzen* ☆☆☆.

GMT
Unimaginatively named Montreal micro(after founders Gravel, Martineau and Thibault). Products have included two golden lagers: the light, perfumery *Tremblay* ☆▷☆☆ and the smooth, malty, *Belle Gueule* ☆☆; the mocha-like *Canon* ☆☆ (actually a Bock but billed as a bière de garde); and the fruity, soft, light, German-style wheat beer *Blanche de L'île* ☆☆▷☆☆☆.

Granite
Now in Toronto (245 Eglington Ave E) as well as Halifax, Nova Scotia (1222 Barrington St). Brewpubs owned by brothers Ron and Kevin Keefe. Products include a flowery *Summer Ale* ☆☆ and a malty, buttery *Best Bitter* ☆☆▷☆☆☆. The latter is also available dry-hopped under the name *Special* ☆☆☆, cask-conditioned and served on hand-pump. A deep, amber-brown ale of 4.5, 5.6, called *Peculiar* ☆☆☆, is clean, soft and fruity. This is a classic old ale, though slightly lighter in body than its Peculiar (sic) inspiration in Britain.

Also to be found on Eglington Ave E are a couple of unrelated brewpubs: the Spruce Goose (at 130) and the sardonically named Vinifera (at 150).

Granville Island

Still doing some small-scale brewing in its original home, the trendy-touristy shopping area of Granville Island, Vancouver, but more at Kelowna, in the Okanagan Valley of the same province. *Island Lager* ☆☆ has a touch of new-mown hay, a sweetish maltiness and a very light hop balance. *Lord Granville Pale Ale* ☆▷☆☆ is lightly malty and textured. *Tenth Anniversary Ale* ☆☆ is firmer, with hints of chocolate-chip and leafy hop. *Island Bock* ☆☆☆▷☆☆☆ is lightly creamy, with notes of malted milk. The brewery shares premises with a winery, and the two are owned by a liqueur and whisky company.

Great Lakes

This name occurs in several places in N American brewing. This micro, originally in Brampton, Ontario, now in Etobicoke, in the Toronto metro area. Great Lakes Lager was at first soft and sweet, drying in the finish. Since been reformulated for "more commercial appeal". (New version not tasted.)

Hart

In the Ottawa Valley, at Carleton Place. Micro producing the beautifully balanced *Hart Amber Ale* ☆☆☆, with a rocky head; creamy malt aroma and palate; lots of American hop aromas and flavours; and a clean, refreshing fruitiness towards its dry finish. A cask version is available at the Barley Mow (1060 Bank St, Ottawa).

Horseshoe Bay

First micro in Canada – founded in 1982, at Horseshoe Bay, near Vancouver. Two owners later, it produces the brassy, dryish, Horseshoe Bay Ale ☆☆ and the creamier, grainy *Nut Brown* ☆☆.

Labatt

National brewer, now owned by Interbrew, of Belgium. Its biggest seller is the bland, sweetish, *Blue* ☆. Its principal ale is the lightly aromatic *50* ☆. Labatt has been a pioneer of *Ice Beer* ☆☆, a dubious achievement. Among several other products introduced in recent years have been the extremely delicate *Classic Wheat* ☆☆; the caramelish, verbose, *Copper Amber Lager* ☆ (in Quebec, a similar brew is called Celtique); and *Alexander Keith India Pale Ale* ☆☆, a very light interpetation of the style. A *Porter* ☆▷☆☆ is sweetish and thin. Local brands include the sweetish *Schooner* ☆, in the Maritimes; and the drier *Kokanee* ☆▷☆☆, in the west.

Lion D'Or

English-style ales at a brewpub in Lennoxville (6 College St, near Bishop's University), in the townships to the E of Montreal. Products include the beautifully balanced *Lion's Pride* ☆☆▷☆☆☆, clearly inspired by the similarly named ale from Fuller's, of London, England.

McAuslan

On Rue St Ambroise (reputedly named after a monk who was Montreal's first brewer), near Griffin Town. Products include

Frontenac ☆☆, a light, clean, flowery, golden ale; *St Ambroise Pale Ale* ☆☆☆, much more assertive, hoppy, and appetising; and a creamy, remarkably smooth *Oatmeal Stout/Bière Noire* ☆☆☆, with a complexity and depth of bitter-chocolate flavours. Under the Griffon name, a *Blonde* ☆☆ (*Extra Pale Ale*) is lightly dry, with some hop bitterness. A *Rousse* ☆☆▷☆☆☆ (identified in English as a *Brown Ale*) is almondy and honeyish. The bilingual *Ale aux Framboises* ☆☆ tastes less obviously of raspberries than blackberries (though none are used).

Molson

National giant which also owns Carling of Canada. A minority share in Molson is held by Miller of the US, and a substantial stake by Foster's of Australia. The regular range of Molson ales includes *Golden* ☆, light in both palate and body; the carbonic, fruity *O'Keefe* ☆; the well-known *Export* ☆▷☆☆ lightly fruity and spicy; *Stock Ale* ☆☆ with more hop character; *Rickard's Nutbrown* ☆☆, thinnish in body, with caramel and coffee flavours; and Brador ☆☆▷☆☆☆, an ale-like malt liquor (5; 6.2). Lagers include *Molson Canadian* ☆☆, clean and well-balanced but rather bland; the slightly tart *Carling Black Label* ☆; the sweetish *Old Vienna* ☆; and the perfumed, fruity, crisp *Molson Ice* ☆☆, introduced in 1993. A toffeeish, apple-tinged, *Scottish Ale* ☆☆ was introduced in some markets in 1996. In the same year, *Signature Cream Ale* ☆☆▷☆☆☆ was relaunched in British Columbia. It returned with a full, golden, colour and a firm, fruity, attack.

Moosehead

Sizable regional brewer, in New Brunswick, exporting widely. Moosehead's beers have a delicate hop character, firm body, and grassy yeastiness. Its local brew, *Alpine* ☆▷☆☆, has a little more character than Moosehead *Canadian Lager* ☆, which is marketed in the USA. *Moosehead Pale Ale* ☆▷☆☆ is drier. *Ten Penny Stock Ale* ☆☆ is slightly more characterful.

Niagara Falls Brewing

In the town of Niagara, on the Canadian side of the Falls. As several of the local vineyards make Eiswein, this micro, established in July 1989, produced in November of that year an Eisbock, certainly the first commercially made "ice beer" in the Americas since Prohibition, and probably the first ever in the New World. *Niagara Eisbock* ☆☆☆▷☆☆☆☆ (15.3; 1060–62; 6.4; 8) has a peachy colour and palate; a light, soft, maltiness; a smooth body and palate; and a dry, estery finish. The brewery's other products include the hoppy *Trapper Premium* ☆☆, a conventional lager; *Maple Wheat Strong Beer* ☆☆☆ (6.8; 8.5), in which the defining ingredient is very evident among nutty flavours and cracker-like crispness; the caramelly, grainy, *Grit-stone Premium* ☆☆▷☆☆☆ (4.7; 5.8), something between an English Brown Ale and a stronger Belgian dark brew; the soft, slightly syrupy, *Olde Jack* ☆☆▷☆☆☆ (5.8; 7.2), which sounds like an old ale, is billed as an extra-strong bitter and might best be styled as a barley wine; and the very rich, tar-like, peppery *Brock's Extra Stout* ☆☆☆ (4.7; 5.8). A cherry *Kriek* ☆☆ is better balanced than the sweet *Apple Ale* ☆☆.

Okanagan Spring

In the lake-side fruit and wine country of the Okanagan Valley, at Vernon, British Columbia. Fast-growing micro whose products include a smooth, firm *Lager* ☆☆, with some hop bitterness; a very light-bodied *Pilsner* ☆☆, with a good Saaz hop flavour; a soft, sweetish, fruity, *Pale Ale* ☆▷☆☆; a very smooth, lightly nutty *Brown Ale* ☆☆; the velvety, coffeeish *St Patrick's Stout* ☆☆▷☆☆☆; the big *Old English Porter* ☆☆☆ (6.8; 8.5), with notes of Oloroso sherry; and the buttery, banana-ish, gold (filtered) *Premium Wheat* ☆☆. Founded by Buko von Krosigk whose grandfather helped establish the Tsingtao brewery, in China. Okanagan Spring is now owned by Sleeman (*see* entry).

Picaroon

Word related to "picaresque" and "pirate". This micro is in maritime new Brunswick at Fredericton. Products include a coffeeish, malty *Irish Red* ☆☆ and a drier, grainy *Best Bitter* ☆▷☆☆.

Rotterdam/Amsterdam

These were originally separate brewpubs, but now they are combined in the premises of the Rotterdam (600 King St W, Toronto). That name is used for the pub, while the brewery upholds the Amsterdam name. Products include a toasty *Amber Lager* ☆☆ and a toffeeish *Nut Brown Ale* ☆☆. A seasonal *Framboise* ☆☆☆ is packed with fruit.

Russell

Family-run micro, in the Vancouver suburb of Surrey. Products include a copper-coloured *Cream Ale* ☆☆, sweetish, toffeeish and lightly spicy; and a fruitier, hoppier, paler *Amber Ale* ☆☆.

Sailor Hägar's

The name arose from the owners' Scandinavian roots. This pub and brewery is on the north side of Vancouver Harbour (86 Semisch Ave). Beers, some on hand-pump, include a very good *Extra Special Bitter* ☆☆☆, with big malt and hop flavours; a smooth, long, orangey *Witbier* ☆☆▷☆☆☆; and a slightly hop-accented *Scandinavian Amber Lager* ☆☆▷☆☆☆.

Seigneuriale

The name remembers Boucherville, near Montreal, as a French colonial estate. This micro in the town produces, in several variations, very dry, strong (6.0; 7.5 or more) pale beers, similar in style to the Belgian Duvel. The basic *Seigneurialle* ☆☆▷☆☆☆ has a rounded, fruity (Seville orange?) dryness. A *Blonde* ☆☆▷☆☆☆ is paler and crisper. A *Reserve* ☆☆☆ version is smoother, with perfumy hop flavours. A marginally stronger *Triple* ☆☆ is lighter-bodied and spicier (lemony, gingery?).

Shaftebury

Named after the town in Dorset, England, but with a proprietary spelling. Fast-growing micro in Vancouver suburb. Malt accented products (broadly English in style) include a flowery, textured *Honey Pale Ale* ☆☆; a tawny, toffeeish, faintly fruity *Cream Ale* ☆☆☆, along the lines of an English Mild; the grainy, dryish, balanced *Rainforest Ale* ☆☆; the fruity, rounded *Original Ale* ☆☆▷☆☆☆; and the rainy-sounding *Wet Coast* ☆☆☆ (6.8; 8.5) winter ale, winey and peppery, with notes of blackstrap molasses.

Sleeman

Having brewed in Cornwall, then in Guelph, Ontario, from the mid-19th century, the Sleeman family lapsed from the industry before World War II, then returned to start this sizable micro in the same town in 1988. Products include dryish *Silver Creek Lager* ☆☆; and *Sleeman Cream Ale* ☆☆, with a perfumy, sweetish, bouquet and a slightly tart, fruity flavour development. The latter is to some extent based on an original Sleeman formulation.

Spinnakers

The first brewpub in Canada (308 Catherine St, Victoria, British Columbia) in 1984. Still producing some excellent ales, with casks on the bar for as long as they last on Thursday, Friday and Saturday evenings. Products have included: a superbly refreshing *Hefe-Weizen* ☆☆▷☆☆ (sometimes rendered Heffe-), spiced with coriander and laced with peach juice; a big, toasty, apple-ish *Dunkelweizen* ☆☆; *Spinnakers Ale* ☆☆, golden and lemony, *Jameson's Scottish* ☆☆☆ (4.8; 6.0) whiskyish and faintly peaty; *ESB* ☆☆☆ (4.4; 5.5), full of earthy, leafy, minty hop character and bitterness; the strong (5.0; 6.2) *Ogden Porter* ☆☆▷☆☆, creamy, roasty and hoppy; and the very soft *Empress Stout* ☆☆▷☆☆ (4.3; 5.2). *Eau de Tabernac* ☆☆☆ was a medicinal-tasting beer made with maple syrup and aged in the style of Rodenbach. *Unusual* ☆☆☆ was an acidic blend of aged beers in the style of a lambic. This was also used as the basis for a light but syrupy, fruity-tart *Pêche*.

Steamworks

Vancouver brewpub, in the Gastown quarter (375 Water St). A massive, carved, stair-well leads to the warehouse-style restaurant which serves some Pacific Rim dishes. Early brews started malty but finished dry. *Not So Pale Ale* ☆☆ was claret in colour, with leafy hop notes. *Nutbrown Nirvana* ☆☆ was slightly medicinal and soothing. *Rastabolter* ☆☆▷☆☆ (4.8; 6.0) was malty and peppery

Swan's

Second brewpub in Victoria (506 Pandora St), with bedrooms. Products include: a malty *Bavarian Lager* ☆☆▷☆☆; a coffeeish, long, *Dark Lager* ☆☆▷☆☆; a flowery, heathery, (American-style) *Wheat Beer* ☆☆; a honeyish *Pale Ale* ☆☆; a hoppy, dry, *Bitter* ☆☆☆; a smooth, malty-fruity, *Scotch Ale* ☆☆▷☆☆; nutty *Appleton Brown Ale* ☆☆▷☆☆; a light but oily, roasty, *Porter* ☆☆; and a relatively light, sweetish, *Oatmeal Stout* ☆☆.

Storm Brewing

Punning micro, in an Italian-accented warehouse district in Vancouver. Products include the ale-like *Altbier Red Sky* ☆☆; the hoppy *Hurricane India Pale Ale* ☆☆▷☆☆, with notes of flowering currant; and the assertive *Continental Coffee Ale* ☆☆☆ (arabica, at the end of the boil and in secondary fermentation).

Tall Ship

In the waterside town of Squamish, N of Vancouver. This micro produces *India Pale Ale* ☆☆ (6.0; 7.5), strong, amber-red with restrained hop character but good flavour development; the very smooth *Black Ship Ale* ☆☆▷☆☆☆, with notes of hazelnut and dark chocolate (a top-fermenting Schwarzbier?); and a *Smoked Porter* ☆☆☆ with sweetish, sappy, flavours.

Taylor and Bate
Revivalist brewery in Elora, Ontario. *Elora Pale Ale* ☆☆☆▷☆☆☆ is smooth, malt-accented and beautifully balanced. *Grand Porter Ale* ☆☆ is smooth and chocolatey.

Thames Valley
Newish micro producing lager in London, Ontario.

Tin Whistle
The name belongs to a loco on the Kettle Valley railroad, in the Okanagan region. The micro, in lakeside Penticton, occupies a western storefront building that was formerly a museum of gold mining. Products include *Rattlesnake* ☆☆☆▷☆☆☆, a bronze ale with a good, lingering, lemony, bitterness; and *Black Widow* ☆☆, tawny, smooth, malty and sweetish.

Trafalgar
The amber, nutty, dryish *Red Hill Mild* ☆☆, at a modest 2.3;2.6, is a pleasant entrant from this tiny micro in Oakville, Ontario.

Tree
The name? "Symbol of nature and of British Columbia." The micro in the Okanagan Valley at Kelowna began with an *Amber Ale* ☆☆, malt-accented with good balancing fruit and hop bitterness.

Unibroue
In the Montreal suburb of Chambly, a Belgian-accented micro. Products include the very pale, heavily sedimented, lemony *Blanche de Chambly* ☆☆, a Belgian-style "White"; the medicinal, spicy, peppery *Maudite* ☆☆▷☆☆☆ ("Damned"), a Belgian-style strong (6.4; 8) russet ale; and *La Fin du Monde* ☆☆▷☆☆☆, a very pale, slightly stronger brew with suggestions of honey and anise. *Raftman* ☆☆☆▷☆☆☆ is a woody, smoky, Bière au Malt de Whisky. *Quelque Chose* ☆☆☆▷☆☆☆ (6.4–8.0) is a port-like kriek, intended to be served heated like a *Glühwein*.

Upper Canada
Interesting, well-made brews from a sizable micro in Toronto. Its flagship *Dark Ale* ☆☆▷☆☆☆ is malt-accented, with a soft fruitiness and a dry, hoppy, finish. The pleasant, easy-to-drink, *Publican's Bitter* ☆☆ is actually on the sweet side, but with some tartness and hop in the finish. The *Wheat Beer* ☆☆▷☆☆☆ is golden and bright, refeshing, slightly tart. The *Lager* ☆☆▷☆☆☆ is soft, clean and spritzy, with good hop character in both bouquet and finish. *Rebellion* ☆☆ is a malty, substantial, strong, golden lager. *True Bock* ☆☆▷☆☆☆ has a good malt character, a warming finish and a full amber colour.

Vancouver Island
Early micro now in Victoria. Its *Victoria Lager* ☆☆ is fresh, sweetish and smooth. *Hermann's Dark Lager* ☆☆▷☆☆☆ is less chocolatey than it once was. *Piper's Pale Ale* ☆☆ is smooth and fruity. *Weizen* ☆☆☆ has excellent banana, clove and light smokiness.

Wellington County
English-style ales, sometimes cask-conditioned, from a classic micro in the old brewing town of Guelph, in a region with con-

nections with the British brewing family Arkell. Hence *Arkell Best Bitter* ☆☆☆ (3.2; 4.0), which has in its cask form an earthy aroma of Goldings hops; a deft balance of malty dryness and restrained fruitiness; and a long, hoppy, finish. A good, honest ale. The same beer filtered for the bottle tastes slightly less hoppy. *Wellington SPA* ☆☆ (Special Pale Ale), at 3.6; 4.5, is sweeter and fruitier. *County Ale* ☆☆☆ (4; 5) is bigger-bodied, complex, well-rounded, with a very hoppy finish. *Iron Duke* ☆☆☆ (5.3; 6.5) is malt-accented but beautifully balanced, with great depth of flavour and a dry finish. *Imperial Stout* ☆☆▷☆☆☆ is roasty, chocolatey, syrupy, alcoholic and warming. *Wellington Premium Lager* ☆☆ (3.6; 4.5) is rounded and flavoursome.

Whistler

A mountain known as Whistler gives its name to a ski resort N of Vancouver. The resort's micro is known for *Black Tusk Ale* ☆☆, light-bodied, with notes of coffee and treacle-toffee. The witty *Whistler's Mother* ☆☆ is a firm, dry, lively, Pale Ale.

Yaletown

Warehouse-district brewpub and pizza restaurant, with touches of style (110 Hamilton St, Vancouver). Beers include a banana-ish *Hefeweizen* ☆☆▷☆☆☆, with lightly smoky touches; a soft, hoppy, *Bitter* ☆☆☆; a raisiny but dryish *Nut Brown Ale* ☆☆, and a grainy, coffeeish *Stout* ☆☆.

THE UNITED STATES

THE NEW WAVE OF BREWPUBS and micro-breweries has brought with it styles of beer not made in America since the earlier days of European settlement and much more. Today, there are more than 1,200 breweries, making a wider range of styles than can be found anywhere else in the world. A couple of decades ago, only five or six American beers deviated from the mainstream of light-bodied, bland lagers. Not every new brewery survives, and the second half of this decade is seeing some settling-out, but flavoursome beers are here to stay.

Almost every town has a micro (sometimes with a tasting room) or a brewpub. What follows is a selection. Many of these will display a pile of free newspapers aimed at beer lovers. The newspapers list new small breweries in their region, and are a valuable source of information.

THE NORTHEAST

WHERE TO DRINK

Boston: An excellent selection of brewpubs: Back Bay, Brew Moon, Commonwealth; across the river, Cambridge and John Harvard (*see* entries). Microbrews and ribs at Redbones (55 Chester St, Somerville). More micros, and rooms devoted to the

Kennedys and Michael Collins, at Doyle's (3484 Washington St, Jamaica Plain, near the Samuel Adams brewery). Downtown, Jacob Wirth (31 Stuart) is the city's oldest tavern. The Bull and Finch (84 Beacon) was the inspiration for Cheers. Look out for the free paper *Yankee Brew News*.

New York: West Side (340 Amsterdam, at 76th), A.J.Gordon's (between Amsterdam and Broadway, on W79), Carnegie Hill (1600 3rd Ave and 90th St) and Yorkville (1359 1st Ave at 73rd) are all pleasant, relatively mainstream brewpubs. Upper East Side beer bars include Kinsale (1672 3rd Ave) and Ruby's (1754 2nd).

Midtown brewpubs include a Commonwealth (try the flavoursome *ESB* ☆☆☆ (Rockefeller Plaza and W48, between 5th and 6th Aves). Typhoon (22 E 54th, between 5th and Madison) offers upscale Thai food with moderately hoppy beers. The Beer Bar at Café Centro (MetLife building, 200 Park Ave, at 45th) is a smart lunch spot. After a shaky start, Hansen's brewpub, on Times Square (160 W 42nd St), has begun to find its feet. The Chelsea Brewing Company (where W23 meets the Hudson, at Pier 59) has a whiskyish *Barley Wine* ☆☆▷☆☆☆

On Union Square, Heartland is a lively brewpub (see entry). Not far away, in a building that has been a Yiddish theatre and a German beer hall (190 3rd Ave, between 17th and 18th Sts), The Highlander has offered an authentically malty *80/-* ☆☆▷☆☆☆, cask-conditioned, from the Middle Ages brewery, of Syracuse.

In the West Village, The Blind Tiger (Hudson and 10th) is a pubby place for micros. So, with its literary and political history, is hard-to-find Chumley's (86 Bedford, at Barrow).

In the East Village, DBA (1st Ave, between 2nd and 3rd Sts) is a specialist beer bar. Between 2nd and 3rd Aves, on 7th St, are another speciality beer bar, Brewsky's (with a Ukrainian flavour), the Rabelaisian Belgian café Burp Castle and the city's oldest saloon, McSorley's.

Look for *Ale Street News*.

Philadelphia: The famous beer-list at Copa, Too! (263 S 15th St) was built by Tom Peters, who now has Monk's (264 S 16th), specialising in Belgian beers. The same theme appiles at Cuvée Notredame (1701 Green St). Chef-patron Michel Notredame was formerly at Belgian-accented, Irish-spelled, Bridgid's (726 N 24th). The London Grill (2301 Fairmount Ave) has beers from well beyond the British Isles. Samuel Adams' speakeasy-like brewpub (above the Oyster House, at 1516 Sansom) does some outstanding specials, recently a Rodenbach-style *Tart Ale* ☆☆☆▷ ☆☆☆☆. See also entry for the ritzier Dock St.

Look out for *Beer Philadelphia*.

Washington, DC: The Brickskeller (1523 22nd NW nr Dupont Circle) has the biggest bottled selection in the US and regular tutored tastings. Beers have been pleasant but unexciting at Capitol City, a brewpub in a restored Art Deco bus station (1100 New York Ave NW and H St; and branches) In Alexandria, Virginia Beverage (607 King St) is pubbier, and has been known to make a very hoppy *Strong Ale* ☆☆▷☆☆☆; several good bars within walking distance. Arlington has Bardo Rodeo (2000 Wilson Blvd), a huge, neo-pyschedelic bar making eccentric and sometimes excellent beers. Also in Arlington, Blue 'n' Gold (3100 Clarendon Bvd) is much glitzier; a very flowery, cask-conditioned, *IPA* ☆☆☆ in an otherwise malt-accented range. In Centreville, Virginia, the Sweetwater Tavern (behind the Multiplex Theater) has complex beers by Nick Funnell. Try his chocolatey *Oscura* ☆☆☆.

Look out for *Barleycorn*.

Back Bay
On Boston's busy Boylston St (No 755). Well-run brewpub owned by Commonwealth. The hoppy *Frisian Helles* ☆☆☆ is a remarkable springtime special.

Baltimore Brewing Company
A member of the Grolsch family privately launched this establishment, in order to make and serve lagers, unfiltered but bright nevertheless, in what was once the brewery neighbourhood (104 Albemarle). Lightly smooth, hoppy, *Pils* ☆☆☆; beautifully balanced *Dark* ☆☆▷☆☆☆; spicy fruity *Weizen* ☆☆☆; and outstanding seasonals.

Boston Beer (Samuel Adams)
Wide and adventurous range of beers, with some made in a tiny micro in the former Haffenreffer brewery (tour and sample: ☎617-522-9080), at Jamaica Plain. Boston Beer also owns Hudepohl-Schoenling, in Cincinnati, and uses several other breweries under contract. The newish *Golden Pilsner* ☆☆ is light and well-balanced. *Samuel Adams Boston Lager* ☆☆☆ is much more flowery and flavoursome. A so-called *Boston Beer* ☆▷☆☆ produced in Britain is far less interesting. *Boston Ale* ☆☆☆ is oily, perfumy and appetising. Some very good seasonal and speciality beers. A *Scotch Ale* ☆☆☆ is big, rounded, and lightly smoky. *Old Fezziwig* ☆☆▷☆☆☆ is a toffeeish, orangey, spiced, ale. *Honey Porter* ☆☆ has toast-and-marmalade (Concorde grape?) notes. *Cherry Wheat* ☆▷☆☆ seems to have become heavy and cloying. *Cranberry Lambic* ☆☆☆ is lightly tart, with some strawy aromas (all the yeast is pitched, but a Brettanomyces is used). *Triple Bock* ☆☆☆▷☆☆☆☆, really a barley wine, is made with a champagne yeast, primed with maple syrup and matured in whisky casks. It is liqueur-ish, with notes of vanilla and minty esteriness, and its alcohol content has been know to reach 14; 17.5.

Boston Beer Works
Industrial chic brewpub (61 Brookline Ave), handy for Fenway Park and the Red Sox. Wide range includes *Boston Red* ☆☆ with a sweetish fruitiness enwrapped in an earthy hop; the flavourful, flowery *Beantown Nutbrown* ☆☆▷☆☆☆; the perfumey, very hoppy and dry *Back Bay IPA* ☆☆☆; and a smooth, chocolatey, roasty *Oatmeal Stout* ☆☆▷☆☆☆.

Brew Moon
Good food (try the steamed artichoke) and restrained beers in a post-modernist brewpub in the theatre district of Boston. Best brews are *Nutcracker* ☆☆▷☆☆☆, with a fruity maltiness; and big *Stout* ☆☆☆. (115 Stuart St, in the Transportation Building and branches).

Brimstone
Baltimore micro, noted for its lightly smoky *Stone Beer* ☆☆☆. In part of the old National Bohemian brewery.

Brooklyn Brewery
The dry-hopped, fresh, flowery, firm, flavourful, *Brooklyn Lager* ☆☆☆▷☆☆☆ started well, in 1988, and has gained in character since. It is fermented with the yeast of Schaefer, which departed in 1976, leaving Brooklyn without a brewery. *Brooklyn Brown* ☆☆☆ is a relatively strong (13.5–14; 1054–6; 4.8; 6.0) and more complex counterpart to the Northern English style. *Black Chocolate Stout* ☆☆☆ is the beer world's answer to a warming malted milk with a shot of Bourbon. It contains chocolate malt, but no Hershey bars. *East India Pale Ale* ☆☆☆ is extremely dry, with the aroma of a hop-pocket and flavours remniscent of lemon-grass. *Brooklyner Weisse* ☆☆☆▷☆☆☆ has a light interplay of fragrant hop, clove and banana. The brewery, in Brooklyn's Williamsburg district, has as a neighbour the beer bar Mugs (125 Bedford Ave). Elsewhere in Brooklyn, the Park Slope brewpub (356 6th) takes its name from that arty neighbourhood. Try the *IPA* ☆☆, which has good hop flavours.

Cambridge Brewing Company
From downtown Boston, head across the river to 1 Kendall Square, at Broadway and Hampshire, Cambridge to this conservatory-style bar-restaurant. Sweetish, fruity *Golden* ☆▷☆☆ ale; hoppy *Pale* ☆☆; spicy *Amber* ☆☆; very fruity, leafy *IPA* ☆☆; *Porter* ☆☆ with notes of treacle-toffee and roasted chocolate beans; and some characterful seasonal specialities. In Cambridge see also the unrelated John Harvard.

Catamount
The classic example of a regular golden ale in the East Coast tradition comes from this Vermont micro. *Catamount Gold* ☆☆☆ (10.5; 1042; 3.6; 4.5) has a good American hop character in both bouquet and finish, between which is a clean, lightly malty palate, with flavour development towards fruity notes. *Catamount Amber* ☆☆☆▷☆☆☆ (12; 1048; 4.0; 5.0) is more assertive all round, with a polite nod towards an English Pale Ale. *Catamount Porter* ☆☆☆ (13; 1052; 4.2; 5.3) is remarkably smooth, creamy and chocolatey in flavour and is the most outstanding porter on the East Coast. Catamount is at White River Junction.

Climax
"Peak of pleasure" micro in Roselle Park, New Jersey. Honeyish *ESB* ☆☆☆ especially recommended.

Commonwealth
Original Burton Unions decorate this pioneering brewpub in Boston (138 Portland and Merrimac) between Boston Gardens (home of the Celtics) and the Faneuil Hall tourist area. Products include *Best Burton Bitter* ☆☆☆, with plenty of hop in its aroma and long finish; the soft, sweetish *Amber Ale* ☆☆; the complex, rummy, *Stout* ☆☆☆▷☆☆☆; and seasonal specialities that include a faintly medicinal *Porter* ☆☆☆▷☆☆☆; and a winey *Winter Warmer/Special Old Ale* ☆☆☆. Also in New York.

Dock Street

Much mentioned in a popular TV series, *Thirty-Something*. "Brasserie" food and an astonishingly varied, ever-changing, range of well-made beers in a chic brewpub at 2 Logan Square (18th and Cherry), Philadelphia. Products have included: a soft, aromatic, *Bohemian Pils* ☆☆▷☆☆☆; a hoppy *German Pils* ☆☆; a slightly chocolatey *Oscura* ☆☆☆▷☆☆☆, based on the Mexican dark type; a lightly malty *Dunkel* ☆☆; a very malty *Bock* ☆☆; a lightly spicy *Hefe-Weisse* ☆☆; a grainy *Rye Beer* ☆☆☆▷☆☆☆; a lightly chocolatey *Mild* ☆☆▷☆☆☆; a soft, lightly fruity, *Amber* ☆☆ ale; a dryish *Pale Ale* ☆☆; a very fruity, slightly winey, *Bitter* ☆☆; an *IPA* ☆▷☆☆ somewhat lacking in hop; an oily, firm, *Irish Red Ale* ☆☆▷☆☆☆; a chocolatey *Stout* ☆☆; and a rich *Barley Wine* ☆☆☆▷☆☆☆☆ with an astonishingly spritzy finish. *Grand Cru* ☆☆☆▷☆☆☆☆, a stronger imitation of Rodenbach, was a recent delight.

Geary

This is a highly regarded micro in Portland, Maine. The Anglo-American accent of its ales echoes the early traditions of East Coast brewing. *Geary's Pale Ale* ☆☆▷☆☆☆ (12; 1048; 3.6; 4.5) is a New England classic: copper-coloured, dry, clean, crisp, lots of late-hop taste, with ale fruitiness (from old Hampshire's Ringwood yeast). *Hampshire Special Ale* ☆☆☆☆ (17.5; 1070; around 5.6; 7.0), is tawny and bittersweet, drying to a tremendous hop finish. This beer is produced for winter.

Genesee

The name of the river on which stands the city of Rochester, New York, home of America's biggest regional brewery. Creditably, for a brewery so large, it specializes in ales. Sad to say, neither its *Twelve-Horse Ale* ☆☆ (3.8; 4.7) nor its *Genesee Cream Ale* ☆▷☆☆ (3.7; 4.6) has much character.

Gritty McDuff's

Brewpub in the Old Town area of Portland, Maine (396 Fore St). Products include a well-balanced *Bitter* ☆☆☆; a *Brown Ale* ☆☆▷☆☆☆, the palate on the light side, but with some maltiness; a coffeeish *Stout* ☆▷☆☆; and many seasonal specials.

Hartford

Brewpub in town of same name (35 Pearl St, in a former ice-cream parlour in the financial district). Lively-tasting brews include the unfortunately named *Pitbull Gold* ☆☆, a fruity, perfumey, hoppy, dryish, ale; *Arch Amber* ☆☆ (named after a Civil War memorial), sweeter, but well balanced. Specials have included a *Brown Ale* ☆☆☆▷☆☆☆ which is chocolatey, but again very well balanced.

Heartland

The most metropolitan of brew-restaurants, on the west side of Union Square, New York. Beers include the very soft, spicy (coriander), fruity (orange peels) *Indian River Ale* ☆☆▷☆☆☆; the nutty, malty, *Red Rooster* ☆☆; the toasty, marmaladey, *Cuyahoga Brown* ☆☆; the witty, bitter, *Indiana Pale Ale* ☆☆☆; *Farmer Jon's Oatmeal Stout* ☆☆, creamy and coffeeish; and the spritzy, fruity, *Harvest Wheat* ☆▷☆☆.

Independence
Philadelphia micro. Fruity, dry, *Gold* ☆☆. Full-flavoured, malty but dry, amber *Independence Ale* ☆☆☆▷☆☆☆. Lightly malty, well-balanced, satisfying, Märzen-style, *Franklinfest* ☆☆☆▷☆☆☆.

Ipswich
Earthy, hoppy, fruity *Ipswich Ale* ☆☆, from a micro in the town of the same name, in Massachusetts. The brewery also has a fruity, slightly tannic, brown ale called *Pilgrim* ☆▷☆☆ and a flavoursome, sweetish *Stout* ☆☆ .

John Harvard
Reminiscent of a gentlemen's club, though women are most welcome. Chicken pot pie a speciality but much more ambitious fare, too. British-accented beers. Best are the lightly dry, citric-tasting Old Willy *IPA* ☆☆☆▷☆☆☆ and the beautifully balanced *Mid Winter Strong Ale* ☆☆☆▷☆☆☆. (33 Dunster St, off Harvard Sq, Cambridge; ☎868-3585)

Lion
Old-established brewery in the former coal town of Wilkes-Barre, Pennsylvania. Products include *Stegmaier 1857* ☆☆, malty but dryish, with a good hop note in the finish; and *Stegmaier Porter* ☆☆▷☆☆☆, dry, firm, chocolatey, slightly oily, and now an all-malt brew. Stegmaier was once a rival brewery across town.

McNeill's
Cask-conditioned ales at a brewpub in Brattleboro, Vermont (90 Elliot St). Robust, malty and sometimes with notes of Madeira. A sweetish, creamy, golden *Bitter* ☆☆; a fuller-coloured, hoppier *Special* ☆☆; a dryish, tasty *Nut-brown* ☆☆; a flavour-packed *Double Brown* ☆☆☆; and a hugely aromatic *IPA* ☆☆☆. Products have also included a soft, pale *Bock* ☆☆ which has a good malt character.

Magic Hat
Lively micro in Burlington, Vermont. Beers generally have big, well-rounded, flavours. Blind Faith *IPA* ☆☆▷☆☆☆ is a firm, hoppy example.

Mass Bay
Abbreviated micro on Boston Harbor, Massachusetts Bay. Principal product is *Harpoon Ale* ☆☆, fruity, with a firm, cookie-like maltiness and a perfumy, hoppy finish. Bottled beers are brewed at F X Matt.

F X Matt/Saranac
From the Black Forest, the Francis Xavier Matt family emigrated to the Mohawk River valley and built a brewery in Utica, under the Saranac name. Today, the fourth generation of the Utica Matts works in the company. Its many products range from flowery, notably crisp *Saranac Golden Pilsner* ☆☆ to nutty buttery, dark *Chocolate Amber* ☆☆▷☆☆☆.

Middlesex Brewing Company
Micro established in 1993 in the high-tech town of Burlington, near Boston, Massachusetts, Early products include the chocolatey, dark, *Middlesex Brown Ale* ☆☆▷☆☆☆ and a very roasty, firm *Oatmeal Stout* ☆☆.

The Mountain Brewers

Near skiing country at Bridgewater, Vermont. Micro making *Long Trail Ale* ☆☆, light, soft, fruity, with a gentle bitterness in the finish.

Mountain Valley/Ruffian

In the Ramapo Mountains, but actually commuting distance from Manhattan, at Suffern (122 Orange Ave), New York. This brewpub produces a wide range of well-made beers, from a *Pils* ☆☆☆ with very good hop flavours, by way of a fruity, tart, Belgian-accented, *Copper Ale* ☆☆, to a complex , whiskyish, chocolatey, *Porter* ☆☆▷☆☆☆.

Neptune

A bridal-wear manufacturer shares premises and ownership with this uniquely New York phenomenon: a rag trade microbrewery. Products include a vaguely Scottish Ale, malty and rounded, curiously called *Neptune U* ☆☆; a sweeter, more complex, brew, *Neptune 66* ☆▷☆☆☆; and *Black Sea Stout* ☆☆, with lively dark-chocolate flavours.

New Amsterdam

New Amsterdam Amber ☆☆ is a fruity lager/ale hybrid. A hoppier version is called *New Amsterdam Ale* ☆☆☆▷☆☆☆. These were briefly brewed in Chelsea, Manhattan, but are now made under contract at F. X. Matt.

New England Brewing Company

Smart brewpub and restaurant in Norwalk, Connecticut. Products include *Atlantic Amber* ☆☆▷☆☆☆, a medium-bodied, malt-accented, creamy, earthy, fruity brew; *Gold Stock Ale* ☆☆☆, with an oily-malty body, lots of flavour development and a long, hoppy, finish; and a dry, firm, smooth, palate-arousing *Oatmeal Stout* ☆☆▷☆☆☆.

New York Harbor

New York Harbor Ale ☆☆ is golden in colour, starting soft and malty, but with a crisp, hoppy, almost tart, finish. *New York Harbor Porter* ☆▷☆☆ is a light, well-balanced, coffeeish, interpretation of the style. These beers were created by New Yorker Sal Pennachio, and are brewed under contract at Stevens Point, Wisconsin.

Northampton Brewery

Bar and grill making lagers and ales, at Brewster Court, Northampton, Massachusetts. Products have included a Saaz-accented Pilsener called *Gold* ☆☆; a relatively light Vienna-style *Amber* ☆☆; and some excellent seasonal specials, including a dark, smooth, *Bock* ☆☆▷☆☆☆.

Old Dominion

Virginia, the first English colony, is sometimes known as the Old Dominion. This sobriquet was taken as a corporate name by a micro established in 1990 in the Virginia suburbs, near to Washington's Dulles Airport. The "old" is dropped in the name of the beers. Very well-made beers, mainly German in style, ranging from the Dortmunder-ish *Dominion Lager* ☆☆☆▷☆☆☆ to a well-lagered *Spring Bock* ☆☆☆ and clovey *Summer Wheat* ☆☆☆. Also produces the astonishingly aromatic, dry, *Tuppers' Hop Pocket* ☆☆☆▷☆☆☆☆ ale.

Olde Town
Busy lunch and dinner spot in the Washington outer suburb and former town of Gaithersburg, Maryland. This brewpub, in a smartly converted general store, offers whisky sausages with a fruity *Scottish Ale* ☆☆; a hoppy, creamy, oily *Porter* ☆☆▷☆☆☆ and a well-rounded *Stout* ☆☆.

Ould Newbury
Commercial home-brewery in Newbury, on the North Shore of Massachusetts. *Yankee Ale* ☆☆ is soft and sweetish, with a hoppy dryness in the finish. It is marketed unfiltered.

Otter Creek
Psycho-pharmacologist Lawrence Miller studied the effects of alcohol on the brain before establishing this micro, in Middlebury, Vermont. Complex, malty, beers, notably a very drinkable, golden *Helles Alt* ☆☆☆.

Oxford Brewing
A Briton founded this micro, in Baltimore. Its *Oxford Class* ☆☆▷☆☆☆ is a very English-tasting ale, malt accented but very well balanced. Sometimes found cask-conditioned as *Oxford Real Ale*. Also produced is a smooth, chocolatey *Porter* ☆☆▷☆☆☆.

Penn Brewing
Handsome beer-hall, making its own excellent products in the 1880 Eberhardt & Ober brewery building in the "German town" of Pittsburgh (800 Vinial St, at Troy Hill, Allegheny). Products include a clean, malty Helles called *Penn Light Lager* ☆☆▷☆☆☆; a hoppy *Kaiser Pils* ☆☆☆; the Munich-style chocolatey, slightly roasty *Penn Dark* ☆☆; an aromatically malty, smooth *Märzen Fest* ☆☆☆; and a very malty, delicious *Bock* ☆☆☆▷☆☆☆.

Portsmouth Brewery
Brewery-restaurant in Portsmouth, New Hampshire (56 Market St). Products include the malty, fruity (figgy?) ale *Old Brown Dog* ☆☆▷☆☆☆.

Potomac River
Micro established in Chantilly, Virginia, in 1993. First product, adopting an earlier spelling, was *Patowmack Ale* ☆☆, with a firm body and a touch of maltiness in the finish. Also a fruity *Red* ☆☆ and a medium-dry chocolatey *Porter* ☆☆.

Ram's Head/Fordham
A 1740s tavern invoking the memory of a colonial brewer in Annapolis, Maryland. A brewpub since 1995, but with German style beers: a soft but complex *Helles* ☆☆☆; a very authentic *Alt* ☆☆☆ and a layered, malty *Doppelbock* ☆☆☆

Ramstein
German-style wheat beers, malt-accented, in *Blonde* ☆☆☆ (actually tan) and *Dark* ☆☆☆, versions, from the High Point micro, Butler, New Jersey.

Red Bell
In an 1895 brewery among the relics and ghosts of four or five others, in what was once the beer-making quarter of Philadelphia. This micro produces the light but malty Philadelphia *Original Lager* ☆☆ and a textured *Scotch Ale* ☆☆▷☆☆☆, among others.

Rohrhbach
A church occupies part of this former school building in an old German quarter of Rochester (315 Gregory St), New York. The rest is a brewpub. Good malt accent in all the beers, especially a *Scotch Ale* ☆☆▷▷☆. Elsewhere in Rochester, The Old Toad Pub (277 Alexander St) cask-conditions ales from Geary.

Rolling Rock
Long-established lager with a cult following, though it has no great character beyond a touch of new-mown hay. *Rolling Rock* ☆▷▷☆☆ is brewed in the monastery town of Latrobe, near Pittsburgh, Pennsylvania. A more interesting range, notably a *Bavarian Black* ☆☆ is produced under the Latrobe brand.

Shipyard
Miller now has a stake in this Portland micro, noted for its hoppy, fruity, tasty ales – including a complex version of the British beer *Old Thumper* ☆☆▷☆☆☆. There is an associated brewpub in Kennebunkport called Federal Jack's.

Sisson's
Pubby downstairs; cosy, well-regarded, restaurant upstairs. Beers include the toasty, *Stockade Amber* ☆▷☆☆; the buttery, peppery, *Irish Red* ☆☆▷☆☆; the dark, deep, *Edgar Allan Porter* ☆☆ and the orangey-tasting, Belgian-style, *Frère Jaffe* ☆☆☆▷☆☆☆. Sissons is at 36 E Cross St (opposite the market), Baltimore; ☎ 539-2093.

Stoudt
Not a style but a surname. Mrs Carol Stoudt's brewery constantly wins awards, confirming its status as one of the finest in the East. Products include a *Pilsener* ☆☆☆ with a delicate bouquet, good hop flavours and a dry finish; a well-balanced *Export Gold* ☆☆☆ with a superbly aromatic malt character; several seasonal interpretations of malty Bocks (one with clover honey) and spicy wheat beers, as well as more Anglophone top-fermenting styles such as a hoppy *IPA* ☆☆☆▷☆☆☆; and a *Belgian Double* ☆☆☆▷☆☆☆ and *Triple* ☆☆☆▷☆☆☆ with clovey notes The brewery is at Adamstown, Pennsylvania, between Reading and Lancaster, on Route 272. There is a steak restaurant, beer garden, and Sunday antiques market.

Straub
Smallest of the old-established breweries in the USA. Family-owned and a part of the local folklore in St Mary's, in the Allegheny Mtns, 100 miles N of Pittsburgh. *Straub Beer* ☆▷☆☆ has a sweet aroma and palate, a light body and a dry finish.

Sunday River
Ski resort brewery and restaurant at Sunday River, near Bethel, Maine. Well-made beers include a malty but well-balanced *Alt* ☆☆▷☆☆☆; the sweeter, fruitier, hoppier *Redstone Ale* ☆☆; the slightly syrupy *Barons Brown Ale* ☆☆☆▷☆☆☆; and *Black Bear Porter* ☆☆, coffeeish, liqueur-like: perhaps more like a sweet stout.

Tremont
Boston micro making a fruity ale, occasionally available cask-conditioned, as *Best Bitter* ☆☆☆▷☆☆☆

Vermont Pub and Brewery

Nancy Noonan, wife of beer-writer Greg, runs this vaguely Irish brewpub in a cosy Italianate restaurant (144 College St) in downtown Burlington (a college town and tourist spot on the US side of Lake Champlain. A wide and constantly changing range has included a full-bodied but dry *Kellerbier* ☆☆▷☆☆☆; the sweetish, perfumey, *Burly Irish Ale* ☆☆; a hoppy *Winter Ale* ☆☆; and a very dry *Smoked Porter* ☆☆☆, the latter made at various times with maple, hickory or applewood.

Victory

West of Philadelphia, at Downingtown. Two veterans of the micro movement make beers that are well-balanced and very expressive in their hop and malt character, from the notably Saaz-accented *Prima Pils* ☆☆☆ to the creamy, slightly smoky, *St Victorious Doppelbock* ☆☆☆.

Wharf Rat

With family origins in Kent, owner Bill Oliver makes English-accented beers. His best is his lightly syrupy, malty, *ESB* ☆☆. His establishment has the atmosphere of a true pub, right down to its stone cellars. It is in a row of 1860s merchants' buildings in Baltimore (206 W. Pratt St; ☎244-8900), opposite Camden Yards, where trains once shunted, and now the home of the Orioles' baseball park. Oliver also has a Wharf Rat, but without a brewery, at Fell's Point.

Wild Goose

The geese that give their name to this micro visit its home turf each October, and take their chance with hunters. The brewery is at Cambridge, Maryland. Its *Amber Beer* ☆☆ has a malty start, with hoppy dryness in the finish. Its *Porter* ☆☆▷☆☆☆ is full of flavour, with fruit, chocolate, vanilla, and Bourbon-like notes.

Woodstock

The festival was not quite in Woodstock, and neither is this micro, though the owner lives there. The Woodstock Brewing Company is nearby, in the Hudson Valley town of Kingston, once the state capital of New York. The brewery was founded in 1992. Products include spicy *Hudson Lager* ☆☆; the light, fruity, dry *St James Ale* ☆☆; and smooth, dry *Porter* ☆☆.

Yards

The Philadelphia "village" Manayunk (Native American: "where we go to drink") is the home of this micro. Very assertive beers, including a stingingly peppery *IPA* ☆☆☆ and a sweetish, firm, smooth, gingery *Saison* ☆☆▷☆☆☆.

Yuengling

The oldest brewery in the United States, and thriving. Yuengling, founded in 1829 and still owned by the family, is best known for its *Porter* ☆☆, which has a soft, medium, body, a hint of liquorice and a dash of roasty dryness. *Lord Chesterfield Ale* ☆▷☆☆ is light, but with a nice touch of hops.

THE SOUTHEAST

Breweries are springing up throughout the South, despite heat that favours beer as simply a quencher, social attitudes that deem anything but a national beer un-American, and the Bible belt. Only Mississippi is wholly without a beer to call its own. Look out for *Southern Draft.*

WHERE TO DRINK

Miami: Tobacco Road, 626 S Miami. Brewpubs: Thai Orchid, 9565 Sunset Drive; and, in Miami Beach: The Abbey, 1115 16th St; Clevelander, 1020 Ocean Drive; South Pointe Seafood; 1 Washington Ave.

New Orleans: Bulldog, 3236 Magazine St; Cooter Brown's (509 S Carrollton), and Carrollton Station (8140 Willow St), both on the Charles St streetcar line. Brewpubs: Acadian, 201 N Carrollton. See entry for Crescent City.

Orlando: Cricketers Arms, 8445 International Drive, Mercado Village. See entry for Beach.

Abita

New Orleans' local micro, albeit across Lake Ponchartrain, with a brewpub in Abita Springs (72011 Holly St). This deservedly successful southern pioneer brews lagers, including a nutty *Amber* ☆☆ and the whiskyish *Andygator* ☆☆☆ (1080; 20; 7.0; 8.5). The tawny to dark *Turbodog* ☆☆▷☆☆☆ is grainy, toffeeish, brew on the lines of an Altbier. In New Orleans, also look out for flavoursome beers from the Rikenjaks micro, of Jackson, Louisiana.

Atlanta Brewing

Spring water is brought 60 miles by tanker truck from Blue Ridge, Georgia, to this new micro in urban Atlanta. Perhaps this touch contributes to the smoothness of the malty, chocolatey, fruity, *Red Brick Ale* ☆☆. The city also has the Marthasville Brewing Company, which produces the nutty, slightly medicinal, *Sweet Georgia Brown* ☆☆. Good selections of beer at the local Taco Mac chain of bars.

Beach Brewing

Micro opposite Universal Studios, Orlando, Florida. Sweetish *Red Rock* ☆▷☆☆☆ and tawnier, nuttier, *Magic Brew* ☆▷☆☆. Part of the Mill group (*see* entry).

Big River

Chattanooga, Tennessee, brewpub, in 1903 trolley barn. For a light-bodied ale, *Fool's Gold* ☆☆☆▷☆☆☆ is outstandingly hoppy.

Birmingham Brewing Company

Alabama micro. Products include the malty, nutty, fruity *Red Mountain Red Ale* ☆☆. Birmingham also has the unconnected Magic City brewpub (420, 21st St S); best beer is the rummy *Old Oxmoor Stout* ☆☆. Magic City also has a brewpub in Mobile.

Blackstone

Nashville, Tennessee, restaurant and brewery. Mahogany interior matches the colour of the silky *Saint Charles Porter* ☆☆. Also black, chocolatey, *Oatmeal Stout* ☆☆▷☆☆☆. Subtle, complex. beers. (1918 West End Ave).

Bluegrass

Louisville, Kentucky brewpub. Has a hoppy *Pils* ☆☆▷☆☆☆, good despite the use of a top-fermenting yeast. *St Matthew's* ☆☆ is a treacle-toffeeish strong ale. (3929 Shelbyville Rd).

Bohannon/Market Street

   Lindsay Bohannon's family was in the tobacco business, but he prefers beer. His micro is in what were the elegant offices and warehouse of the Green Briar whiskey distillery, on 2nd Ave (formerly Market St), Nashville, Tennessee. The brewery's *Pilsener* ☆☆▷☆☆☆ is smooth and dry, with a spicy hop finish; its *Wheat* ☆☆ soft and fruity; its *Golden Ale* ☆☆ fruity and sweetish.

   Among seasonal specialities, the *Oktoberfest* ☆☆ (15; 1060; 4.5; 5.6) has a beautifully sustained aromatic hop character but perhaps too roasty a malt note.

Bosco's

The name comes from the Italian for "wood". This stylishly Italianate restaurant-pub also uses its wood-burning pizza oven to heat stones to make a brew inspired by the German Rauchenfels Steinbeer. *The Famous Flaming Stone Beer* ☆☆☆ is surprisingly light but firm, with a toffeeish palate and a late smoky dryness on the finish. The brewery also has a wide range of well-made beers. It is located at 7615 W Farmington Boulevard, Germantown, an affluent suburb of Memphis, Tennessee. Also in Nashville.

Brewbakers

West Virginia, brewpub, in a former department store (857 3rd Ave, Huntington). German-style beers include a very malty, banana-ish, *Weizen* ☆☆☆▷☆☆☆.

Carolina Brewery

At Chapel Hill, the third town of the Raleigh-Durham area, in North Carolina. This cafe-style brewpub has good food and well-made beers, including a well-balanced, aromatic, Bohemian-style Pilsener called *Franklin Street Lager* ☆☆▷☆☆☆.

Crescent City

New Orleans brewpub on Decatur Street, facing Jackson Square (where the old Jax brewery is now a shopping mall). A German owner offers a very hoppy, dry, *Pils* ☆☆☆; the bronze coloured *Red Stallion* ☆☆, which has a cookie-like maltiness; and a dark lager, *Black Forest* ☆☆▷☆☆☆, with coffeeish notes.

Dilworth

Brewpub in Charlotte (1301 E Bvd), N Carolina. Products include *Albemarle Ale* ☆☆, bronze, buttery, and slightly sharp in the finish, and a malty, grainy, very sweet, *Scottish Ale* ☆☆▷☆☆☆ and a coffeeish *Porter* ☆☆.

Dixie

New Orleans' colourful survivor. This much-loved 1907 brewery, with its domed building and cypress fermenters, now makes a far greater range of beers. The basic *Dixie Beer* ☆☆ is a light lager with a touch of malt character. *Blackened Voodoo Lager* ☆☆▷☆☆☆ has a deep, tawny colour and a malty, treacly, palate (4.3; 5.4); really a respectable Kulmbach-style lager? *Crimson Voodoo Ale* ☆☆▷☆☆☆ has a complex, malty-fruity character. A "white chocolate" beer is as sickly as its inspiration.

Hilton Head
First brewpub in South Carolina, at Hilton Head (7C Greenwood Drive). Products include a toffeeish *Scottish Ale* ☆☆.

Irish Times
Mock-Irish pub with brewery, in Palm Beach Gardens (9920 Alternate A-I-A), Florida. Products include a sweet, toffeeish, *Irish Red Ale* ☆▷☆☆.

Jack Daniel's
The famous whiskey distillery, at Lynchburg, Tennessee, has turned its former bottling hall into a small brewery. Jack Daniel's *Amber Lager* ☆☆ is clean, simple, and lightly toffeeish. A raspberry-flavoured, spiced *Winter Brew* ☆☆, aged over oak chips, was everything and nothing.

McGuire's
Big, bustling brewpub in Pensacola (600 E Gregory), Florida. Principal product is a malty, buttery, vanilla-scented, *Irish Red* ☆☆. A grainier, fruitier, version called *Irish Ale* is produced by Oldenberg for bottling.

Miami Brewing
With a sampling bar for guests, this micro in 1995 ended Miami's status as a beer desert. First beer was the pleasantly dry, all-malt, *Hurricane Reef Lager* ☆☆, followed by a sweetish *Raspberry Wheat* ☆☆. 9292 NW 101 St; %305-888-6505.

Mill Bakery and Brewery
Chain (a baker's dozen) in Florida and the South. Each managed separately, so products vary from the disappointing to the delightful (for example, a rich *Scottish Ale* ☆☆☆), at Winter Park, a suburb of Orlando, Florida.

Nail City
Celebrating the local industry in Wheeling, West Virginia. Opposite the Civic Center, this handsome brewpub offers a muscular, hoppy, *ESB* ☆☆☆.

Oldenberg
A Southern brewery by virtue of its location in Fort Mitchell (400 Buttermilk Pike), Kentucky, but just across the river from the Midwestern city of Cincinnati. It looks authentically like an 1880s German brewery, but was built in the 1980s. Has an entertainment hall and pub-restaurant. Oldenburg's chief product is a soft, malty pale lager *Premium Verum* ☆☆.

Ozark
Arkansas brewpub-restaurant, opposite the Walton Arts Center in Fayetteville. Beers include an *India Pale Ale* ☆☆☆ heady with East Kent Goldings.

Ragtime
Brewpub and seafood grill, in Atlantic Beach, near Jacksonville, Florida (207 Atlantic Bvd). Products include *Redbrick Ale* ☆☆, light, soft and malty-fruity.

Richbrau
The old capital of the South, Richmond, Virginia, has a brewpub at the Queen's Arms (1214 Cary St, in the 19th-century part of the town). Products have notably included a creamy, winey, barley wine called *Poe's Tell Tale Ale* ☆☆☆. Richmond also has a

microbrewery with a taproom called Legends. Look out for their smooth *Pilsner* ☆☆▷☆☆☆ which has a spicy hop character. (321 W 7th St).

River City
Overlooking yacht harbour and riverfront at Jacksonville, Florida. Big brewpub with good kitchen. Brews include a *Barley Wine* ☆☆▷☆☆☆ with a good malt character. (835 Gulf Life Drive).

Tomcat
Brewer Thom Tomlinson makes the complex, long, *Bengal IPA* ☆☆☆ in a micro in Raleigh, North Carolina.

Vino's
Winey-sounding pizza restaurant making flavoursome beers in Little Rock, Arkansas. *Rainbow Wheat* ☆☆☆ has notes of toffee, banana and lemon, (923 W 7th St).

West Virginia
Main street (1291 University Ave) brewpub in Morgantown. *Appalachian Ale* ☆☆ is nutty and long.

Ybor City
The name refers to the Cuban neighbourhood of Tampa, Florida, where this micro operates in a former cigar factory. Early products have included the malty but spritzy *Ybor Gold* ☆☆ lager and the reddish-brown *Gaspar's Ale* ☆☆▷☆☆☆. The latter, named after pirate Joe Gaspar, is almost an Old Ale available round the corner at The Oak Barrel Tavern (1901N 13th St).

THE MIDWEST
Once the best-known brewing region in the US, but the initiative had gone west long before Pabst and Schlitz closed their Milwaukee breweries. The region is fighting back with micros. Two of the livelies, Lakefront and Sprecher, are in the old brewing capital.

WHERE TO DRINK
Chicago: Just a couple of blocks from the Water Tower is the Clark Street Ale House, near the corner with Chicago Ave. Quenchers, at Fullerton and Western Ave, is a more established speciality beer-bar. A former brewing family owns The Berghoff (17 W Adams and State St, in The Loop), perhaps the best of the surviving old beer taverns in the US; it is well-run, with a carefully chosen, if limited, selection of beers, and its lunch counter's halibut sandwiches are justly famous.

Milwaukee: It sounds ironic, but the Water Street brewpub takes its name from the thoroughfare on which it stands, at number 1101, one block N of the Performing Arts Center. The brewery makes commendable ales from extract. At the former Schlitz brewery tap, the Brown Bottle (221 W Galena Court), there is a long beer-list, and a splendid 1930s interior.

No city has as many famous old German restaurants. These include the grand, vaulted dining rooms of Maders (1037–41 3rd Ave), with a long list of beers and a museum of steins. Look out for *Midwest Beer Notes* and *Great Lakes Brewing News*.

Minneapolis: Several brewpubs, including The District, with the very malty, anis-tinged, witty, *Grateful Red* ☆☆☆ (430 1st Ave N, near the Target Center). Among those in St Paul is Shannon Kelly's (downtown, at 395 Wabasha), with a soft. roasty, *Stout* ☆☆ and a sweetish, nutty, *Brown Ale* ☆☆▷☆☆☆.

Adler of Appleton
An 1858 brewery in Appleton, Wisconsin, converted into a mall that accommodates two restaurants served by a single small brewhouse (1004 S Old Oneida). Products, which seem somewhat variable, have included a sweetish *Amber* ☆, a creamy, rooty, *Oatmeal Stout* ☆☆ and a rich *Bock* ☆▷☆☆. A pumpkin beer (unfortunately, not tasted) has won plaudits.

Anheuser-Busch
The St Louis-based brewer of *Budweiser* ☆ and the better-balanced *Michelob* ☆▷☆☆ produces 30 or so other beers. The Michelob Specialty range includes a fruity, sherbety *Hefe Weizen* ☆☆▷☆☆☆ and a lightly toffeeish *Amber Bock* ☆☆. A more assertive American Originals selection has a crisp, tinglingly hoppy, golden lager called *Faust* ☆☆▷☆☆☆ and a licorice-tasting, creamy, *Black and Tan* ☆☆▷☆☆☆. An *American Hop Ale* ☆☆☆ is grassy, fruity, appetizingly bitter and robust. *Red Wolf* ☆☆ is a sweet, syrupy, lager. A similar product has been marketed in Britain under the name *Roscoe's Red*.

Boulevard
Well-run micro in Kansas City, Missouri, producing a dry, clean, peachy-citric, refreshing *Wheat Beer* ☆☆▷☆☆☆; a *Pale Ale* ☆☆▷☆☆☆ with a rounded, fruity, palate, moving to a hoppy finish; and *Bully!* ☆☆▷☆☆☆, a chocolatey, fruity, roasty, earthy, dry porter. Also in Kansas City, Mo: 75th St brewpub, with an aromatic *Oatmeal Stout* ☆☆ (520 W 75th).

Brewmasters Pub
Housed in a former monastery building in Kenosha (4017 80th St), between Milwaukee and Chicago. *Kenosha Gold* ☆ is a well-balanced lager; *Amber Vienna* ☆☆ has good malt flavours; *Royal Dark* ☆☆ has a touch of chocolate; and a *Smoked Porter* ☆☆☆ balances mesquite and hickory with East Kent Goldings.

Broad Ripple
Brewpub in the Broad Ripple entertainment district of Indianapolis (840 E 65th St). The owner, John Hill, is from Yorkshire, England. Products have included an *IPA* ☆☆▷ ☆☆☆ with a sharp smack of hop in the finish; a British-accented *ESB* ☆☆☆, with lots of flavour development; and a light, smooth, malty-coffeeish *Porter* ☆☆.

Capital
Its beer-garden gave the rubric Garten Bräu to beers from this micro in Middleton, which adjoins Madison, state capital of Wisconsin. At their best, the beers are very good. They include a malty *Lager* ☆☆ broadly in the Munich Helles style; a hoppy Pilsener called *Special* ☆☆▷☆☆☆; a malty, coffeeish, slightly oily *Dark* ☆☆▷☆☆☆; an enjoyably spicy *Weizen* ☆☆☆ (served with yeast) and seasonal specials.

Cherryland

Close to the cherry-growing country of Door County, Wisconsin. This micro is in a turn-of-the-century train station, at Sturgeon Bay. Its malt-tinged *Golden Rail* ☆ and hoppier *Silver Rail* ☆ are brewed from extract. Both are thinnish with light fruitiness throughout. The brewery also makes cherry and apple beers.

Chicago Brewing Company

Born in a former pickle factory in 1989. Aggressive micro producing *Legacy Lager* ☆☆☆, starting firm and malty and becoming perfumey and hoppy; *Legacy Red Ale* ☆☆, its syrupy maltiness balanced by a touch of tart hoppiness; *Big Shoulders Porter* ☆, with a suggestion of liquorice; and *Heartland Weiss* ☆☆▷☆☆☆, with a hint of clove.

Cold Spring

This old (1874) regional in Cold Spring, Minnesota, has become very marketing-oriented under new owners. The revived *Gluek's Pilsner* ☆ is sweetish and bland.

Columbus

Promising ales, made with a mix of whole grain and malt extract, at a very small micro in an old brewery complex in Columbus, state capital of Ohio. Products include a *Pale Ale* ☆☆☆ in very much the British style and a *Nutbrown Ale* ☆☆▷☆☆☆ with a malty palate and a "winter warmer" character. The beers are available at the adjoining Gibby's Tavern and Hagen's, a restaurant serving hearty American food.

Crane River

Brewpub in Lincoln, Nebraska (200 N 11th). Products include the somewhat roasty *Sod House Altbier* ☆▷☆☆☆.

Crooked River

Micro founded in 1994 in Cleveland, Ohio. Products include *Black Forest Lager* ☆☆▷☆☆☆, with a good malt character and a late, hoppy, dryness; and the malty, fruity, strong (16; 1064; around 5.3;6.4) *Yuletide Ale* ☆☆▷☆☆☆.

Dubuque Star

Lovely late 1800s brewery overlooking the Mississippi at Dubuque, Iowa. Its many products include the reddish-brown lager *Big Muddy* ☆☆, with a crisp maltiness remniniscent of peanut brittle.

Firehouse

In the 1915 firehouse of Rapid City, S Dakota (610 Main St). Products have included a very hoppy *Bitter* ☆☆ and a very sweet *Barley Wine* ☆☆.

Flatlanders

Large brewpub, with striking, Prairie-style architecture, north of Chiacgo. Products include an excellent, lightly peaty, Scottish-style *Eighty Shilling Ale* ☆☆☆. Try it with the pheasant. (Route 45 and Milwaukee Ave, in the village of Lincolnshire).

Free State

Between Kansas City and Topeka, the town of Lawrence was associated with the anti-slavery Free State Party. Today, it is the home of a well-regarded brewpub in an old trolley depot (tram-shed) at 636 Massachusetts, just north of Liberty Hall Opera House. Products include a hearty *India Pale Ale* ☆☆☆ with excellent hop flavours.

Golden Prairie
In the pre-Prohibition Michael Brand brewery, in Chicago. This micro has a local following for inventive brews like its Bourbon-tasting *Maple Stout* ☆☆▷☆☆☆ and *Buckwheat Beer* ☆☆☆, with a grainy note reminiscent of poppyseed cake.

Goose Island
An encyclopedic range of specialities rotates at this brewpub, on a goose-neck of land near Chicago's Halsted nightlife area (1800 N Clybourn). From an unfiltered, pale, Slavic *Pivo* ☆☆▷☆☆☆ to the huge, oaky *Bourbon County Stout* ☆☆☆▷☆☆☆☆. Goose Island's separate micro concentrates on the rounded *Honker's Ale* ☆☆▷☆☆☆.

Great Dane
State capital brewpub in Madison (Dane County), Wisconsin. Excellent beers, including a subtle and complex *IPA* ☆☆▷☆☆☆ and a *Barley Wine* ☆☆▷☆☆☆ with suggestions of oak and oloroso sherry. (123 East Doty St; ☎608-284-0000). The town's Angelic brewpub (322 W. Johnson St) has more restrained, but well-made, beers.

Great Lakes
In an 1860s saloon (complete with genuine bullet holes), Jungian academic Patrick Conway and his brother Dan established Cleveland's first brewpub and subsequently micro, with a modestly serious restaurant downstairs (2516 Market St). Products include a soft, perfumy, dryish *Dortmunder Gold* ☆☆▷☆☆☆; and a rounder, deeper, Vienna-style lager named after local gangbuster *Eliot Ness* ☆☆▷☆☆☆. Additions include a beautifully balanced hoppy-fruity bitter called *Moondog Ale* ☆☆☆; the bravely named (after an incident in local folklore) *Burning River Pale Ale* ☆☆▷☆☆☆, full of malt and hop flavours, with a long finish; the aromatic, hoppy, fruity *Commodore Perry IPA* ☆☆▷☆☆☆; and very dark, dense, coffeeish but dry and clean *Edmund Fitzgerald Porter* ☆☆▷☆☆☆ that might be better termed a stout.

Great Northern
In the former Great Northern railroad station at Fargo, North Dakota. This brewpub's range notably includes the creamy, figgy, spicy, *Pullman Porter* ☆☆▷☆☆☆.

Hoster
Revival of old brewery name, near its original premises, in Columbus, Ohio. The new Hoster's is an excellent brewpub, in an old trolley barn (tram-shed), at 550 S High St Brews, all bottom-fermented, include well-balanced *Gold Top* ☆☆▷☆☆☆, a little lighter than it once was; an *Amber Lager* ☆☆▷☆☆☆, quite dry for the style; and the smooth, espresso-ish *Eagle Dark* ☆☆☆, a year-round Bock. The Bologna sandwiches are also recommended.

Huber
This old-established brewery in Monroe, Wisconsin, includes in its portfolio several beers originally made for the Berghoff tavern, in Chicago. *Original Lager* ☆☆ has a light, malty nose and

an American hop character; *Famous Red Ale* ☆☆ is malty and whiskyish, with a touch of butterscotch. *Genuine Dark Beer* ☆☆ is sweetish and mild, again with a hint of whisky.

Hudepohl-Schoenling
Cincinnati's regional brewery is now a Midwest outpost for Boston Beer (Samuel Adams). It continues to produce *Little Kings* ☆☆▷☆☆☆, a classic American Cream Ale, and the lightly malty *Christian Moerlein* ☆☆ range of lagers for its previous owners.

Indianapolis Brewing Company
In German immigrant days, there was a brewery of this description using the brand Duesseldorfer. The name is reminiscent of Altbier, but the new micro has revived the rubric for several ales. These include a pale, perfumy, malty *Amber* ☆☆ and a thinnish but smooth and roasty *Dark* ☆☆.

Joe's
An occasional, spicy, and tart *Gueuze* ☆☆☆, made with cultures from a bottle of Boon, is a rare treat at this student brewpub in Champaign, Illinois (706 S 5th St).

Jones Street
New brewpub in the old beer-and-brewing neighbourhood of Omaha, Nebraska (1316 Jones). Products include *Ryan's Irish Stout* ☆☆▷☆☆☆, smooth, with treacle-toffee and burnt flavours.

Kalamazoo Brewing Company
The sober-suited Larry Bell delights in brewing eccentricity. His wide range of fruity brews, with intense flavours, includes no fewer than four or five stouts. His strong (10; 12.5) *Expedition Stout* ☆☆☆▷☆☆☆☆ tastes like beef braised with prunes and port wine. Brewery and café at 315 E Kalamazoo Ave.

Lake Superior
In the 1856 former Fitger's brewery in Duluth, Minnesota. This micro has produced the sweetish *Kayak Kölsch* ☆▷☆☆; a malt-accented, slightly roasty *Alt* ☆; and hop-accented *Special Ale* ☆☆▷☆☆☆. There is an adjoining restaurant (600 E Superior).

Lakefront
Robust brews in a wide range from a lively Milwaukee micro. A very bitter *Organic ESB* ☆☆ is a newish product. The longer-established *East Side Dark* ☆☆☆ is rich, malty, chocolatey and perilously drinkable at almost a Bock strength (around 4.75; just under 6.0). On St Valentine's Day, a *Cherry Lager* ☆☆☆ is released. This has recently gained a fuller fruitiness, but still has a good balance of cherry-skin tartness. Door County cherries are used.

Leinenkugel
Frequent new products in recent years, such as a flowery, creamy, (but not particularly wheaty) *Honey Weiss* ☆☆; a rounded, fruity, *Auburn Ale* ☆☆; a toffeeish *Bock* ☆▷☆☆; and a molasses-tasting Doppelbock called *Big Butt* ☆▷☆☆, the goat-inspired name perhaps a joke that rebounds. This old-established enterprise, in Chippewa Falls, Wisconsin, now also operates a brewery in Milwaukee. Leinenkugel is owned by Miller.

Mickey Finn's
A hundred-year-old tavern, now a brewpub, at Libertyville (412 N Milwaukee Ave), in prosperous Lake County, north of Chicago. Good beers, notably a clovey *Hefe-Weizen* ☆☆▷☆☆☆ and a juicy, malty, peaty *Wee Heavy* ☆☆☆.

Miller
In an intensely competitive market, Miller has been obliged to turn its attention back to its light, sweetish, mainstream beers after a period of more interesting brews. Such experimentation is now being left to Leinenkugel, Celis and Shipyard.

Millstream
By a mill stream in the main village of the Amana Church colonies of Iowa. These villages are better known for fruit wines, but this micro adds beer to their offerings. *Millstream Lager* ☆▷☆☆ is sweetish, soft and light; *Schildbrau* ☆☆ is a malty, amber lager in broadly the Vienna style.

Mishawaka
Brewpub in the Indiana town whose name it bears. The pub, in a former fitness centre (3703 N Main St), is less than four miles from the University of Notre Dame. Products include the smooth, dry, complex *Founders' Stout* ☆☆▷☆☆☆.

New Glarus
Excellent micro in the Wisconsin-Swiss town of the same name. Its oustanding brew is an almondy, bittersweet, *Belgian Red* ☆☆☆▷☆☆☆☆ made with cherries from Brussels, Wisconsin, and yeasts from Flanders.

Page
In the old brewery quarter of Minneapolis, a new-generation micro, which is named after its founder. *James Page Private Stock* ☆☆▷☆☆☆ is a hearty, American-accented, Vienna-style lager, with plenty of malt and hop. Page pioneered the use in beer of wild rice, which is native to the Minnesota lake country. The brewery has two products in this style, both taking their name from a natural park on the borders of Minnesota and Canada. *Boundary Waters Wild Rice Beer* ☆☆☆ is light, clean and dry, but with plenty of flavour. *Boundary Waters Bock* ☆☆ is amber, with a clean, sweetish, palate.

Pavichevich
There is truly a Czech accent to the Pilsener with the odd name *Baderbräu* ☆☆☆ produced by this micro in the suburbs of Chicago. When fresh, it has a delightfully flowery bouquet of hops, and some malty sweetness, and both characteristics are sustained through the palate to a gentle, elegant finish. A Bock (not tasted) has proven popular.

Point
Under new ownership in recent years, and with more diversity of products. This small regional brewery, in Stevens Point, Wisconsin, has a light dry, toffeeish, *Pale Ale* ☆▷☆☆ and a creamy, sweetish, *Maple Wheat* ☆☆.

River West
Newish Chicago brewpub in the River West warehouse district. A *Berliner Weisse* ☆☆☆▷☆☆☆ with appropriately lactic flavours wins points for adventurousness, but lacks really acidic sharpness.

Toasty, malty *Doppelbock* ☆☆▷☆☆☆; hoppy-lemony *Red Fox Ale* ☆☆; and chewy, licorice-tinged *Stout* ☆☆. (925 W Chicago Ave. Owner also has Weinkeller brewpubs in Berwyn and Westmont).

Schell

Not only the prettiest location of any brewery in the USA, but also some interesting beers. August Schell, founded in 1860, in New Ulm, Minnesota, has a deer park and gardens open to the public. Products include a hoppy *Pils* ☆☆☆; a lightly malty *Export* ☆☆; a tawny, rummy *Bock* ☆☆; a *Weizen* ☆☆▷☆☆☆ with an apple-pie fruitiness; and the malty-chocolatey *Schmaltz's Alt* ☆☆. The brewery also makes many beers under contract.

Schlafly/Tap Room

Tom Schlafly's brewpub, in downtown St Louis (2100 Locust, at 21st; ☎314-241-2337). Restrained but well-made beers include a cask-conditioned *Pale Ale* ☆☆☆▷☆☆☆.

Sherlock's Home

Outstanding cask-conditioned ales at a brewpub in a suburb of Minneapolis (11000 Red Circle Drive, Minnetonka). *Bishop's Bitter* ☆☆☆, soft but well hopped with Fuggles and Kent Goldings, and with a touch of acidity in the finish, is perhaps America's most English-tasting example of the style. *Piper's Pride* ☆☆☆ is a malty but beautifully balanced Scottish ale, with a dash of oats and of quassia, a bittering made from tree bark. During the period from Thanksgiving to the first week of January, there is a malty, wonderfully oily, *Winter Warmer* ☆☆☆ in a "pin" (small wooden cask) on the bar. This last is dry-hopped, and sometimes tips the odd blossom into the glass. *Palace Porter* ☆☆ is more on the lines of a strong Mild; and *Stag's Head Stout* ☆☆☆ dry and faintly medicinal. The owner, Bill Burdick is distantly related to the late Peter Maxwell Stuart, of the Traquair House brewery, in the Borders in Scotland. The pub also keeps a good selection of single malt Scotches.

Sioux Falls Brewing

In the town of the same name, in South Dakota (431 N Phillips). This brewpub's products include a fruity, hoppy, very drinkable, *Pale Ale* ☆☆; a more complex, slightly Bourbon-ish *Red* ☆☆ and a toasty, roasty, *Stout* ☆☆.

Sprecher

Hearty beers, evoking the traditions that Milwaukee almost forgot. Products have included *Special Amber* ☆☆, a malty but dryish brew broadly in the Vienna style; *Black Bavarian* ☆☆☆ (15; 1060; 4.8; 6.0), smooth and intense, with hints of treacle-toffee, and a huge finish; *Irish Stout* ☆☆▷☆☆☆ (15; 1060; 4.8; 6.0), hoppy, roasty, fruity and enwrapping; *Milwaukee Weiss* ☆☆▷☆☆☆, a lovely pale-amber colour, with both sweetness and acidity; and *Hefe-Weiss* ☆☆☆, an unfiltered version that is full of flavour. The beer can be bought at the brewery (701 W Glendale Ave).

Stroh

National brewer, headquartered in Detroit (though no longer making beer there). Now owns Heileman (of La Crosse, Wisconsin), and brews Pabst. Recent speciality products have included smooth, dryish, brews under the Red River brand (notably a gingery, spiced, *Sunflower Wheat* ☆☆▷☆☆) and classic styles with the Augsburger label. Among the latter, a lightly tart *Weiss*, ☆▷☆☆ a toffeeish *Red* ☆☆, a faintly roasty *Dark* ☆☆, a well-balanced *Bock* ☆☆ and a smokier *Doppelbock* ☆▷☆☆.

Summit
Well-established micro in St Paul, twin city to Minneapolis. A summertime *Sparkling Ale* ☆▷☆☆ is light, dry and faintly yeasty. *Extra Pale Ale* ☆☆ has a malty middle, a good development of perfumed fruitiness and a dry finish. *Great Northern Porter* ☆☆☆ is smooth, with herbal and bitter-chocolate notes. Excellent seasonal specials are also produced by the brewery.

COLORADO AND THE SOUTHWEST

Few Americans would nominate Colorado as the nation's biggest brewing state but, in volume terms, it is. More importantly, it now has one of the liveliest populations of brewpubs and micros.

In large part its best-known brewery, Coors, in Golden, accounts for Colorado's high output of beer. Without Coors, Golden would be a Wild West town, and some consumers still think of Coors as a folksy brewery in the hills, yet its capacity is 15–20 million barrels. There is no bigger single brewery plant in the world. Not far away, in Fort Collins, Coors' rival Anheuser-Busch now has a large brewery. It is curious that, with a further three micros and five or six brewpubs, the 87,758 people of Fort Collins have nine or ten local beer-makers. Fort Collins is the home of the tabloid *Rocky Mountain Brew News*. Austin, Texas, puts out *Southwest Brewing News*.

WHERE TO DRINK

Denver: In recent years, Denver has been the location of the Great American Beer Festival. With about 1,500 beers from more than 300 breweries, all of them American, this event offers a larger selection than any in the world. It is usually held in September or October (details from the Association of Brewers, Box 287, Boulder, Colorado 80306–0287, ☎303–4470816). Denver has about a dozen brewpubs, plus two or three micros. Several of these follow as entries. Pints Pub (221 W 13th Ave, near Denver Library) has a good selection. So do branches of Old Chicago. Even less beer-friendly southwestern states like Nevada, Utah and Oklahoma are beginning to bubble with brewpubs, but the real contest is between Colorado and Texas (reviewed in brief below).

Austin: As well as the Celis (see entry) and the Hill Country micro (making the toasty *Red Granite* ☆☆▷☆☆ ale), Austin has a remarkable collection of brewpubs. The 6th St area, where the young flock to hear music and to drink, has at 502 Trinity, the Copper Tank, a singles bar with decent beer (notably the hoppy *White Tail Ale* ☆☆ and an occasional *IPA* ☆☆▷☆☆). Across Congress, the newly fashionable warehouse district has the pubbier Waterloo (with the most characterful brews, including a long, clean, dry *IPA* ☆☆☆ and a huge *Imperial Stout* ☆☆☆) at 4th and Guadalupe; and, at 4th and Colorado, the more restaurant-orientated Bitter End, with blander beers, though the *IPA* ☆☆▷☆☆☆ has a good surge of hops.

Dallas: The Yegua Creek brewpub (2920 Henderson) has post-modern decor and *Pale Ale* ☆☆☆ with plenty of flavour development. *Vail Pale Ale* ☆☆☆, very bitter and flavourful, recalls the Colorado origins of Hubcap, now also in Dallas (1701 N Market). The Texas/Dallas/West End micro has had another change of name, not to mention change of management. It is now St Andrew's, with the sweetish *Friar's Lager* ☆▷☆☆ and a malty *Friar's Ale* ☆☆.

Houston: One of America's best beer bars is The Gingerman, at 5607 Morningside (and now in other cities). A lively rival (also in other cities) is Timberwolf (2511 Bissonnet, Rice Village). Houston's first brewpub, The Village (2415 Dunstan, nr Rice University) has some very good beers, notably a hoppy, long, *Pale Ale* ☆☆☆ and a big *Raspberry Imperial Stout* ☆☆☆. Nearby, the hoppy *Bad Czech Ale* ☆☆ is served in a former bank. (Bank Draft Brewing, 2424 Dunstan). The offerings at Houston Brewing (6228 Richmond) include a well-balanced *Steam Beer* ☆☆▷☆☆☆ and a fruity *IPA* ☆☆ more on the lines of an ESB. St Arnold's is a newish micro making a good *Kristall Weizen* ☆☆▷☆☆☆, albeit with an ale yeast, a complex, hoppy *Amber* ☆☆▷☆☆☆ and a dry, lightly toffeeish *Brown* ☆☆.

San Antonio: The Boardwalk, at 4011 Broadway, is a health-orientated bistro with some vegetarian offerings; its tiny brewery's products include the flavourful but variable *Extra Special Supersonic Bitter* ☆☆. Joey's (2417 N St Mary's) is a pubby bar with the hoppy *Big Bob's Ale* ☆☆. Frio is a micro making a flavourful *Lager* ☆☆▷☆☆☆. Yellow Rose is also a micro, with a wide range, within which the best beer is the coffeeish *Wildcatter's Stout* ☆☆.

Avery

Micro in Boulder (which has eight or nine breweries). Avery has a nicely nutty, hoppy brew called *Redpoint Ale* ☆☆.

Assets

Brewpub, bakery and grill in Albuquerque, New Mexico (6910 Montgomery NE). Products include the malty *Duke City Amber Ale* ☆▷☆☆ and *Ol' Avalanche* ☆☆▷☆☆☆, with notes of Madeira and allspice.

Bandersnatch

Near the Phoenix Cardinals football stadium and Arizona State University, Bandersnatch (125 E 5th Ave, in the suburb of Tempe) is a brewpub with a well-balanced, English-style bitter called *Premium* ☆☆▷☆☆☆; a flavoursome *Milk Stout* ☆☆; and seasonal specials.

Beaver Street/Whistle Stop

Brewpub in Flagstaff, Arizona. At 11 S Beaver St, near the Amtrak station. Beers include *Railhead Red* ☆☆, reminiscent of an English Bitter. Flagstaff Brewing, at 16 E Highway ("Route") 66, is more studenty. Its offerings include the dry-hopped *Ganouj Pale Ale* ☆☆.

H C Berger

A collector of John Dillinger memorabilia, and keen home-brewer, Sandy Jones established this microbrewery in Fort Collins in 1992. Beers include the clean, light, sweetish *Whistlepin Wheat* ☆☆; the maltier, more complex *Indego Pale Ale* ☆☆; and a dry-hopped *IPA* ☆☆▷☆☆☆ which is aged on oak chips.

Black Mountain

In the fake Wild West town of Cave Creek, near Phoenix. A micro, with the beers featured next door at The Satisfied Frog (6245 E Cave Creek Rd). *Black Mountain Gold* ☆▷☆☆ is a lager with a touch of malt and hop. The very hot *Cave Creek Chili Beer* ☆▷☆☆, containing a whole pod, is produced under contract in Evansville, Indiana.

Breckenridge

The Continental Divide provides a magnificent backdrop for this ski-resort (9,600ft/3,200m) brewpub, at the old gold-mining town of Breckenridge, Colorado (600 S Main). Products have included *Avalanche Ale*☆▷☆☆, fruity, tart and refreshing; the fuller-coloured *End of Trail Ale* ☆☆, which is drier; a notably creamy *Oatmeal Stout* ☆☆☆; and a soft, fruity, unfiltered, *Mountain Wheat* ☆☆. Branches in Denver and other cities.

Bricktown

Oklahoma city brewpub, in the well-restored warehouse district (1 N Oklahoma). Products include a golden, lightly dry *English Ale*☆▷☆☆☆. The state also has some remarkably English-tasting beers, including an excellent *Mild* ☆☆☆, at the Cherry Street brewpub, in Tulsa (15th and Peoria).

Carver

Bakery and brewery in Durango, Colorado (1022 Main). Products include the firm, nutty, toffeeish, malty, *James Brown Ale* ☆☆▷☆☆☆.

Celis

Pierre Celis revived "white" wheat beers in his native Belgium by establishing the Hoegaarden brewery there. After being bought out by national giant Interbrew (Stella Artois), he left for America. He built a brewery there, then sold a controlling interest to Miller. His *Celis White* ☆☆☆☆ is perhaps lighter, certainly softer and fuller in flavour, than today's Hoegaarden. Other products include the creamy, perfumy, flowery *Golden* ☆☆▷☆☆☆; the fruity, dry, almost woody-tasting *Bock* ☆☆ (misnamed; it is a bronze ale, of 4.0; 5.0); the very aromatic, spicy, golden *Grand Cru* ☆☆▷☆☆☆, a less strong (4.0; 5.0) counterpart to Hoegaarden Grand Cru; a toffeeish, spicy *Dubbel* ☆☆☆ (4.4; 5.5).

Champion

Sport bar and brewpub in Denver (1442 Larimer Sq). Products have included the golden, light, sweetish *Sports Ale* ☆▷☆☆ (with a touch of wheat) and the grainy, nutty (peanut brittle?) *Home Run Ale* ☆☆.

CooperSmith's

Smart, successful brewpub in former bakery in Fort Collins (5 Old Town Sq). Wide range of beers has included the very long *Punjabi Pale Ale* ☆☆; the soft, light, dry *Albert Damm Bitter*

☆☆▷☆☆☆; the smooth, nutty *Not Brown Ale* ☆☆▷☆☆☆ (with a tawny colour); and the smoky, peaty, whiskyish *McScooter's Scottish Ale* ☆☆☆.

Coors/Sandlot

In addition to the regular *Coors* ☆☆, the national giant produces the malty, rounded, *Winterfest* ☆☆☆; the slightly buttery *George Killian's* ☆☆, inspired by an Irish ale; the more toffeeish *Killian's Brown* ☆▷☆☆; and, under the Blue Moon name, a lightly flowery, sweetish *Honey Blonde Ale* ☆☆; a cinnamon-tinged *Harvest Pumpkin Ale* ☆☆; and thinnish *Belgian White* ☆☆. and a sweetly malty *Abbey Ale* ☆☆▷☆☆☆. Coors' Field, the Colorado Rockies' baseball park, is the only sports stadium in the world with its own brewpub, called Sandlot. It has made some more assertive brews.

Coyote Springs

Phoenix brewpub, with beer garden on main thoroughfare (4883 N 20th and Camelback). Beers include a very aromatic Belgian-style Triple called *Three Blind Monks* ☆☆▷☆☆☆.

Crested Butte

Brewpub in the Colorado town of the same name (226 Elk Ave). Very fruity, dryish products include *Red Lady Ale* ☆☆.

Denver Chop House

A golden *Mild* ☆☆▷☆☆☆, on handpump, was an interesting entrant at this smart steak restaurant and brewpub in Denver (1735 19th St). Owned by Rock Bottom.

Estes Park

Micro founded in 1993, and immediately acclaimed for its golden *Miners' Pale Ale* ☆☆ and its *Renegade Red* ☆☆☆. To taste the first was like biting on hops, to sample the second like chewing them. Began in Boulder (as High Country); now in Estes Park.

Flying Dog

In the chic mountain resort of Aspen, Colorado (424 E Cooper). *Doggie Style* ☆☆ is a bronze ale with lots of hop. *Wolfhound* ☆☆ is an Irish Stout, very creamy.

Great Basin

In the restored Victorian Avenue district of Sparks, twin town to Reno. This brewpub's specialities include *High Desert Harvest Ale* ☆☆☆ aromatised with pinon nuts, juniper and sagebrush.

Great Divide

Denver micro. Products include the orangey *Bee Sting Honey Ale* ☆☆▷☆☆☆ and a dry, chocolatey, rounded *Porter* ☆☆▷☆☆☆.

Holy Cow!

Casino brewpub in Las Vegas (2423 Las Vegas Bvd S), making better beers than the context suggests. The golden *Pale Ale* ☆☆ is soft and perfumy, while the *Amber Ale* ☆☆ is rich and rounded.

Hops

Café-style brewpub in the Phoenix area. A wide range of products has included a dryish *Pilsner* ☆▷☆☆☆; a malty *Amber Ale* ☆☆; a rather stout-like *Bock* ☆▷☆☆; and orangey-tasting *Barley Wine* ☆☆.

Hubcap

In the ski resort of Vail, Colorado. Brewpub (143 E Meadow Drive) producing a wide range of products, with a creamy house character. These include the aromatic, hoppy, soft, beautifully rounded *Solstice Ale* ☆☆☆ (which has a reddish colour); the almost whiskyish *Beaver Tail Brown Ale* ☆☆☆; and the gentle *Rainbow Trout Stout* ☆☆▷☆☆☆.

Irons
Very small micro in Lakewood, Colorado. Products, all unfiltered, include the dry, hoppy, resiny, almost chewy *Green Mountain Ale* ☆☆▷☆☆☆.

Judge Baldwin's
Colorado Springs brewpub (Antlers Doubletree Hotel, 30 S Cascade). Early products have included a pale but well-balanced *Amber Ale* ☆▷☆☆☆ and a dryish *Porter* ☆☆.

Lonetree
Bottle-conditioned ales from a Denver micro established in 1993. They include a *Cream Ale* ☆☆▷☆☆☆ with a hint of honey-dew melon and a perfumy, dry finish; *Sunset Red* ☆☆, light sweet and fruity; and *Iron Horse Dark* ☆☆, syrupy and chocolatey.

Macfarlane
Family-owned micro in Phoenix. Excellent beers include an orangey, clovey *Hefe-Weizen* ☆☆▷☆☆☆.

New Belgium
Hugely succesful micro. Products have included a soft, malty, fruity, Belgian-style amber ale called *Fat Tire* ☆☆▷☆☆☆ (the name honours mountain-bikers); a tart, well-rounded *Old Cherry Ale* ☆☆▷☆☆☆, with a tempting orange-pink colour, made from locally grown Montmorency sour pie cherries; an *Abbey* ☆☆☆, in the Belgian "Dubbel" style, with lots of malt and fruitiness and a touch of demerara sugar (16.5; 1066; 5.2; 6.5); and a hugely flowery *Trippel* ☆☆☆ (18.5; 1074; 6.4; 8.0).

Oasis
Brewpub in Boulder (1095 Canyon Bvd). Products notably include the soft, complex, hoppy *ESB* ☆☆▷☆☆☆; and the solid, almost tar-tasting *Zoser Stout* ☆☆▷☆☆☆.

Odell
This fast-growing micro in Fort Collins has made, among other products: a perfumy, fruity, *Wheat Beer* ☆☆▷☆☆☆; a malty-fruity *Golden Ale* ☆☆; and a smooth, nutty, Scottish-style *Ninety Shilling* ☆☆☆.

Pike's Peak
Colorado Springs micro. Early products have included golden, hoppy *Jack Rabbit Pale Ale* ☆☆ and tawny, malty, tongue-enwrapping *Red Granite Amber* ☆☆.

Prescott
The historic Western town of Prescott, Arizona, has a lively brew-pub of the same name (130 W Gurley St). Enjoyable, dryish, beers include the very coffeeish *Petrified Porter* ☆☆▷☆☆☆.

Preston
Tiny brewery, operating sporadically in the warmer months. It adjoins the Embudo Station restaurant, where the "Chili Line" railroad once ran between Santa Fe and Taos, New Mexico (State Highway 68). *Ristra* ☆☆☆ is a beautifully rounded chili Brown Ale. Original brewer Steve Eskeback makes a peppery *Green Chili Beer* ☆☆☆ at his own pub in Taos (106 Des Georges Lane).

Rio Bravo

Smart restaurant-brewery in the small, revived downtown of Albuquerque (515 Central Ave NW). At the lighter end, *Coronado Gold* ☆☆▷☆☆☆ has an excellent hop character. So does the fruitier *High Desert Pale Ale* ☆☆▷☆☆☆.

Rock Bottom

Industrial chic brewpub in Denver (1001 16th St). *Premium Draft* ☆▷☆☆ is a light, golden ale; an occasional *Arapahoe Amber* ☆☆ has good, leafy, hop character; *Red Rocks* ☆▷☆☆ is lightly malty; *Falcon* ☆☆ Pale Ale fruit-accented but well-balanced; *Molly's Titanic* ☆☆ a perfectly sinkable Brown Ale that starts sweet and malty but finishes deliciously fruity and tart; *Black Diamond Stout* ☆☆ is full-bodied, with an emphatic bitter-chocolate note. Branches in Cleveland, Minneapolis, Houston, Portland (Oregon), San Jose (California).

Rockies

The original owners of Boulder Brewing, founded in 1979, moved their operation to the present, purpose-built site but left before the company changed its name to Rockies. Based on that connection, it can still claim to be America's longest-established operating micro. Products include a malty-fruity *Amber Ale* ☆☆; a very malty, attractively tawny *Wrigley Red* ☆☆▷☆☆☆, in broadly the style of a Scottish ale; and a roasty *Porter* ☆☆ that seems to have lost some of its edge.

San Juan

Restored rail station brewpub in the resort of Telluride (300 S Townsend). Products include the sweetish *Little Rose Amber Ale* ☆☆; the aromatic, hoppy *Tomboy Bitter* ☆☆; and the winey *Boomerang Brown* ☆▷☆☆.

Santa Fe Brewing Company

On a horse ranch at Galisteo, in the High Mountain Desert near Santa Fe, New Mexico. This micro began with *Santa Fe Pale Ale* ☆☆▷☆☆☆, soft and smooth, malt-accented, with some fruit and a long, gentle, hoppy finish. Later products have included a beautifully balanced *Porter* ☆☆▷☆☆☆.

Schirf/Wasatch

In unlikely Utah, a company whose products include *Wasatch Premium* ☆☆, a hoppy but well-balanced ale, and the flavoursome *Wasatch Weizen* ☆☆. Micro in Salt Lake City and brewpub 25 miles east in the ski resort Park City.

Spoetzl

Bohemian and Bavarian settlers founded this brewery, which in the early 1990s restored its original name. It is in the tiny town of Shiner, about 70 miles S of Austin, and slightly further from St Antonio and Houston. It is a lovely mission-style building, but its beers are more mainstream: the light *Shiner Premium* ☆; a dark counterpart described as a *Bock* ☆▷☆☆; the slightly drier *Kosmas* ☆☆, named after Mr Spoetzl; and a light *Wheat* ☆☆.

Squatters

Salt Lake brewpub (147 W Broadway). Products include the lemony, gingery, refreshing *Rocky Mountain Wheat* ☆☆; the grainy *Cole's Special Bitter* ☆▷☆☆; the perfectly described *Hop*

Head Red ☆☆▷☆☆☆; and the smooth, malty *Parley's Porter* ☆☆. The company has opened a second brewpub, bakery and deli one block S of the Delta Center (home of the Utah Jazz basketball team).

Tabernash
Mystical Native American name for a Denver micro making outstanding German-style brews. Its *Weiss* ☆☆☆ has an excellent clove character. Its *Denargo Lager* ☆☆☆ is a dark, Munich-style classic.

Walnut
Boulder brewpub (1123 Walnut). Products have included a lightly tart *Swiss Trail Wheat Ale* ☆☆; the soft, dry, hoppy *Big Horn Bitter* ☆☆☆; the smooth, clean, *Old Elk Brown Ale* ☆☆▷☆☆☆; and the creamy, roasty *Devil's Thumb Stout* ☆☆▷☆☆☆.

Wynkoop
The biggest beer-sales of any brewpub in the world, yet quality has been maintained and the ambience is still pubby. The brewpub is on a street named after one of Denver's founders, Edward Wynkoop, whose Dutch surname indicates a wine merchant. The establishment is in the old warehouse district of Denver (Wynkoop and 18th). Products have included the remarkably Bavarian-tasting *Wixa Weiss* ☆☆☆; *IPA* ☆☆▷☆☆☆, fruity, perfumy and oaky; a hoppy, well-balanced *ESB* ☆☆▷☆☆☆; a hoppier *Special Bitter* ☆☆☆; a chocolatey *Scottish Ale* ☆☆; a malty-fruity, warming Old Ale called *Churchyard* ☆☆☆ sometimes aged in Jack Daniel's casks. The dryish, malty *Mile High Lager* ☆☆▷ ☆☆☆ is dedicated to Kurt Vonnegut – a brewer's son.

CALIFORNIA
There are more breweries by far in California than in any other state – about 150. This is a new phenomenon. There were just four national giants, plus Anchor Steam, when America's first new-generation micro-brewery, New Albion, fired its kettle in Sonoma, California, in 1977.

New Albion did not survive, but its crew and yeast went on to start the Mendocino County Brewing Company, which thrives in the appropriately named town of Hopland.

That first micro-brewery was in wine country, and the grain has been greatly assisted by the grape. Viticulture is a thirsty business, and winemakers enjoy a quenching beer, but their industry also has a more fundamental contribution. Much of northern California is touched by viticulture, and this means that people are not embarrassed to discuss the aromas and flavours of drinks and foods. The blossoming of boutique wineries set an example that made it easier for micro-breweries to find funding, equipment and credibility.

Anchor Steam's principal, Fritz Maytag, grows renowned Cabernets (and olives, and has a share of his family's cheese business); the founders of the Santa Cruz Brewing Co were originally wine-growers; the brewer at Butterfield formerly made wine at Heitz; there are many similar examples.

WHERE TO DRINK

The largest combined festival of American and imported beers to be held anywhere takes place in San Francisco on a weekend in early to mid-July under the auspices of the local public broadcasting station, KQED. In eclectic San Francisco, Belgian beers are featured at Le Petit Café (2164 Larkin) and the New Wave club Toronado (547 Haight). The East Bay has many places, including a Belgian bistro called Mrs Coffee (Nob Hill Shopping Center, Livermore), and Lyon's (7294 San Ramon Rd, Dublin). Notable shops are The Cannery Wine Cellars (2801 Leavenworth, San Francisco) and The Wine Exchange, on the town square in Sonoma. America's first brews-paper, *The Celebrator*, is published in the East Bay, at Hayward.

Brewpubs aside, southern California's favourite spot for an off-beat beer may be a sandwich shop. Between downtown Los Angeles and Pasadena, at San Gabriel (413 W Las Tunas Drive; an appropriate-sounding address), The Stuffed Sandwich has about 750 beers, four of them on draught, and a caring proprietor. Highly recommended in Santa Monica: The Library (2911 Main) and Father's Office (1018 Montana).

Anchor

Serious beer-lovers worldwide know Anchor as the inspirational "Small is Beautiful" brewery. It was founded in the 1890s, in San Francisco, and given a new life in the late 1960s by its present owner, Fritz Maytag. Its principal product, *Anchor Steam Beer* ✩✩✩✩, is made by a process unique to the United States (and, for more than 60 years, to this brewery) Anchor Steam Beer is not only a (protected) brand-name but also a style. Before refrigeration reached the West, pioneering brewers used lager yeasts at natural temperatures in unusually shallow vessels that resemble coolers as much as fermenters. Anchor Steam is still made in this type of vessel. The result is a beer that has some of the roundness of a lager but the fruitiness of an ale, with a characteristically high natural carbonation. It is also an all-malt beer, with a very good hoppy dryness (the varietal accent being clearly Northern Brewer). It is made to conventional gravity, of around 12 (1048; 4.0; 5.0). The brewery also makes a rich, creamy, faintly herbal, *Porter* ✩✩▷✩✩✩ (1068; 17; 5.0; 6.25) that might better be described as a bottom-fermenting medium stout. Anchor's intensely aromatic, hoppy-tasting (Cascade), dry, top-fermenting *Liberty Ale* ✩✩✩✩ (4.8; 6.0) is an American classic, widely copied. Its *Old Foghorn Barley Wine* ✩✩✩▷✩✩✩✩ (25; 1100; 7.0; 7.0; 8.75) is beautifully rounded, soothing and warming. Its *Wheat Beer* ✩✩, the first in America since Prohibition, is very light, clean and delicate, with a hint of honey and apple; 70 percent of the grist is wheat. From Thanksgiving through Christmas and New Year, *Our Special Ale* is a spiced brew produced for the holiday season. This brew is different every year.

Anderson Valley

The valley has grown grapes, hops and marijuana, and its "secret language" provides the slightly odd names for the beautifully rounded beers of the Buckhorn brewpub (14081 Highway 128), in

Booneville, Mendocino County. They include *Poleeko Gold* ☆☆, soft, lightly citric and dry; *Boont Amber* ☆☆☆, starting sweet and fruity, finishing dry and hoppy; *Belk's ESB* ☆☆▷☆☆☆, with lots of American hop flavours; *Deep Enders' Dark* ☆☆, a chocolatey but dry Porter; the silky *Barney Flats Oatmeal Stout* ☆☆☆; and the fruity *High Rollers Wheat Beer* ☆☆, among many others.

Belmont

Beach brewpub at the beginning of the pier at Belmont Shore, Long Beach. Beers have included the tart, dry-hopped *Marathon Ale* ☆☆; the fruitier, amber-red, *Top Sail Ale* ☆▷☆☆; and a soft, roasty Porter, *Long Beach Crude* ☆☆.

Bison

Colourful brews range from a fragrant, herbal, soft *Honey Basil Ale* ☆☆☆ to a dusty-tasting, bakery-smelling *Gingerbread Ale* ☆☆▷☆☆☆ and a big, toasty *Pumpernickel Ale* ☆☆☆. Brewpub at 2598 Telegraph, Berkeley.

Boulder Creek

Mainstreet brewpub in Boulder Creek, which is between Santa Cruz and Saratoga. Products have included a very hoppy *Kölsch* ☆☆; a malty-fruity, but slightly tart, *Scottish Ale* ☆▷☆☆; and a grainy *Oatmeal Stout* ☆☆.

Brewski's

One of the more elaborate among the brewpubs that feature in almost every beach community in Los Angeles. In a wide and varying selection at Brewski's (73 Pier Ave, Hermosa Beach) a piney, minty *India Pale Ale* ☆☆☆▷☆☆☆ has been the most memorable.

Buffalo Bill

Pioneer pub-brewer "Buffalo Bill" Owens established this brewpub (1082 B St, Hayward, in the East Bay). It is now owned by brewer Geoff Harries. Products include a very well-balanced *ESB* ☆☆, with good flavour development; and a grapefruity IPA called *Tasmanian Devil* ☆☆▷☆☆☆ (originally, but no longer brewed with hops from Australia).

Burlingame Station

Assertive beers from a brewpub in the San Francisco suburb of Burlingame (333 California, opposite the railroad station). *Ryzberry* ☆☆☆ was an early speciality, employing wheat, rye and raspberry. The nearby Barley & Hopps (201 South "B" St and 2nd, San Mateo) has won praise for its *Rye PA* (not tasted).

Butterfield

Ex-winemaker Kevin Cox created the reddish-amber, soft, slightly chewy, hoppy-fruity *Bridal Veil Ale* ☆☆ (named after a waterfall in Yosemite); a clean, well-balanced, light, roasty *Brown Ale* ☆☆; the dry, malty, textured *Tower Dark* ☆☆▷☆☆☆ (somewhere between a strong dark Bitter and a Porter) and a very hoppy-tasting *IPA* ☆☆☆. Butterfield is a brewpub and grill in Fresno (777 East Olive Ave).

Calistoga Inn/Napa Valley Brewing

Italianate chalet-style bed-and-breakfast, restaurant, brewpub and beer-garden at Calistoga (1250 Lincoln Ave), Napa Valley. Products include a richly malty, spicy *Red Ale* ☆☆▷☆☆☆ with a suggestion of sassafras root.

Crown City

The city is the old winter resort of Pasadena, where the foothills of the San Gabriel Mountains meet Greater Los Angeles. Crown City is a brewpub in a renovated china pottery, now a shopping mall (300 S Raymond). Early products have included a sweetish, fruity *Amber* ☆☆ and a *Porter* ☆▷☆☆ with a hint of blackcurrant. The range continues to develop.

Dempsey's

An *Irish Ale* ☆☆, smooth, slightly oily, soft and malty, and a *Stout* ☆☆☆▷☆☆☆ that starts creamily and surges to a powerful espresso finish, are among the products of this brewpub in the Golden Eagle Shopping Center, Petaluma. Dempsey's has an excellent kitchen.

Downtown Joe's

The town of Napa has its own brewpub and garden, at 902 Main. It is to be hoped that a new brewer retains the Scots-accented *Golden Thistle Bitter* ☆☆☆, with its sweetish, malty, softness. Predecessor Brian Hunt now has his own nearby micro, Moonlight, producing a coffeeish Black Beer called *Death and Taxes* ☆☆☆.

Etna

Revival of an 1870s brewery (closed during Prohibition), on the site of its bottling hall, by Andrew Hurlimann, the stepson of the founding family (who came from Alsace-Lorraine). Etna (population 770) was a gold-mining (and hop-growing) town. It is north of Mount Shasta, near Yreka. Early products, unfiltered, have included the soft, fruity, dry *Etna Ale* ☆▷☆☆ and the hoppier *Export Lager* ☆☆.

Fremont

Golf course brewpub at Fremont (3350 Stevenson Bvd). Best beer is a malt-accented, slightly grainy *ESB* ☆☆.

Golden Pacific

Located between San Francisco and Oakland, at Emeryville. Microbrewery, whose products include the aptly named *Bitter-sweet Ale* ☆☆, with a malty chewiness and a balancing dryness; *Cable Car Lager* ☆☆, with a good hop aroma and firm, malty texture; *Golden Gate* ☆☆, is fuller in colour, body and strength; and further variations of the theme are also produced by Golden Pacific.

Gordon Biersch

Serious German-style lagers and excellent food in a stylish brewpub in Palo Alto (640 Emerson), with branches in San Francisco, San Jose, Pasadena and Hawaii. Products include a malty but firm *Export* ☆☆☆; a smooth, malty, amber *Märzen* ☆☆☆, slightly dry for the style; a soft, chocolatey, slightly roasty *Dunkles* ☆☆☆▷☆☆☆ a chocolatey, clovey *Dunkel Weizen* ☆☆▷ ☆☆☆; and a rummy, treacly *Bock* ☆☆☆▷☆☆☆.

Hogshead

In the Old Town of Sacramento (114 J St). This cellar brewpub was founded by micro pioneer Jim Schlueter, and is now under new ownership. Products have included the malty, sweetish, *Hogshead Lager* ☆☆ and the dark, chocolatey *McSchlueter* ☆☆.

UNITED STATES | **161**

Hubsch

See Sudwerks.

Humboldt

On Humboldt Bay, at Arcata (856 10th St). A "frontier" brewpub, whose founders included Mario Celotto, former linebacker with the Oakland Raiders. Products, all top-fermented, include *Gold Rush* ☆▷☆☆, soft, fruity and dry; *Red Nectar* ☆☆▷☆☆☆, smooth, sweetly malty, with a good complex of hop flavours; *Storm Cellar Porter* ☆☆, with a bitter-chocolate character; and the aromatic, big-tasting, coffeeish, dryish *Oatmeal Stout* ☆☆▷☆☆☆.

Lind

In the East Bay town of San Leandro, veteran micro-brewer Roger Lind produces the dry, hoppy *Drake's Gold* ☆☆; the hoppy but smoother *Drake's Ale* ☆☆▷☆☆☆; and the big, chocolatey, spicy *Sir Francis Stout* ☆☆☆.

Los Gatos

Lavishly-fitted brew restaurant: well-made lagers and ambitious food, in the town of the same name (130G N Santa Cruz). The malty, warming *Oktoberfest* ☆☆☆ is especially good.

Lost Coast

Humboldt Bay brewpub, at Eureka (617 4th St). Wide range includes *Downtown Brown Ale* ☆☆, tawny, soft, smooth and lightly malty, with chocolatey sweetness and coffeeish dryness.

Mad River

Just inland of Eureka and Arcata, at Blue Lake. Veteran micro-brewer Bob Smith makes the refreshing, appetizing, dry, citric-tasting *Steelhead Extra Pale Ale* ☆☆, with an emphatic American hop character. His creamy *Extra Stout* ☆☆▷☆☆☆ is full of flavour, with suggestions of toffee, chocolate, coffee and figs, and a long, oily, clinging finish.

Marin

A ferry ride from San Francisco, at 1809 Larkspur Landing Circle, in Marin County. Wide range includes *Mount Tam Pale Ale* ☆☆▷☆☆☆, with a fruity start and a very hoppy finish; the sweetish *Albion Amber* ☆☆; the malty *St Brendan's Irish Red* ☆☆▷☆☆☆; an aromatic *Imperial-style Stout* ☆☆▷☆☆☆; the herbal-tasting, dry-hopped *Old Dipsea Barley Wine* ☆☆☆; a syrupy, delicious, *Wheat Wine* ☆☆☆; and several beers made with fruit extracts.

Mendocino

"Son of New Albion", and one of the country's first brewpubs, is in a 100-year-old saloon at Hopland, about 90 miles N of San Francisco, on Highway 101, in Mendocino County. Amid vineyards, the revivalist brewers planted the town's earlier crop, hops, around their ornamental kiln. Their beers include *Peregrine Pale Ale* ☆▷☆☆, lightly fruity, and sweetish; *Blue Heron Pale Ale* ☆☆, fuller in colour, body and hop character; the justifiably renowned *Red Tail Ale* ☆☆☆, copper coloured, with anise notes; seasonal specialities like the spicy *Eye of the Hawk* ☆☆▷☆☆☆, a strong, malty ale; and *Black Hawk Stout* ☆☆, medium-dry, fruity and chocolatey. The company plans an additional, free-standing micro.

Murphys Creek

About 100 miles E of San Francisco, at the small town of Murphys, in the Sierra foothills. Products include an ESB called *Murphys Red* ☆☆, fruity and dry, with good hop flavours; a light, crisp *Stout* ☆☆▷☆☆☆; and a very sweet *Barley Wine* ☆☆.

Nevada City

Despite its name, Nevada City is in California. It has become a retreat for writers and artists. The brewery makes, unfiltered, the malty-fruity pale lager *Nevada City Gold* ☆▷☆☆ and a Vienna-style *Dark* ☆☆, with a clean, sweetish palate. This micro has family links with a brewpub at Pizza Junction (11401 Donner Pass Rd), in Truckee, further up the road to Reno.

North Coast

Rightly well-regarded ales from a brewpub in a former Presbyterian church and chapel of rest at the old port of Fort Bragg (444 N Main) in Mendocino County. *Alt Nouveau* ☆☆ is golden-to-bronze, and malty-peachy; *Ruedrich's Red Seal Ale* ☆☆▷☆☆☆ is fresh, fruity and creamily soft, beautifully balanced, with an appetizingly dry finish; *Old No 38 Stout* ☆☆☆ is creamy and chocolatey, with lots of flavour development. *Rasputin* ☆☆☆ is a brandyish Russian Imperial Stout. North Coast now has a micro across the street.

Old Columbia

A German-born veteran of American brewing, Karl Strauss helped set up this brewpub in San Diego (1157 Columbia, near the trolley). Products include *Columbia Amber Lager* ☆▷☆☆, lightly malty, with some hop in the finish; Downtown *After Dark* ☆▷☆☆, vaguely like a British ale; *Black's Beach* ☆▷☆☆, dryish and Porter-like; and *Red Trolley* ☆☆▷☆☆☆, a fruity "ESB". The Karl Strauss Brewery Gardens opened in 1994, in the San Diego Tech Center.

Pacific Coast

Beer-lovers visiting San Francisco should take the BART train to Oakland to sample the ales of this brewpub in a city-centre Victorian building (906 Washington). Products include an excellent, English-style dark *Mariners' Mild* ☆☆☆; the hoppy *Gray Whale Ale* ☆☆▷☆☆☆; the assertive *Blue Whale Ale* ☆☆☆, matured over oak chips; and the dry, herbal-tasting, *Killer Whale Stout* ☆☆▷☆☆☆.

Pacific Hop Exchange

Tiny micro in Novato making unfiltered beers. These include the soft, yeasty, dryish, hoppy *Gaslight Pale Ale* ☆☆.

Pete's Wicked

California-based enthusiast Pete Slosberg created these products, which were originally made at a now-defunct micro in Palo Alto. They are now produced in Minnesota. *Pete's Wicked Ale* ☆☆▷☆☆☆ has a chestnut colour, a rich aroma, and a depth of fruitiness. A wide range of specialities is produced.

River City

Sacramento (Downtown Plaza) brewery-restaurant with good lagers, notably a well-rounded *Pilsner* ☆☆☆. Try the salmon with basil in a green-onion sauce.

Riverside
Brewpub in the former Fruit Exchange, in old citrus country, at
Riverside (3394 7th St), E of Los Angeles. Products have included
the smooth, hoppy *Golden Spike Pilsner* ☆☆▷☆☆☆, the well-
balanced *Pullman Pale Ale* ☆☆, which has an attractively pinkish
colour; and the coffeeish, roasty *7th Street Stout* ☆☆☆.

Rubicon
Well-regarded brewpub in Sacramento (2004 Capitol). Products
have included a *Summer Wheat* ☆☆ with a lot of hop in the
finish; an *Amber Ale* ☆☆▷☆☆☆ that is also well hopped;
an intensely hoppy *IPA* ☆☆☆; the coffeeish, burnt-tasting
Ol' Moe's Porter ☆☆▷☆☆☆; and a spectacular *Winter Wheat
Wine* ☆☆☆ which is fruity, smooth and very warming.

St Stans
Stanislaus County, abstemiously Baptist, gave birth to this micro in
1984, and it moved to a brewpub site in Modesto (821 L St) in
1990. A German-accented range began with two brews in loosely
the Düsseldorf style: the pale *Amber Alt* ☆☆, with a malty accent
and some apple-and-fig fruitiness; and *Dark Alt* ☆☆, which is
ruby-coloured and chocolatey, with a touch of roastiness.

San Andreas
On the fault line, in the town of Hollister (737 San Benito). This
brewpub suffered only minor damage in the 1989 'quake, but
close neighbours were less lucky. Some thought the brewery had
tempted providence with its *Earthquake Pale Ale* ☆☆▷☆☆☆,
extremely dry, but hardly vengeful. *Kit Fox Amber* ☆☆, named
after an endangered species, is maltier but still dryish. *Survivor
Stout* ☆☆ is coffeeish and dry. *Plum Nut Amber* ☆☆▷☆☆☆
smelled of Slivovitz and tasted of almonds. A wintergreen-tasting
Woodruff Ale ☆☆▷☆☆☆ is among other eccentricities.

San Diego Brewing
Suburban brewpub (10450 Friars) with an excellent Old Ale,
called *Three Ninety Five* ☆☆☆. The same company has a second
brewpub, Callahan's (82889-A Mira Mesa Bvd). See also Old
Columbia and Riptide.

San Francisco
Where downtown San Francisco meets the North Beach restaurant quarter (155 Columbus, at Pacific), a 1907 saloon houses the
city's oldest brewpub (est. 1986). Products have varied, but are
good at their best. The golden *Albatross Lager* ☆▷☆☆ has lots of
American hop character, as well as some Saaz; *Emperor Norton*
☆☆ is broadly in the Vienna style, nutty, with touches of vanilla
and apricot; *Gripman's Porter* ☆☆ is chocolatey and medium-dry.

Santa Cruz
This seaside resort on Monterey Bay gives its name to a brewpub at
516 Front St. Products include the lightly hoppy *Lighthouse Lager*
☆▷☆☆; an *Amber* ☆☆ that is well-rounded with a dry finish;
sometimes a slightly roasty, medicinal *Dark Lager* ☆☆; and a dry,
assertive, coffeeish *Porter* ☆☆▷☆☆☆. Other seasonal specialities
have included a smooth, chocolatey *Pacific Stout* ☆☆▷☆☆☆; a
rich but hoppy *Beacon Barley Wine* ☆☆▷☆☆☆; and an intensely
aromatic Christmas beer called *Hoppy Holidays* ☆☆☆.

Santa Rosa

This college town in Sonoma now gives its name to the brew-pub, formerly called Kelmer's (458 B St). The beers are now more assertive and the sports theme has gone since new owners arrived. Products include a grainy, dry, hoppy, fruity *IPA* ☆☆ and a somewhat medicinal *Barley Wine* ☆☆ with a warming finish.

Seabright

Outstanding beers from the second brewpub established in Santa Cruz (519 Seabright Ave). Products include *Pelican Pale* ☆☆, lightly malty with a dry finish; *Seabright Amber* ☆☆☆▷☆☆☆, fruity and hoppy, with a long finish; *Amber Banty Rooster IPA* ☆☆☆, with a hoppy nose and palate, very dry, especially on the finish; *Pleasure Point Porter* ☆☆☆, with a coffeeish, malty start and a dry finish; and a smooth, winey *Oatmeal Stout* ☆☆☆▷☆☆☆.

Sierra Nevada

One of the earliest new-generation breweries in the US, started in 1981, and now established as the Château Latour among American micros. *Sierra Nevada Draught Ale* ☆☆☆ is very slightly sweeter in palate than its companion bottled *Pale Ale* ☆☆☆☆. This American classic has an teasing balance between the piney, juniper-tasting Cascade hops and the fruitiness of the top-fermenting yeast. The *Porter* ☆☆☆ is among the best brewed anywhere in the world: firmly dry, but with a gentle, coffee-toffee finish. The strong *Stout* ☆☆ (4.8; 6.0) is very smooth, with a powerful roastiness in the finish. A *Celebration Ale* is brewed for the winter holiday period, to a different specification each year, sometimes with experimental new varieties of hops. In late winter and early spring, Sierra Nevada has its *Big Foot Barley Wine* ☆☆☆☆, with a huge hoppiness in its earthy aroma and chewy palate. This is among the strongest beers in the United States, at 8.0–10.0 by weight; 11–12.5 by volume. This beer is bottle-conditioned for four weeks at the brewery, and becomes winier if kept for a further three months. Properly cellared, it should remain in good condition for a year or two. There is also a range of characteristically well-made seasonal lagers.

SLO

The town of San Luis Obispo gives its initials, and a location, to this brewpub (1119 Garden St). Products include a *Pale Ale* ☆, with a dry maltiness and some fruit; a smooth, fruitier *Amber Ale* ☆☆; and a fruity, chocolatey, sweetish *Porter* ☆☆.

Stoddard's

Brewery-restaurant at Sunnyvale (111 S Murphy), on the peninsula south of San Francisco. Beers include a malty, textured *Porter* ☆☆☆. Try the gnocchi with fennel sausage.

Sudwerk/Hubsch

From *Sudhaus*, German for "brewhouse". Hubsch is a family name. Robustly German beers at a pub in Davis (2001 2nd St), home town of the University of California's beer and wine departments. Hubsch beers include a soft, malty *Lager* ☆☆▷ ☆☆☆; a *Pilsner* ☆☆☆ with a beautiful balance of malt and hop; a deftly malt-accented *Märzen*; and a *Dark Lager* ☆☆☆ with a good bitter-chocolate character.

Tied House

The name first manifested itself at a brewpub in Mountain View (954 Villa St), a town S of San Francisco. The description, the British term for a pub "tied" to one brewery, implied a planned chain. There are now further Tied Houses in Alameda and San Jose, but they have their own breweries. Principal beers are a lightly fruity *Pale* ☆; a fruitier, pleasant *Amber* ☆▷☆☆; and a fuller-flavoured *Dark* ☆☆ in broadly the style of a soft English Bitter.

Triple Rock

Well-established, studenty brewpub in the college town of Berkeley (1920 Shattuck Ave). Principal products are *Pinnacle Pale Ale* ☆☆▷☆☆ dry, lightly hoppy and fruity; *Red Rock Ale* ☆☆ sweeter, still fruity, with more hop in a late finish; and *Black Rock Porter* ☆☆ light to medium in body, but dry and quite complex.

Twenty Tank

San Francisco brewpub (316 11th St, S of Market, near Folsom) established by Triple Rock. Products include the robust, perfumed, full-coloured *Hi-Top Ale* ☆☆☆.

HAWAII

Big Island: In Kailua, the Kona micro (named for the district, better known for coffee) has malty beers, including a spicy-tasting *Pale Ale* ☆☆ and *Lilikoi Wheat Ale* ☆☆▷☆☆☆, reminiscent of flowering currant and apricot but made with the local passion fruit whose name it bears.

Honolulu: Good selection of beers at Murphy's (2 Merchant St). Gordon Biersch has a lively branch on the harbour (101 Ala Moana Bvd). The micro Ali'i has a dryish *Porter* ☆☆, a slightly sharp *Stout* ☆☆ made with Kona coffee; and a cocoa-ish *Brown Ale* ☆☆▷☆☆☆ flavoured with local macademia nuts.

Maui: Sharktooth is a brewpub hidden in the upstairs of the Kaahumanu shopping centre, in Kahului; beers include a fruity, peppery *ESB* ☆☆. The micro Trade Winds has enjoyable beers, including a *Sunset Ale* ☆☆▷☆☆☆ with a lemony hop character, and a malty, toffeeish Old Ale called *Paniolo* ☆☆☆ (Hawaiian for "Cowboy").

THE NORTHWEST

No American city can match Portland, Oregon, in numbers of breweries. The metro area has 20-odd, and the state as a whole three times that number. The neighbouring state of Washington has a similar number, with a good dozen in the Seattle area.

Portland specializes in brewpubs, while Seattle has more free-standing "ale houses", but in both cities micro-brewed beers are more widely available in ordinary bars and restaurants than anywhere else in America.

Both states grow barley for malting, and between them possess the principal regions for the cultivation of hops in America (the

Willamette Valley in Oregon and Yakima in Washington State).

The two major cities are small enough to have a local pride in their beers but sufficiently large to offer a worthwhile market to their brewers. With their relatively cool weather, both states favour indoor drinking in taverns, and draught beer is more widely served here than elsewhere in the USA. This has helped micros begin without the expense of a bottling line. The climate also favours the fuller-flavoured speciality beers, as opposed to light quenchers.

Seattle is known for its interest in food and drink, and Portland quietly shares the same enthusiasm for civilized living. Seattle also has America's most adventurous importer of beer, Merchant Du Vin.

With the economic growth of the Pacific Rim, Seattle – longtime the gateway to Alaska – has become a commercial capital for a wider region. Its beery influence crosses the border into Idaho, Montana and, at a pinch, Wyoming.

WHERE TO DRINK

The Oregon Brewers' Festival, a major public tasting, has been a model for similar events elsewhere in the USA. It is usually takes place on the third weekend in July, in Portland. For information, check any of the city's three old-established micros (BridgePort, Portland Brewing, and Widmer).

Each of these has a pub/tasting room on its premises (see also Full Sail entry for details of the Pilsner room). The Horse Brass (4534 SE Belmont) is a long-established speciality beer bar.

The elegant Heathman Hotel (SW Broadway and Salmon) is the place for the well-heeled beer-lover. Its two bars offer differing selections of micro and imported beers, and the hotel also owns the nearby B Moloch bistro, which has its own associated brewery (see entry for Widmer).

In Seattle, the best place for beer gossip is The Pike Pub and Brewery (1415 1st Ave), with bookshop and museum. The most central of the city's famous ale-houses is The Pioneer Square Saloon (73 Yesler Way). Across the ship canal is the pioneering Cooper's Ale House (8065 Lake City Way NE). The Red Door Alehouse (33401 Fremont) is in the same part of town as RedHook's Trolleyman pub. Serious beer lovers favour The Latona, at 6423 on the avenue of the same name.

The Blue Moon, famous as a picturesque and vaguely literary tavern (712 NE 45th), has a better range of beers than might have been expected. F X McRory (419 Occidental Ave S), a bar-restaurant near the Kingdome, has a large selection of micro-brews available on draught. Cutters (2001 Western Ave) is a beer-aware establishment, with sister restaurants in other cities.

Look out for *The Pint Post*.

Alaskan Brewing

The first (founded 1986) new-generation micro in Alaska. Famous for its Christmas seasonal *Smoked Porter* ☆☆☆☆. The malt is smoked over alder twigs at an establishment that normally provides this service for salmon. For the past four or five years, the beer has been unfiltered, and will develop with age. Fresh, it has almost the seaweediness of an Islay malt whisky. With age, first the fruity wood notes come to the fore; then the cocoa-ish, roasty malt character; and finally the creamy texture. The brewery, in the state capital Juneau, makes variety of excellent beers, including the remarkably smooth, malty *Alaskan Amber* ☆☆.

Bayern

The name is German for Bavaria, and Jurgen Knoller's products have an authentic character judging from his *Pilsener* ☆☆▷☆☆☆: firm-bodied, with a tasty malt character and a delicately hoppy finish. An *Amber* ☆☆☆▷☆☆☆ also has excellent malt flavours. This brewpub is in a former rail-road building in Missoula, Montana (North Higgins and Railroad).

Big Time

Some of Seattle's best young brewers have, over the years, worked at this pubby spot (4133 University Way NE), and it is to be hoped this tradition can be maintained. Known for citric, grape-fruity IPAs like *Bagwan's Best* ☆☆☆; the dazing *Old Woolly* ☆☆▷☆☆☆ barley wine; and pioneering rye brews. *Mud in Your Rye* ☆☆☆ featured the grain in roasted form.

Bird Creek

Named for Ike Kelly's birthplace, but his micro is 25 miles away in Anchorage, Alaska. *Old 55* ☆☆ commemorates the year of his birth. It is a Pale Ale, well balanced but accented towards perfumed hoppiness and late dryness.

Black Star/Great Northern

By the Great Northern tracks in the Montana railroad town of Whitefish. This micro's most interesting product has been the smooth, beautifully balanced *Big Fog Amber Lager* ☆☆▷☆☆☆ (5.4; 6.75). *Black Star* ☆☆ is a smooth, dryish, malty lager with some flowery hop.

Blitz Weinhard

This brewery is best known for *Henry Weinhard's Private Reserve* ☆☆ an aromatic lager that was one of America's most distinctive beers before microbrews became readily available. A recent addition was a *Porter* ☆☆ with a touch of malty dryness on the finish.

BridgePort

Founded by winemakers Dick and Nancy Ponzi in 1984, this is the oldest of Portland's new brewpubs and micros, making malt-accented ales. Its signature *BridgePort Ale* ☆☆☆ is ruby-coloured, soft and Scottish-accented. *Pintail* ☆☆ is a very fruity (blueberries?), hoppy ESB in broadly the English style. Since a change in ownership, the brewery has been emphasising its refreshing, appetising *IPA* ☆☆▷☆☆☆, with notes of peach sherbert and garden mint. There is much more pepperiness to *Old Knucklehead* ☆☆▷☆☆☆ (around 7.4; 9.2). On its own premises (1313 NW Marshall), BridgePort offers cask-conditioned ale.

California and Alaska

The state names are also streets in Seattle. Where they meet, this brewpub offers, among other beers, the smooth, dryish *Fauntleroy Stout* ☆☆.

Coeur d'Alene

A resort in Idaho. The Coeur d'Alene brewery and T W Fisher pub (204 2nd St) produce a *Pale Ale* ☆▷☆☆ and a *Festival Dark* ☆▷☆☆ that are both somewhat grainy and acidic.

Deschutes

The town of Bend, Oregon, takes its name from a twist in the Deschutes River. Its Deschutes Brewery and Pub (1044 Bond St NW) produces an extensive range of beers. These have included the enjoyably dry *Pils* ☆☆; a hop-accented *Kölsch* ☆☆; the soft, sweetish *Cascade Golden Ale* ☆☆, with an appropriate dash of hops in the finish; the firm, fruity, hoppy *Bachelor Bitter* ☆☆☆; the aromatic *Mirror Pond Pale Ale* ☆☆▷☆☆☆; the smooth, well-balanced *Anniversary Alt* ☆☆☆; a coffeeish *Scotch Ale* ☆☆ that was almost a sweet stout; the slightly burnt-tasting *Bond St Brown Ale* ☆▷☆☆; the dry, oily, chewy, nutty, complex *Black Butte Porter* ☆☆☆; and the fruitier, sweeter, smokier *Obsidian Stout* ☆☆▷☆☆☆, among others.

Elysian

Poetic pints on Pike. Star young brewer Dick Cantwell produces a smooth, malty, Dortmunder-style *Lager* ☆☆☆; a hoppy *ESB* ☆☆▷☆☆☆; a clingingly malty pale *Bock* ☆☆; and a viscous, relatively hoppy *Stout* ☆☆▷☆☆☆ at this highly regarded brewpub in Seattle (1221 E Pike).

Eugene City Brewery

One of half-a-dozen brewpubs in the Oregon city of Eugene (pop 112,000). This establishment (844 Olive St) offers aromatic, fruity brews, including the dry *Orca Pale Ale* ☆☆▷☆☆☆.

Fish

A seductively hoppy *IPA* ☆☆☆ and an outstanding *Old Scotch Ale* ☆☆☆ full of earthy peatiness are among the products of this micro and taproom at 515 Jefferson, Olympia, Washington.

Full Sail

Brewpubs at "The Pilsner Room" in Portland (307 SW Montgomery) and in Hood River, Oregon (506 Columbia St), the latter also serving as a micro. The name "Full Sail" was inspired by the popularity of wind-surfing near the confluence of the rivers Hood and Columbia. Beers have included a Saaz-accented *Pilsner* ☆☆▷☆☆☆; a fruity *Red Ale* ☆☆; a very flowery, earthy *IPA* ☆☆☆▷☆☆☆ (E Kent Goldings); a beautifully rounded *Amber* ☆☆☆▷☆☆☆ (inspired by Samuel Smith's); a big, malty-fruity *Nut Brown* ☆☆☆; a soft, smoky *Stout* ☆☆▷☆☆☆; a peaty, sappy *Wassail* ☆☆☆; and a rich *Doppelbock* ☆☆☆.

Grant's

Hop country micro and pioneering brewpub, known for its distinctive products, and making liberal use of the Yakima Valley crop. The beers are created by the equally characterful Scottish-born brewer and hop expert Bert Grant. The fruity *Celtic Ale* ☆☆☆, with an Irish-looking label, has the original gravity (1034) and appearance of an English dark Mild but much more hop. The medium-amber *Grant's Ale* ☆☆☆, smooth and malty, is billed as being Scottish in style, but again has more hop than that would suggest. The *IPA* ☆☆☆ takes full advantage of that description and permits itself to be very dry indeed, with a powerful, lingering, hop finish. The modestly titled *Perfect Porter* ☆☆☆ is firm and rounded, with a cocoa-powder flavour. The *Imperial Stout* ☆☆☆ (5.8, 7.2) is fruity and honeyish, but still dry. The oddly spelled *Weis* ☆☆, made with 30 percent wheat, is light, dry, smooth and tart.

Grant's, of Yakima, Washington, originally had a brewery and pub in the town's former opera house. It now operates The Brewery Pub across the street, at 32 North Front, in the old railroad station, and also runs a micro-brewery elsewhere in the town.

Hale's

Early ale revivalist Mike Hale now has a pub and brewery in Fremont, Seattle (4301 Leary Way NW) and a micro in the eastern Washington city of Spokane. Products have included a hop-accented but well-balanced *Pale American Ale* ☆☆; a malty but rounded *Special Bitter* ☆☆▷☆☆☆ (inspired by George Gale's); and a smooth *Stout* ☆☆ with toasty, toffeeish flavours.

Hair of the Dog

A jammy, warming, Belgian-style Triple called *Golden Rose* ☆☆▷☆☆☆ and the outstanding *Adambier* ☆☆☆ (red peppers in chocolate?) based on the 19th-century dark style of Dortmund are among the products from this lively new Portland micro.

Harrison Hollow

At 2455 Harrison Hollow Boulevard, Boise, Idaho. This brewpub makes a whiskyish *Western Ale* ☆☆ and a very refreshing, lemony, clean-tasting *Ginger Wheat* ☆☆▷☆☆☆.

Hazel Dell

Brewpub just across the river from Portland in the Washington town of Vancouver (8513 NE Highway 99). The general manager is called Joe Moran. Products include the hoppy but well-balanced *Red Zone Pale Ale* ☆☆.

Kessler

Dryish, malty beers from a brewpub in Helena, Montana (1439 Harris St). Examples include a full-bodied ale that is relatively low in alcohol (2.8, 3.5), called *Number Seven* ☆☆, and a rich, malty-spicy *Doppelbock* ☆☆☆▷☆☆☆.

Lang Creek

In an aircraft hangar in remote Marion, Montana. This micro is run by flying buff John Campbell. Products include *Trimotor* ☆☆☆, broadly an ESB, with a nutty malt character and fresh hop flavours.

Leavenworth

In the mock-alpine tourist town of Leavenworth, Washington (636 Front St). This brewpub has produced has a Frisian-style *Pilsner* ☆☆☆, perfumed, dry and assertive (loosely modelled on Jever, but using St Christoffel yeast); a hoppy *ESB* ☆☆; a rummy *Porter* ☆☆▷☆☆☆ and a malty *Stout* ☆☆☆, both big and complex; and the splendidly malty Doppelbock *Procrastinator* ☆☆☆, well worth waiting for.

McMenamins

Grateful Dead "heads", whose repertoire of brewpubs is now well into two figures, with more than 150 beers. There is a parent brewery (with restaurant, cinema and bedrooms) at a former "poor farm", Edgefield, at Troutdale (2126 SW Halsey), 20 miles E of Portland. A wide range of beers includes a flavoursome bitter called *Hammerhead* ☆☆☆, well-balanced but with a lingering emphasis on American hops; the roasty, grainy *Terminator* ☆☆▷☆☆☆ (not a Double Bock but a Stout); and *Ruby* ☆☆, a refreshing, tart, spritzy, raspberry beer.

Maritime Pacific
Seattle micro. Products have included the malty, smooth *Night-watch Ale* ☆▷☆☆ and the coffeeish *Bosun's Black Ale* ☆☆.

Milestown
Tiny micro in Miles City, in the Yellowstone Valley of Montana. Products include an assertive Munich Helles called *Old Milestown* and the fruity, tart, indeed witty *Coal Porter*. Too early to rate.

Mount Hood
Brewpub in ski country at the town of Government Camp, Oregon. Products have included the hoppy-spicy *Pinnacle ESB* ☆☆ and a lightly hoppy *IPA* ☆☆.

Onalaska
Midwife Susan Moorehead and husband Dave run this tiny micro-brewery and tavern, in the old sawmill town of Onalaska, Washington (248 Burchett Rd). Their robust, earthy products include the bronze, nutty, perfumed *Onalaska Ale* ☆☆ (4.0, 5.0), the maltier, slightly stronger *Red Dawg* ☆☆ (4.25, 5.3); and the mild, chocolatey *Howlin' Stout* ☆☆.

Otto Brothers
Charlie and Ernie Otto, and their partner Don Frank, brew in the town of Wilson, in Jackson Hole, Wyoming, and have a tasting room (1295 West St). They make very acceptable beers from extract. *Teton Ale* ☆☆, modelled on an English Bitter, is malty and fruity. *Old Faithful* ☆☆ an American Pale Ale, is drier and more fruit-accented.

Pacific Northwest
Brewpub right in the heart of downtown Seattle (322 Occidental Avenue S). Beers, with a hop accent, have included the perfumed *Blonde* ☆☆; a fuller-coloured, hoppier *Gold* ☆☆; an English-accented *Bitter* ☆☆▷☆☆☆; a well-balanced *Amber* ☆☆▷☆☆☆; a very fruity dry *Stout* ☆☆; and an aromatically malty *Winter Warmer* ☆☆☆.

Pike
Lively shrine to beer (1415 1st Ave), adjoining Pike Place Market, in Seattle. Principal products are a creamy, nutty, beautifully balanced *Pale Ale* ☆☆☆ and the soft, smooth, toasty, dryish *5X Stout* ☆☆☆. Specialities have included an astonishingly refreshing *East India Pale Ale* ☆☆☆; *Birra Perfetto* ☆☆☆, heavily seasoned with oregano; *Cerveza Rosanna* ☆☆▷☆☆ a lightly peppery chili ale; a rich, salty *Oyster Stout* ☆☆☆ flavoured with the liquid from the shellfish; *Old Bawdy* ☆☆☆ an oak-aged barley wine made from peated malt, finishing with a tantalising whiff of smoke; and a delicate, appetising *Rauchbier* ☆☆▷☆☆☆.

Portland Brewing
Classically Northwestern-style ales from a cosy brewpub (1339 NW Flanders St) and a grander newer micro and tasting

room (2730 NW 31st). Products include *Oregon Honey Beer* ☆☆▷ ☆☆☆, primed in the kettle and emerging with just the faintest hint of clover in its smooth palate; the light, dryish *Portland Ale* ☆▷☆☆☆; *Mount Hood* ☆☆, aromatized with that variety of hop, and with a late dryness in the finish; the hoppier, yet fairly sweet, Scottish-accented *McTarnahan's* ☆☆☆; a smooth, dryish, iron-tinged *Porter* ☆☆▷☆☆☆; and a strong *Stout* ☆☆▷ ☆☆☆ with a touch of cookies and burnt currants. The Portland Brewery has also produced a honey-primed strong brew called *Pollinator* (not tasted).

Pyramid/Thomas Kemper

Ever-new seasonal styles and well-made beers are produced in a brewpub/micro in Seattle, and Kalama, Washington; there is also a branch located in Berkeley, California. Pyramid may have avoided upsetting the brewers of Cologne by dedicating its Kölsch-style beer to Kalama. *"Kälsch"* ☆☆☆, which is smooth and finely balanced, is perhaps the best example of this style currently brewed in America. Among other recent tastings, an *Apricot Ale* ☆☆ was iron-ish and tart; a *Hefeweizen* ☆☆ very hazy and grapefruity; a *Rye Ale* ☆☆☆ was pithy, lemony and pepperminty; a *Best Brown* ☆☆▷☆☆☆ was richly malty, with notes of cotton candy; a *Scotch Ale* ☆☆☆ had notes of creamy coffee and port wine; a seasonal *Porter* ☆☆▷☆☆☆ was fruity, with notes of applewood smoke; the regular *Espresso Stout* ☆☆▷☆☆☆ contains no coffee but has a fittingly oily dryness. The wintry *Snow Cap* ☆☆☆ barley wine is long, lingering and aromatically hoppy. Tastings of Thomas Kemper include a sherbety, orangey, grassy, Belgian-style *White* ☆☆▷☆☆☆; a malty, Munich-style *Pale Lager* ☆☆▷☆☆☆; an appropriately licorice-like *Bohemian Dunkel* ☆☆☆; an *Oktoberfest* ☆☆☆, with an outstanding peachy/malty character; a *Maibock* ☆☆☆, with a delicately flowery (parma violets?) hop aroma; a lemony, creamy *Hefeweizen* ☆☆▷☆☆☆; and a *Roggen* ☆☆ rye lager that is syrupy, with notes of orange skins and cedar. (Seattle brewpub: 1201 1st Ave S).

Rainier

Once dubbed "The Green Death", but *Rainier Ale* ☆☆ today seems a shadow of its former sins. Even the regular *Rainier Beer* ☆ seems sweeter and less firm-bodied than it was.

Redhook

Early micro, now partly owned by Anheuser-Busch. Breweries with attached pubs in the Seattle area at 3400 Phinney Ave N (Fremont) and 14300 NE 145th St (Woodinville), and another planned on the opposite coast at Portsmouth, New Hampshire. *Ballard Bitter* ☆☆, named after the original brewery site, has regained some of its hop emphasis and is now sub-titled IPA. *Redhook ESB* ☆☆ is smooth, honeyed and fruity. *Blackhook Porter* ☆☆ is toffeeish and roasty. *Double Black Stout* ☆☆☆, made with Starbucks' coffee, has a remarkable balance of roastiness and creamy fudginess. *Wheat Hook* ☆☆ has a tart suggestion of orange juice. Special editions have included the lightly spicy *Redhook Rye* ☆☆▷☆☆☆ and a nutty *Honey Stout* ☆☆☆.

Rogue

The old coastal resort of Newport, Oregon, boasts a busy micro, with a separate tasting room (748 SW Bay Bvd). Although its name is taken from a river in Oregon, "Rogue" suits a brewery making some devilishly assertive products. Most of the brews exhibit a big, layered maltiness balanced by a late hop attack. Rogue is renowned for brewer John Maier's specialities. These include the neatly named *Maierbock* ☆☆▷☆☆☆ (4.8; 6.0): bronze, smooth, toasty; *Mogul* ☆☆ winter ale: treacly, fruity and coffeeish; the chewy *Nutbrown Nectar* ☆☆☆, with extract of hazels from the nearby Willamette Valley; *Smoke* ☆☆▷☆☆☆: light and dry but aromatic (alder is used); *Imperial Stout* ☆☆▷☆☆☆: whiskyish and licorice-tinged, like a Sazerac cocktail; and *Old Crustacean* ☆☆☆, which needs 12-18 months to reveal its remarkable balance.

Roslyn

The television series *Northern Exposure*, set in Alaska, was filmed in the Washington town of Roslyn, once a mining community. Thirsts can be quenched at the tap-room of Roslyn Brewing (33 Pennsylvania Ave). Products include the sweetish, spritzy *Brookside Beer* ☆▷☆☆ and *Roslyn Beer* ☆☆, reddish-brown, with a light, chocolatey sweetness and herbal, hoppy dryness.

Saxer

Pleasant beers, including an unusual, sherbety *Lemon Lager* ☆☆; a well-balanced, Vienna-style *Amber Lager* ☆☆; a toffeeish, cedary *Doppelbock* ☆☆☆▷☆☆☆ and a *Hefe-Dunkel* ☆☆☆ with a tasty, delicate, malt character.

Spanish Peaks

Mountain brewpub in Bozeman, Montana (120 N 19th Ave). Early products include a somewhat medicinal, dry *Porter* and a sweeter, oilier *Oatmeal Stout*. Too early to rate.

Steelhead

Hugely characterful and impeccably well-made beers from a brewpub in Eugene, Oregon (199 E 5th). Products include an explosively hoppy IPA called *Bombay Bomber* ☆☆☆; the complex *Finnegan's Wake Stout* ☆☆☆ dryish, with notes of passion fruit; and a warming, medicinal, syrupy *Barley Wine* ☆☆☆▷☆☆☆. Similar ranges in California, at affiliated Burlingame Station, near San Francisco (see entry) and at another Steelhead (not reviewed) in Irvine.

Sun Valley

Ski-country brewpub on Main St, Hailey, in Sun Valley, Idaho. Products include the sweetish *White Cloud Ale* ☆☆; complex, appropriately hoppy *Galena Bitter* ☆☆☆. The Galena hop variety is named after a nearby peak.

TableRock

Near the mountains, in Boise, Idaho. This brewpub (705 Fulton). Beers include the hoppy *Goathead Bitter* ☆☆☆ and the pleasantly fruity *Orange Blossom Special* ☆☆☆.

Umpqua

The name is native American. This brewpub is in Roseburg, Oregon (328 SE Jackson). Fruity beers in a wide variety of styles, ranging from a herbal-tasting Belgian-style *White* ☆☆☆ to a medicinal *Imperial Stout* ☆☆.

Widmer

German-style beers from a family-run pioneering micro in Portland. In recent years, Widmer has enjoyed great success in the Northwest with its (intentionally) densely sedimented *Hefe-Weizen* ☆☆☆, which tastes somewhere between a beer and a fresh, sweetish grapefruit juice, but deserves points for that curious distinction. The brewery's outstanding product is its hard-to-find *Altbier* ☆☆☆ – firm-bodied, with excellent malt and hop characters, in perfect balance. *Ur-Alt* ☆☆☆ is yet hoppier in style.

Other products have included a smooth, licorice tinged *Black Bier* ☆☆☆ and the lightly tart *Widberry* ☆☆☆▷☆☆☆, which is made with black raspberries. Widmer has a Gasthaus at its main brewery (929 N Russell) and a smaller brewery at the bakery-based restaurant B Moloch (901 SW Salmon).

Wild River

Sophisticated beers from a brewpub in the S of Oregon, near the California state line, at Cave Junction (249 N Redwood Highway). Wide range has included a *Hefeweizen* ☆☆▷☆☆☆ with banana and plum notes; a very good example of an *ESB* ☆☆☆; and a fruity (reminiscent of cherries), creamy, whiskyish *Barley Wine* ☆☆▷☆☆☆.

Winthrop

In the Cascade mountain town of the same name. Brewpub (155 Riverside) with a malty-fruity *Brown Ale* ☆☆; a plummy *Porter* ☆☆; and a gentle *Scottish Ale* ☆☆▷☆☆☆.

THE CARIBBEAN

EMIGRANTS FROM THE Caribbean have helped to spread the popularity of several beers that originate in the region. The best-known internationally is *Red Stripe* ☆▷☆☆, a light-tasting, soft-bodied lager that is brewed in Jamaica. Other examples include the maltier and fruitier *Banks Lager* ☆▷☆☆ from Barbados; and the malty, but drier *Carib Lager* ☆☆, which hails from Trinidad. Gravities are typically in the classical Pilsener range of 11.5–12 Plato (1046–1048); units of bitterness low (15–19); and lagering times short (two weeks is common). In Caribbean ethnic markets in Britain, Red Stripe has an extra-strong lager called *Crucial Brew* ☆.

Several Caribbean breweries also produce sweet or medium-dry stouts, often bottom-fermented, and usually made at "tropical" gravities, in the range of 15–20 Plato (1060–1080), with alcohol contents of between 4.5 and 6 percent by weight, 5.75–7.75 by volume. One such is Red Stripe's grainy, cakey *Dragon Stout* ☆▷☆☆ Some of these stouts are produced in the most unlikely places. Haiti, for example, has the dry, fruity *Prestige Stout* ☆☆.

LATIN AMERICA

ALL THE COUNTRIES of Latin America have brewing industries, some very large. All produce beers distantly derived from
the Germanic tradition, including the occasional dark speciality.
Peru, for example, has *Cusqueña Malta* ☆☆. The latter term
often means a malt-extract drink, but this one is a strongish (4.5;
5.6) lager, almost black, very sweet and coffeeish.

Brazil has *Xingu* ☆☆▷☆☆☆, purportedly originating from the
Indians of the Amazon but more like a Kulmbacher lager. Brazil
also has the odd Bock beer and Dortmunder-style lager. There is
also a lagerish character and extreme sweetness to the same country's *Caracu Stout* ☆☆, which is decidedly lacking in roastiness.

In Brazil, the newish São Paulo Brewery is a micro with a Pilsner called *Mass* (not tasted), said to be brewed according to the
German Beer Purity Law. A red lager is planned. São Paulo also
has the new brewpub Dadobier (Av Juscelino Kubischeck at Av
Faria Lima), selling unfiltered beer – and seating 3,000 people.
There is also a Dadobier in Porto Alegre (Av Nilo Pecanha), and
more brewpubs are opening.

In Argentina, the Patagonian town of El Bolsón has two newish
small breweries. One produces lagers and fruit beers. The other,
the oddly-named Rowanbräu, makes something more ale-like,
conditioned in the bottle. In February, the town has a beer festival
to celebrate the hop harvest.

The Latin American beers best known outside the sub-conti-
nent are those from Mexico. The success in the US of Corona
(from the Modelo group; see below) has done a disservice to
Mexican beer. Corona is a cheaply made, watery, sweetish beer,
originally intended simply as a thirst-quencher for manual
workers in Mexico. Each of the brewers in Mexico has such a
product, usually bottled in plain glass, with an enamelled name
instead of a label. By a freak of fashion, and initially with very
little promotion, Corona became a cult beer among sub-Yuppies
in the southwest of the USA. This has encouraged Mexican
brewers to concentrate on such products, at the expense of their
several more interesting beers. It has also encouraged Americans
to believe that all Mexican beer is light and bland. The way
things are going, that will, regrettably, soon be true.

Cuauhtémoc
Second-largest of the Mexican brewing companies. Also owns
Cruz Blanca. (It is itself owned by the same holding company as
Moctezuma.) The Cuauhtémoc products are lightened by a high
proportion of corn, and tend to have a dry, slightly tannic, finish.
The company has a typically Mexican range. The "clear-glass"
brand is *Chihuahua* ☆. The dry, crisp quencher *Tecate* ☆ began as
a regional brand. *Carta Blanca* ☆ and (in the US market) the
smooth *Carta Blanca Dark* ☆▷☆☆☆ are mainstream brands.
Bohemia ☆☆ is a pleasantly hoppy Pilsener with a high gravity

for the style (13; 1052; 4.2; 5.4). *Indio Oscura* ☆▷☆☆ is a reddish lager, broadly of the Vienna type but a little thin and dry for the style. *Commemorativa* ☆☆▷☆☆☆ (14.3; 1057; 4.3; 5.6) is a medium-dark Christmas beer.

Moctezuma

Biggest exporter, but smallest in the Mexican market. Uses a lower proportion of adjuncts and makes a point that they include rice. Its beers tend to be relatively smooth, with a spritzy finish: kräusening is another point of policy. *Sol* ☆ is another sub-Yuppie quencher; *Superior* ☆▷☆☆ is a lightly fragrant, spritzy Pilsener-type (11.5; 1046; 3.6; 4.5). Then comes the rather confusing Equis range. *Tres Equis* ☆▷☆☆ is a marginally fuller Pilsener-type. *Dos Equis Lager Especial* ☆▷☆☆ is fractionally fuller again (12; 1048- 3.7; 4.6). The best-known version, simply called *Dos Equis* ☆☆, is amber-red in colour, and made broadly in the Vienna style. It, too, has a gravity of 12 Plato. The dark-brown *Noche Buena* ☆☆☆ Christmas Beer (4.8; 6.0) is very smooth, with both malt and hop in its long finish. *Tres Equis Oscura* has been discontinued, because the company has more faith in its less interesting beers.

Modelo

Biggest of the Mexican brewing companies, also owning Yucatan. Its most noteworthy product is the *Negra Modelo* ☆☆☆, on the dark side for a Vienna-style beer, creamy in body, with a hint of chocolate (just the thing with chicken molé). Its least-noteworthy, but biggest-selling brand is *Corona* ☆. The Yucatan brands include a dryish, slightly salty *Montejo* ☆▷☆☆ and lightly malty *León Negra* ☆☆ (not so much black as brownish-red).

JAPAN

AN ASTONISHING DIVERSITY of beers is now being made in Japan, and brewpubs are opening at the rate of more than one a month. With its high disposable income and keen awareness of fashion, Japan has taken up small beer with a fervour rivalling that of the United States. At some brewpubs, there can be a long wait for a table.

This revolutionary change follows the repeal two years ago of a law that made it impossible to open a small brewery. This law effectively maintained a cartel for the four national brewers: Kirin, Asahi, Sapporo and Suntory.

With Japan's opaque system of addresses (employing block numbers rather than streets), even the brewpubs are hard to find, and it helps to have a good hotel concierge, tour guide or Japanese friend. The key phrase, comparable to "micro-brew" in the US, is *ji-biru* (local beer). Like many phrases applied to beer in Japan, this derives from an expression normally used in respect of sake. *Ji-biru* is often unfiltered, and a very hazy approximation of Kölsch is especially popular.

WHERE TO DRINK

Tokyo: A small chain called Beer Bar Brussels offers about 100 Belgian specialities, including some imported directly from tiny breweries. These are small, unpretentious bars. The most central, not far from the Imperial Palace, and on the Hanzomon metro line, is in the Kanda bookstore district (3-16-1 Kanda Ogawamachi, Chiyoda-ku; ☎3233-4247). There are other branches in the Kagurazaka, Kayabacho and Harujuku districts. Jazz pianist Masaharu Yamada has a piano bar and Belgian-accented restaurant called Bois Cereste, in a fashionable dining area (2-13-21 Akasaka, ☎3588-6292).

Sapporo: This major city, on the island of Hokkaido, has a long-established beer bar run by Japanese-speaking American Phred Kaufman, something of a local personality. It is right behind the Excel Hotel, and is called The Beer Inn (Onoda Building, South 9, West 5, Chuo-ku (☎512-4774). This basement bar has only four or five tables, but it is crammed with beer memorabilia and stocks about 250 brews. Among them are some produced for Kaufman by the Rogue brewery, in Oregon. One is flavoured with the tart hascup berry, which is found only in Hokkaido and Siberia.

Arai

Sony founder's son Hideo Morita pursues the family's original industry sake - and beer, in the Arai mountain resort, developed for the winter Olympics. Arai is near Nagano, in the Japanese Alps.

This upscale resort's brewery produces two ales, a fresh, appetizing *Blonde* ☆☆ and a crisp *Dark* ☆☆, both slightly lighter in character than those of consultant Choju-Gura.

Asahi

Despite the dubious distinction of having given the world "dry" beer, Asahi does have some products of substance. Its *Super Premium* ☆☆ is said to be made with water trucked from Mount Fuji, and is hopped entirely with Saaz; whatever its origins, it is a perfumed, smooth and beautifully balanced golden lager. Asahi's *Black Beer* ☆☆☆, already an enjoyable beer, has recently gained in character, swapping some of its caramel-malt richness for a slightly drier, bitter-chocolate note and a darker colour. The brewery also produces its outstandingly traditional strong (6.4; 8.0) *Stout* ☆☆☆▷☆☆☆☆, which is made with a Brettanomyces culture. This beer has notes of sherry and whisky, especially on the nose.

In the company's Tokyo riverside offices and a couple of adjoining post-modernist buildings designed by Philippe Starck, Asahi has half-a-dozen restaurants and bars, including a brew-pub. The latter, its equipment divided between two floors, is in a curiously cylindrical building. Although the brewpub makes three beers, the full range is available only on the third floor, served from two showcased red tanks in the Sumida River Brewery Pub. A mildly toffeeish Altbier, named after the *Azuma Bridge* ☆▷☆☆ and a Kölsch known simply as *River Beer* ☆▷☆☆, both lacking in hop, are served lightly hazy (some of the yeast having been removed by centrifuge). A fuller, tarter, version of the latter, *Zwickelbier* ☆☆, is served without this treatment. (23-1, Azumabashi 1-Chome, Sumida-Ku; ☎5608-3831).

Beer Station

Railway station beer halls under this name are being developed by Sapporo together with a restaurant group. The one in the Garden Place development at Tokyo's Yebisu station began with a lightly malty, amber-red *Dunkel* ☆☆ brewed by Sapporo and decanted into large tanks on the premises. The one at Ryogoku station (1-3-20 Yokozuna, Sumida-ku. ☎03-3623-5252), near Tokyo's sumo stadium, is a genuine brewpub. Beers include a smooth, lightly dry *Pilsner* ☆☆▷☆☆☆; a truly dark lager called *Praha Dunkel* ☆☆☆ (inspired by U Fleku, of Prague); and a mildly fruity *Weizen* ☆☆ made with an ale yeast. Very good sushi, too. Round the corner is the Popeye pub, specialising in Japanese micro-brews (2-18-7 Ryogoku. ☎03-3633-2120).

Choju-Gura

The name means "Long Life Warehouse". It is applied to a 300-year old warehouse of Shirayuki sake, in Itami, just outside Osaka. The warehouse now accommodates a museum, mini sake and beer breweries and a restaurant with hints of Belgium. Sake-making Itami is twinned with the Belgian gin town of Hasselt. Shirayuki's owner, Shintaro Konishi, first imported Belgian beers (still sold in his shop next door), then started to make his own versions. To a soft, fragrantly fruity *Blond* ☆☆▷☆☆☆ and a malty, spicy, cocoa-tinged *Dark* ☆☆☆, he has now added a sweetish, perfumed, Belgian-style *Blanche* ☆☆☆. (Chuo 3-4-15, Itami. ☎0727-73-1111).

Csarda

The name, Hungarian for inn, took the fancy of the owner (who works in the clothing industry) on his travels in Europe. The adobe-like interior of this brewpub, with beams painted like wooden toys, suggest eclecticism, but Hungarians would enjoy the giant carp sculpture outside. It is by the earthquake memorial park in Kobe Hatoba-cho, Chuo-ku; ☎078-333-8688). Beers have included a hoppy, perfumed *Pilsner* ☆☆☆; a malty but well-balanced *Bitter Ale* ☆☆▷☆☆☆; an *Amber Ale* ☆☆▷☆☆☆ with a very good malt character; a licorice-tinged *Brown Ale* ☆☆▷☆☆☆; a sweetish *Wheat Beer* ☆; a lightly smoky Rauch-bier, *Paruku* ☆☆☆ (named after the park); and a beautifully rounded *Sweet Stout* ☆☆☆ containing lactose. Also a branch in Yokohama.

Decks/Sunset Beach

Young lovers flock to Tokyo's bayside Daiba district. The Decks shopping centre there boasts this American-accented brewpub. Beers, all unfiltered, are disappointing. They include a fruity, light *Kölsch* ☆; an orangey *Alt* ☆▷☆☆; and a lemony *Special* ☆ wheat beer. (1-6-1 Daiba, Minato-ku. ☎03-5500-5070)

Doppo

Italian-sounding brand-name for German-style beers made by the Miyashita sake brewery in the city of Okayama, in the south of the main island. A *Pilsner* ☆▷☆☆ has a firm, slightly sticky, malt background and quite a bitter finish. A *Dunkel* ☆☆ is a bright reddish-brown in the Vienna style with a sweetish, barley-sugar/ malt character. This is a micro, not a brewpub. Its beers can sometimes be found in Takashimaya department stores in major cities.

Gotenba

Mount Fuji resort town, sometimes rendered in English as Gotemba, 100 km SW of Tokyo. The Gotenba Kohgen ("Plateau") Brewery is in a complex with hot springs and two modern hotels (one Japanese-style), set among cherry trees and pines. The exterior of the brewery is in half-timbered "Old German" style worthy of Disneyland. The hall-like interior is more credible, with an open barbecue preparing sausages, ribs and excellent steaks, and a most impressive brewhouse behind glass. The owning company, in the sausage business, went into brewing in a joint venture with the municipality.

A *Pils* ☆☆ has a light but smooth maltiness and a good, late, hoppy bitterness. The *Dunkel* ☆☆ has an amber colour in the style of a Vienna lager, with a touch of juicy maltiness, but is light and dry for the style. The *Weizen* ☆☆ is hazy, but with no yeast-bite, smooth, dryish and gently fruity, with notes of orange-peel and grapefruit. (719 Kohyama, Gotenba, Shizuoka Prefecture; ☎0550-87-5500).

Grand' Place

A designer of movie sets has re-created the famous Brussels square with astonishing credibility inside a modern warehouse in Nagoya. Eat mussels and fries at an indoor "pavement café". This brewpub is a younger sister to Choju-Gura (see above). Slightly bigger-tasting than their Itami counterparts is a flowery, nutty *Gold* ☆☆▷☆☆☆ and a soft, toffeeish *Brown* ☆☆☆. (1701 Takayanagi-cho, Meito-ku. ☎052-772-0147).

Hoppy Beverage

Making beer at last, after half a century producing a low-alcohol beverage optimistically called Hoppy. This micro, also known as Akasaka Ji-Biru, has its premises in a suburb of Tokyo. Its unfiltered *Pils* ☆▷☆☆ is a tasty beer – but hardly in style, with its syrupy, fruity flavours. Its *Kuro Half* ☆▷☆☆ ("Demi-Black") is similar but fuller and more toffeeish; it is intended as a Munich-style lager. In central Tokyo, the beers can be found, incongruously, at a bar-restaurant bringing a touch of Japanese style to Canadian salmon and crustaceans: the Koji Vancouver, in the the lower-ground level of Kokusai Shin Akasaka Building (☎3583-5414). The owners of this restaurant also have a business in Vancouver, Canada.

Kinokuni Nohan

In English, the Woodland Brewery. In a barn-like (rustic post-modern?) building of local cedar, at Katsuragi, gateway to Kouya-san mountain country, south of Osaka. Unfiltered, top-fermenting beers include a smooth, malty *Altbier* ☆▷☆☆. Capacity problems have limited production of two better-balanced lagers, branded Gunkan (after a Meji-era warship); a *Helles* ☆☆ and a maltier *Dunkel* ☆☆. Eat beef with local pickled horseradish. (702 Sana, Katsuragi-cho. ☎0736-22-1005).

Kirin

Even with a recent drop in hop character, *Kirin Lager* ☆▷☆☆ is pleasantly crisp. The name *Ichiban* ☆▷☆☆ ("First Squeeze") adapts a sake term. This lightly malty, smooth golden lager is made from the first runnings from the mash-run. The *Black Beer* ☆☆▷☆☆☆ has toffee-licorice, rooty, slightly smoky flavours. The strong (6.4; 8.0) *Stout* ☆☆☆ has treacle-toffee notes. The company's smallish brewery in Kyoto has been known to make a malt-accented *Alt* ☆☆▷☆☆. This can sometimes be found in the restaurant at Kirin's remarkable Beer Village, in Yokohama. This tourist attraction, set around the architecturally striking 1990s Kirin brewery, also includes a brewpub in the style of the 1860s, evoking the beginning of the industry in Japan. The brewpub has a firm-bodied, hoppy golden lager called *Spring Valley* ☆☆▷☆☆. (The Beer Village, Tsurumi-ku, Namamugi 1-17-1; ☎045-503-8250).

Kizakura Kappa

In Kyoto, the historic city of temples and gardens. Kizakura means "yellow cherry-blossom", and a tree of that persuasion stands in the courtyard outside this beautifully restored, Kyoto-style building. Kappa is a mythological creature resembling a human with a turtle's shell. A sake brand named Kappa is made by the owners of this brewpub, which has a gallery of art devoted to the creature. An *Alt* ☆▷☆☆ is a little fruity, thin and spritzy for the style. A *Kölsch* ☆▷☆☆ is fruity for the style, too. A beer curiously called *Kölsch Mild* ☆☆ is sweeter and yet fruitier, with fresh apple notes. The latter derives from the interesting use of a sake yeast. (53 Kajiwara-cho, Shimomisu, Yoko-ooji, Fushimi-ku, Kyoto; ☎075-611-4101).

Komi

A block away from Nagoya's Grand' Place (previous page). Komi is a stylish, Italian-accented (Roman?) restaurant and brewery. Beers are more northerly: a lightly clovey *Weizen* ☆☆▷☆☆; a malt-accented, chocolatey *Bitter* ☆▷☆☆; a rich, brownish *Amber Ale* ☆☆; and a strong (5.6; 7.0) *Stout* ☆☆☆, reminiscent of cherries in brandy. (12 Koike-cho, Higashi-ku. ☎052-931-2471).

Kuninocho

Micro near Osaka, at Takatsuki City. Products include a hazy *Kölsch* ☆▷☆☆, with a sweet start and dry finish.

Minami Shinshu

The pretty, wooded resort of Komagane, high in the mountains of the same name, is home to a whisky distillery, adjoining brewery, restaurant (try the horse sashimi) and gift shop. The most interesting beers are a liqueur-ish *Dunkleweizen* ☆☆☆; an *India Pale Ale* ☆☆▷☆☆☆ with a tangy, tobacco-like hoppiness; and a milky, chewy *Sweet Stout* ☆☆▷☆☆☆. (Restaurant: Aji-wai-kobo, 759-447 Akaho, Komagane-shi, Nagano prefecture).

Moku Moku

In Ninja martial-arts country, in the mountains near Ueno, east of Kyoto and Osaka. The name "Moku Moku" refers to the Ninja warriors' technique of vanishing into smoke screens. Despite such excitement – or perhaps because of it – the hill country has been losing population. Local farmers responded by starting a cooperative to process ham, make sausages, grow barley, make their own malt (in a tiny mechanised plant) and brew beer. The brewery also has a tasting bar.

A wide range of robustly yeasty country beers has been produced. They include a full-coloured, spicy, hoppy *Pils* ☆ that lacks the refinement of the style; a smooth, toffeeish, fruity *Amber Ale* ☆▷☆☆; an earthy *Smoked Ale* ☆☆, made with peated malt from Scotland, and an orangey *Biscuit Weizen* ☆☆. The latter is made with "biscuit" malt from Belgium. The brewery is located in the hamlet of Nishiyubune, in the municipality of Ayama, in the prefecture of Mie. ☎0595-43-2011

Nagahama Roman

Between Nagoya and Kyoto, the town of Nagahama is an historic port on Lake Biwa, with a shogun's castle. This brewpub is in a moated building that was once a rice storehouse. Its name implies, with some justification, that it is romantic. *Nagahama Ale* ☆☆☆ has a grapefruity Cascade hoppiness set against a good malt background; it was designed by a Californian. Other characterful products include a medium-sweet *Stout* ☆☆▷☆☆☆, with the flavours of iced coffee, and a slightly chewy *Bock* ☆☆. Local wild ferns, lake fish and duck stew are featured. (14-1 Asahi-cho, Nagahama. ☎0749-63-4300).

Nagara/926

About an hour NW of Nagoya, in the town of Gifu, on the Nagara River where cormorants are trained to fish for the trout-like fish ayu. The number 926 is a Japanese word-play. It is owned by a timber company, and spectacularly features their product, from its parquet floors to its towering pine pillars. Beers include a lemony, sherbety *Weizen* ☆☆; a strongish (4.6; 5.7, "to be different") *Pilsner* ☆☆☆, with herbal Saaz hop flavours; a spicy *Altbier* ☆☆; and a malty *Dunkel* ☆☆▷☆☆☆ with good flavour development. (28 Murasame-cho, Gifu. ☎058-253-9260).

Oh! La! Ho

Such Jinglish exclamations are popular in Japan. This one is attached to a brewpub in dessert-grape and walnut country at Tobu, in Nagano prefecture. Beers include a firm, dry, hoppy *Golden Ale* ☆☆☆ in the American style. (3875-2 Kanou Oaza, Toubu. ☎0268-64-0006).

Okhotsk

Beautiful beer, made with obvious care, in a well-kept brewpub-restaurant that is an unlikely asset to the frontier-ish market town of Kitami, in the east of Hokkaido near the Sea of Okhotsk. Local barley, malted by the Sapporo brewery, is used in single-, double-, and even triple-decoction mashes. In its first year, the brewery produced ten styles. These included the amusingly-named *Bitter Pils* ☆☆☆, with a remarkably long, creamy malt background and a delicate Saaz hop balance. Despite its name, it has only 23 units of bitterness, barely ahead of the 21 in the regular Pils, but it is a delightful beer. A brew called simply *Okhotsk Ale* ☆☆, made with a top-fermenting yeast, has an orangey colour; a firm, smooth, faintly ginger-cookie palate and a lingering subtle dryness. A *Black Beer* ☆☆☆ has an excellent ebony colour, a textured body and dryish, peaty, whisky-like flavours. Hokkaido is noted for its sushi, and the sea-urchin version here is outstanding. (2–2-2 Yamashita-machi, Kitami; ☎0157-23-6300.

Otaru

College town, and historic Hokkaido port, with chunky, stone canalside warehouses. One of these now accommodates a galleried tavern in the style of Bamberg, Germany. Brewer Johannes Braun has decorated nooks and crannies with photographs of two earlier generations of his family, both beer-makers, along with tools of the trade from earlier times, and scenes of German village life. The copper-clad, Bamberg-built brewhouse is open on a plinth in the centre of the bar.

Beers brewed here include a *Helles* ☆☆☆▷☆☆☆ with a firm, malty middle, and good, flowery (almost lemony) Tettnang hop flavours. An orangey-brown *Dunkel* ☆☆☆▷☆☆☆ is firm and smooth, with light but delicious Vienna malt flavours and a fairly dry finish. Seasonal specials (not tasted) have included a *Kölsch*, a *Festbier*, a *Smoked Beer* and a *Weizen*. The menu reflects the owning company's principal business as a chain of steak restaurants – which also has its own ranch. (Otaru Beer, 5-4 Minatomachi, Otaru; ☎0134-21-2323).

Sandaya

Buffet and brewpub on a hillside off the highway between the major city of Osaka and the nearby hot springs area of Nishimoya. Eat sausages, ham, smoked meats with unfiltered, assertive beers. A *Pilsner* ☆ has a yeastily creamy start and a slightly astringent finish. A *Fest-type* ☆☆▷☆☆☆ is reddish and very malty, with a roasty finish. A *Smoked Beer* ☆☆☆▷☆☆☆ has a treacle-toffee start and roasty finish. A *Black Beer* ☆☆☆ has a solid colour and more treacly flavours. This establishment is in the corporate headquarters of a smoked-meat company and restaurant chain, whose president is a passionate beer-lover. He himself roasts the malt (in a wok) and does the brewing. (Sandaya Country Beer, 2-99 Narai, Yamaguchi-cho, Nishimaya, Hyogo Prefecture; ☎078-903-1333).

Sapporo

The post-modernist silver can, known in some export markets, contains the lightly dry, spritzy beer known as "black label" to the Japanese and officially designated *Original Draft* ☆▷☆☆☆. In the town from which it takes its name, Sapporo has a beer garden at its turn-of-the-century brewery, and a firm, sweetish, malty local lager called *Classic* ☆☆☆. Many beer-lovers feel that the aromatically malty, Dortmunder-style *Yebisu* ☆☆☆▷☆☆☆ is the best regular lager from a big brewer in Japan. Yebisu is a Shinto god, but also a Tokyo district where Sapporo once also had a brewery (*see* Beer Station). The company's classic *Black Beer* ☆☆☆, with notes of toffee, figs and coffee, has been made since 1892.

Satsuma

Connoisseurs speak extremely highly of the *Weizen* (not tasted) from this micro, in Kokobu, Kagoshima prefecture in the far S of Kyushu. Products also include the light, dry, rounded *Satsuma Ale* ☆☆.

Suntory

Biggest of Japan's whisky distillers and smallest of the four big brewers, Suntory has been emphasizing a soft brew called *Malt's* ☆▷☆☆, with a gently hoppy finish. Its products have also included a dry, chocolatey *Black Beer* ☆☆▷☆☆☆ and several experimental brews, notably a very soft, malty *Alt* ☆☆ and a clovey *Weizen* ☆☆☆. These speciality beers can be found in the Suntory Malts Club, Times Park, 1-15-1, Tamagawa, Setagaya-ku, Tokyo; ☎3708 3550.

Tambara/Umenishiki

Pavilion-style brewpub, in 200-species herb garden, with Italian-accented restaurant, in town of Tanbara on Shikoku island. Beers include a fruity, pleasantly dry *Pale Ale* ☆☆; a sweetish *Pilsner* ☆▷☆☆; a rather light *Bock* ☆☆; a coffeeish *Double Bock* ☆☆☆; and a fruit beer based on local mandarin oranges. (429-1 Sekiya-ko, Tambara, Ehime prefecture. ☎0898-73-2071).

Uehara/Echigo

The first brewpub in Japan, in church-like, purpose-built premises and offering Italian food. The taste for the latter was acquired by Seiichiro Uehara when he was working as an actor and director in *commedia dell'arte*. His German wife helped further his beery interests and the family's sake business gave him a taste for brewing. The Uehara brewery is at Makimachi, in the prefecture of Niigata, a sake region in the northwest of the main island.

The pub is called Echigo, the old name for the region. A wide range of beers has included a very hazy *Weizen* ☆☆▷☆☆☆, with lemon and bubblegum notes; a hoppy, grapefruity American-style *Pale Ale* ☆☆; a perfumed (fruits gums?) Belgian Tripel (8.0; 10.0), served from a gin crock and confusingly described as *Old Ale* ☆☆☆; a smooth, rounded, licorice-tasting *Stout* ☆☆▷☆☆ and an orangey *Ginjou Beer* ☆☆▷☆☆☆ (Sake Yeast) that was astonishingly light for an alcohol content of 5.6; 7.0. The beers can be found on draught in Tokyo at an upstairs terrace café called Judith, outside the Jingumae metro station in the Harajuku shopping area.

THE REST OF ASIA

SOME ASIAN COUNTRIES have Islamic objections to alcohol, but many have Western-style breweries with the oldest dating from the mid- to late 1800s. In most countries, the climate, culture and standard of living favours nothing more elaborate than straightforward, international-style lagers, but there are some exceptions.

Most international beer-makers have breweries or joint ventures in China, and there are some micros there. China has at least one brewery in every town, but the lack of a beer culture, and of refrigeration in retail outlets, makes for random results. When Germany enjoyed a colonial "concession" in Shantung,

China, hop gardens and a brewery were established in the resort of Tsingtao. This is now one of China's major exporters. *Tsingtao Beer* ☆▷☆☆ is a hoppy, light-bodied Pilsener. The very sweet *Tsingtao Porter* ☆ is harder to find. In 1995, the South China Brewing Company opened as a micro in Hong Kong. Its *Crooked Island Ale* uses English malts but is otherwise a slightly bigger-bodied adaptation of the *Pale Ale* originally created by brewing consultant Ed Tringali for Big Time in Seattle.

A similar ale, paler and less aromatic, is one of several produced at a new brewpub associated with San Miguel, in Manila (The Brewery, Glorieta Mall, Ayala Centre, Makati City). San Miguel, one of the world's major brewers, is Filipino; in a reversal of colonial trade, it had breweries in Spain, but they have now been sold to Kronenbourg of France. The original Filipino *San Miguel Pilsen* ☆ has a light, dryish, maltiness. *San Miguel Dark Lager* ☆☆ is toasty and slightly smoky.

Paulaner of Munich now has a brewpub in Bangkok serving a sweetish unfiltered lager. German technical help was used 60 years ago to set up the Thai brewery that produces the hoppy *Singha Lager* ☆☆☆ (13.8 Plato; 1055; 4.8; 6.0; and a hearty 40 units of bitterness). Local rival *Amarit* ☆▷☆☆ is milder.

While the Singha is a mythical creature resembling a lion, Tiger Beer is a legend in its own lunchtime, perhaps because it entered literature through the pen of Anthony Burgess. *Tiger Lager Beer* ☆☆ is a hoppier cousin to Heineken. The same company produces the creamy, roasty, medium-dry *ABC Extra Stout* ☆☆▷☆☆ (18.2; 1073; 6.5; 8.1). These products are made in Singapore and Malaysia.

India has a large brewing industry. Most of its products are sweetish lagers. Examples are the fairly full-bodied *Cobra* ☆▷☆☆, brewed in India for the British market and *Kingfisher* ☆, brewed under licence in Britain. Another product brewed under licence, *Lal Toofan* ☆, is light and perfumed.

In Sri Lanka, McCallum makes the all-malt *Three Coins Pilsener* ☆☆ and the smooth, chocolatey, bottom-fermenting, *Sando Stout* ☆☆▷☆☆ (15; 1060). The rival Ceylon Breweries has the fruitier, top-fermenting (in wood) *Lion Stout* ☆☆☆, also all-malt, at a similar gravity, producing five percent alcohol by weight; 6.3 by volume. Astonishingly, Ceylon Breweries' lager and stout are available, unpasteurized, from wooden casks, drawn by hand-pump, at The Beer Shop, in the brewery's home town of Nuwara Eliya, and at UKD Silva, in the holy city of Kandy.

AUSTRALASIA

WHILE NEW ZEALAND HAS ENJOYED a blossoming of small breweries, some of Australia's have wilted in harsher economic climes. For the visitor, it is worth noting that most small breweries, and some larger ones, in Australasia have shops on the premises.

Despite their popular reputations, the big brewers in these two countries produce few interesting beers. Heineken has a significant stake in New Zealand's Dominion Breweries, while local rival Lion Nathan also owns Castlemaine, Hahn, South Australian, Toohey's and Swan. Australian rival Foster's owns Cascade, Power's, Tooths and others.

In New Zealand, the description "Draught" refers to a sweetish bronze brew vaguely reminiscent of an ale, but bottom-fermented. "Dark" is usually bottom-fermenting, but occasionally top.

In Australia, "Bitter" is usually a lager, perhaps slightly hoppier than the main stream. "Old" is a dark ale.

Amazulu
African-theme brewpub in Auckland, New Zealand (309 Karangahape Rd). Mainstream New Zealand beers include a toffeeish "Draught" called *Black Magic* ☆▷☆☆.

Australian Pizza Kitchen
An intentionally soured Stout (not tasted) is a new speciality at this malt-extract brewpub (Bailies Corner, London Circuit, Canberra). An earlier smooth, golden *Lager* ☆☆ augured well.

Bays
Mainsteam New Zealand beers from a micro at Tahunanui, Nelson. The *Dark* ☆ has a very full colour but a light (nutty) palate.

Bill Bell's
Long-established pub in south Melbourne (Moray St) making its own beers. Products have included a malt-accented *Real Ale* ☆☆▷☆☆☆ and spicy *Porter* ☆☆.

Boag's
Old-established brewery (tracing its history to 1827) in Launceston, Tasmania. The beers' house character has a touch of new-mown hay. *Boag's Bitter* ☆▷☆☆ has a good dryness in the finish. *Export Lager* ☆▷☆☆ is slightly honeyish. *XXX Ale* ☆▷☆☆ is slightly tart.

Burke's
Stylish brewery building, along the lines of a retro ice-cream parlour, in avocado and capsicum country, N of Auckland, at Helensville. (88 Commercial Rd, adjoining an Italian-accented restaurant overlooking the Kaipara River.) Unfortunately, the beers are very mainstream. The most interesting is a coffeeish *Olde Ale* ☆▷☆☆.

Cascade
Oldest continuously operated brewery in Australia, having first fired its kettles in 1824. Handsome building where the waters cascade off Mt Wellington near Hobart. Beers, with some subtlety of hop character, include: the firm, smooth *Cascade Draught* ☆▷☆☆ ; the slightly crisper *Lager* ☆▷☆☆; the maltier *Premium* ☆▷☆☆; and an oily, roasty *Stout* ☆☆.

Castlemaine
Major brewery in Brisbane, Queensland. Its beers have fractionally more malt character than those of other big Australian brewers, and unusually use hop blossoms rather than pellets or extract. *Castlemaine XXXX* ☆☆ has a touch of new-mown hay in the nose. (Available from the wood at the Breakfast Creek Hotel, Kingsford Smith Drive.) *Carbine Stout* ☆☆ is malt-accented.

Cock & Bull/Steam Brewing

A fruity (apricot?), nutty *Steam Beer* ☆☆▷☆☆☆ a malt-accented, but crisp *Best Bitter* ☆☆▷☆☆☆, the latter on hand-pump, and many other styles, from a British-accented pub and micro (272 Ti Rakau Drive, in the Auckland suburb of Pakuranga). Another British-style pub in Auckland called Speaker's Corner (7 Anzac Rd, Brown's Bay) offers a large range of English, Welsh and Scottish imported beers.

Cooper's

The only small brewery in Australia to have remained independent since the earliest days (founded 1862). Its fruity, sedimented brews are Australian classics. *Cooper's Original* ☆☆ (3.6; 4.5) has touches of apple, pear and banana. The ironically named *Cooper's Sparkling Ale* ☆☆☆▷☆☆☆☆ (4.7; 5.9) has seemed more flowery and citric and less banana-ish of late. *Black Crow* ☆☆▷☆☆☆ has chocolate and toast notes. The coffeeish *Best Extra Stout* ☆☆☆▷☆☆☆☆ (5.5; 6.8) has a good balance of yeastiness and firm smoothness. In home town Adelaide, the range is well-presented at the Earl of Aberdeen (316 Pulteney St).

Cork & Keg

British-style pub (complete with pork pies) in New Zealand's Marlborough wine country (Inkerman St, Renwick) Speciality is a vanilla-ish Old Ale called *Hurricane* ☆☆▷☆☆☆.

Dominion Breweries

National brewer in New Zealand. Mainstream beers with an estery note owed to the continuous fermentation technique. The smallest brewery in the group produces the toffeeish, sugar-and-spice *Monteith's Original Ale* ☆▷☆☆ and the rummier *Trapper's Red* ☆☆.

Dux de Lux

In the old college and arts area of Christchurch, New Zealand (Hereford and Montreal Sts). Brewpub producing a malty *Lager* ☆ ☆▷☆☆☆; a *Bitter* ☆☆ closer in style to a strong Mild; and a well-balanced, strong (5.6; 7.0) Pale Ale called *Nor'Wester* ☆☆☆.

Emerson's

Splendidly complex *Weissbier* ☆☆☆ (in both pale and dark versions), with notes of sherbet, banana and clove, from a micro in Dunedin, New Zealand. Also the fruity, winey *Bookbinder Bitter* ☆☆▷☆☆☆ and the big, spicily hoppy, British-style *1812 IPA* ☆☆☆. On Fridays and Saturdays the beers are hand-pumped from wooden barrels at the Criterion in Tyne St, Oamaru.

Foster's

The internationally known *Foster's Lager* ☆ is sweetish, with notes of banana or pineapple. In its home town, it has recently lost sales to the fractionally drier *Victoria Bitter* ☆ and marginally hoppier *Melbourne Bitter* ☆. *Carlton Genuine Draught* ☆ is lighter, crisper and less fruity. *Abbot's Double Stout* ☆☆ is roasty and coffeeish.

Galbraith's

Public library-turned-brewpub, in Auckland, New Zealand (2 Mt Eden Rd). Very hoppy ales in the southern English style include the Goldings-accented *Bob Hudson's Bitter* ☆☆▷☆☆☆ and the flowery (Fuggles) *Bellringer's Best* ☆☆☆, both on hand-pump.

Geebung Polo Club
A brewpub despite the name. Products include a tasty wheat beer called *Yellow Mongrel* ☆☆ and the creamy *Razorback Stout* ☆☆☆. (85 Auburn Rd, Melbourne.)

Geelong
Micro making lightly hoppy mainstream beers in the Australian town of the same name.

Grand Ridge
Micro in the Strzlecki Hills of the fruit-growing and cheese-making Gippsland region of Victoria. Products have included a well-balanced *Mild* ☆☆ and a fruity, vanilla-tinged, barley wine *Moonshine* ☆☆☆.

Hahn
Sydney micro now owned by Lion Nathan. *Hahn Premium Lager* ☆☆☆▷☆☆☆ has good hop flavours and bitterness.

Harrington's
Related micros, in Christchurch and Richmond, Nelson, New Zealand. Mainstream products but the odd speciality, such as a sweetish *Wheat Beer* ☆▷☆☆.

Kahikatea
The Maori name for a white pine, in this instance indicating a micro in Hamilton, New Zealand. Despite its designation, the fresh, smooth, fruity *Best Bitter* ☆☆ is intended as a more flavoursome version of a New Zealand "Draught". The *Dark* ☆☆ is toasty, with a coffeeish finish.

Lion
Ale micro in Adelaide that developed Two Dogs alcoholic lemonade.

Lion Nathan
National brewer in New Zealand. Its *Steinlager* ☆▷☆☆ has a touch of pollen in the flowery nose, but has lost some character. Specialities include the caramel-tasting *Waikato Draught* ☆▷☆☆ and the sweeter *Speight's Distinction Ale* ☆☆.

Loaded Hog
Post-modernist brewpubs in Auckland, Christchurch and Wellington, New Zealand. *Weissbier* ☆☆ is fruity and perfumed.

Lord Nelson
Well-run hotel, restaurant and brewpub in Sydney's Rocks area (Kent and Argyle Sts). Products include a dryish wheat beer called *Quayle Ale* ☆☆; the soft *Victory Bitter* ☆☆ and the malty-fruity *Old Admiral* ☆☆☆.

Mac's
Pioneering micro in New Zealand. Established in 1981/2 by former All Black rugby player Terry McCashin, in cider-making premises near Nelson. Sweetish, notably fruity beers include the chocolatey *Black Mac* ☆☆ and the newer, golden *Premium Reserve* ☆☆, both lagers. The beers are well-presented at a beachside pub, The Honest Lawyer, 1 Point Rd, Monaco, Nelson.

Malt House
In Auckland, New Zealand, this is the name of a smart brewpub (in an office mall at 501 Karangahape Rd), offering a toffeeish *Stout* ☆☆ and a chocolatey *Dark* ☆▷☆☆. In Wellington, the unrelated Malthouse (Willis St) is a speciality beer bar.

Marlborough
Wine-country micro in Blenheim, New Zealand. Products include the perfumed, hoppy *Marlborough Steam* ☆☆.

Matilda Bay
Pioneering micro in Perth, Western Australia. Best known for *RedBack* ☆☆▷☆☆☆ wheat beer, less spicy than it once was.

Moonshine
Tiny brewery on the Kidepo vineyard, Yallingup, in the Margaret River area of Western Australia. Early brews somewhat astringent.

Old Goulburn
Catholic priest Michael O'Halloran revived this 1830s brewery as a rehabilitation project for disabled people in 1991. Early brews, from malt extract, have included a thinnish, roasty *Stout* ☆▷☆☆, served on the premises. The brewery is in Goulburn, between Sydney and Canberra, Australia.

Onehunga Spring
Formerly Newbegin, now a micro in Auckland. Products include the sweetish, coffeeish *Old Thumper* ☆☆; the well-balanced, lemony *Silver Fern Lager* ☆☆; and (under contract) the more aromatic *Northland Pilsner* ☆☆.

Parrot & Jigger
Rail station brewpub at Lower Hutt, near Wellington. Beers include the fruity, long *Stoker Dark* ☆☆☆; the slightly cedary *Nor'Wester* ☆☆▷☆☆☆, a strong (5.6; 7.0) Pale Ale; and, at the same strength, the creamy, warming *Sou'Wester* ☆☆▷☆☆☆ sweet stout.

Petone
Formerly Strongcroft. In the Wellington suburb of Petone. Lager brewery with an Alt-like *Bitter* ☆▷☆☆ and the treacly *Owd Jim* ☆☆.

Pilot Bay
Very small micro on New Zealand's Bay of Plenty, at the retirement resort of Tauranga. The brewery's *Lager* ☆☆ is hoppy and medium-dry but well-balanced. Its *Amber* ☆☆ is a hoppy ale with an appetisingly dry finish. There is also a *Wee Heavy* (not tasted)

Pink Elephant
Roger Pink, from Kent, England, makes extremely hoppy, elliptically named ales in the vineyard country along Rapuara Rd, near Blenheim, New Zealand. *PBA* ☆☆▷☆☆☆ (Pink's Bitter Ale?) has a late, lingering bitterness. *PDA* ☆☆▷☆☆☆ (Dark Ale?) is a rounded, dryish Mild. *Pachyderm Stout* ☆☆▷☆☆☆ is toasty, with a crisp finish. *Mammoth* ☆☆☆ (5.6; 7.0) has pepper, graininess, cream and strawberry notes.

Polar
Clean, notably malty mainstream beers from a second micro in Petone (see above). Products include fresh, grassy *Lager* ☆☆ and a molasses-tinged *Dark* ☆☆.

Port Dock
Brewpub in Port Adelaide, Australia, producing the malty, golden *Lighthouse Ale* ☆▷☆☆☆; the creamy *Black Diamond Bitter* ☆☆ (closer to a Northern English Brown Ale); and the syrupy *Old Preacher* ☆☆☆ (4.8; 6.0).

Power's
Established in 1987 to fight the giants, but now owned by Foster's. *Big Red* ☆▷☆☆ is a relatively robust lager by Australian standards.

Rangitoto
Volcano-theme sports bar on Auckland's North Shore (134 Hurstmere Rd, Takapuna). *Black Rat Dark Ale* ☆▷☆☆ has some treacle-toffee flavours.

RedBack
Brewpub in Melbourne (75 Flemington Rd) that was an offshoot of Matilda Bay in Western Australia. Both are now owned by Foster's, and the brewpub is used for experimental projects. Products have included the aromatic, fruity *RedBack Hefe-Weizen* ☆☆☆ and a soft, well-balanced *Pils* ☆☆☆.

Roosters
The winemaking Harrison family of Hawke's Bay diversified in 1994 with this brewery, bar and lunch café, in stables-style buildings four miles W of Hastings (1470 Omahu Rd). Beer sometimes direct from the cask. The *Dark* ☆☆☆▷☆☆☆ has a fresh, textured maltiness and good flavour development.

Rifle Brigade
In the old gold-mining town of Bendigo, Victoria, Australia. This brewpub has produced the light *Koala* ☆☆ wheat beer; the assertive *Old Fashioned Bitter* ☆☆▷☆☆☆; and a more flowery, bronze *Premium* ☆☆, among a varying selection.

Sail & Anchor
Pioneering brewpub in Fremantle, Western Australia. Definitely worth a visit. Products have included the fruity *Traditional Bitter* ☆☆☆ and the gently roasty *Brass Monkey Stout* ☆☆☆ (4.8; 6.0).

Scharer's
Hoppy, resiny *Lager* ☆☆▷☆☆☆ and remarkably creamy *Bock* ☆☆☆ most easily found at the Australian Hotel, 100 Cumberland St, The Rocks, Sydney. The original Scharer brewpub is the George IV, in Picton 50 miles SW.

Shakespeare
Former All Black Ron Urlich now owns this city-centre brewpub in Auckland. The *Lager* ☆☆▷☆☆☆ has an excellent hop flavour, *Macbeth's Red Ale* ☆☆▷☆☆☆ a good malt character; *Falstaff Ale* ☆☆☆ has gained in bitterness; *King Lear Old Ale* ☆☆▷☆☆☆ is distinctly rummy and chocolatey; and *Willpower Stout* ☆☆ creamier than in the early days.

South Australian
Major Adelaide brewery. Its beers tend to be marginally drier than those of other big Australian brewers. They include the all-malt *West End Premium* ☆▷☆☆ and a tasty chocolatey *Stout* ☆☆▷☆☆☆.

Sunshine
The outstanding *Black Magic Stout* ☆☆☆ has tobacco and vanilla on the aroma and palate and a praline finish. *Gisborne Gold* ☆☆▷☆☆☆ has a light touch of hop on aroma and flavour, and some length. *Moonshine Strong Pilsener* ☆☆ (5.2; 6.5) is perfumed and smooth. Micro in Gisborne, New Zealand.

Swan
Major brewery in Perth, Western Australia. Products include the lightly hoppy *Emu Bitter* ☆☆ and the slight tart *Swan Draught* ☆.

Toohey's
Once the Catholic, "Irish" brewery in Sydney, now owned by Lion Nathan. *Red* ☆☆ has a dry maltiness and a late touch of hop. *Old Black* ☆☆▷☆☆☆ is fruity and chocolatey.

Tooth's
Once the Protestant, "English" brewery in Sydney; now owned by Foster's. Products include *Resch's Draught* ☆☆, an assertive lager by Australian standards; the sweetish, earthy *Kent Old Brown* ☆☆▷☆☆☆ and the tar-like, almost oaky *Sheaf Stout* ☆☆▷☆☆☆.

White Cliffs
There is a restrained roastiness and smooth, chocolatey dryness to *Mike's Mild* ☆☆, from this micro in Urenui, near New Plymouth, New Zealand.

Wig & Pen
Cask-conditioned ales, reputedly hoppy (not tasted) at a student brewpub in Canberra, Australia (Alinga St/West Row).

AFRICA

THIS CONTINENT MIGHT CLAIM to have had some of the first brewers; Ancient Egyptian communities produced beer at least 3,000 years ago, using barley and an early form of wheat called emmer.

Very similar techniques are still used to produce quick-fermenting, turbid, milky-looking home-brewed "beers" in villages throughout Africa. In some countries, these brews are made commercially and sold in plastic "milk" bottles; *Chibuku* of Zimbabwe is a well-known example. These traditional brews, versions of which are made in other continents, do not resemble modern beers, but are fermented from cereals.

In most parts of the continent, the climate is too hot for barley (Kenya is an exception). Sorghum and cassava flour are among the materials used in traditional beers. As imported barley is expensive for developing nations, and some countries use local cereals as adjucts even in conventional modern beers.

Except for the most fundamentalist Muslim nations, all African countries have their own breweries. Some, like Nigeria and Zaire, have many. Most were set up by European international brewers, often in joint ventures with state governments, and the beers are usually standard golden lagers. The majority are produced for refreshment rather than taste, but there are exceptions. From Kenya, a super-premium version of *Tusker* ☆☆ lager is much more aromatic and hoppy than the usual domestic products. In Uganda, Nile Breweries produces a beer called *ESB* ☆☆ which in this instance means Extra Strong Brew (5.6; 7.0). This is a lager, with some vanilla-like maltiness and a drier, lemon-rind finish.

In Zimbabwe, the newish Digby Nesbit brewery employs a Czech to produce its *Hunter's Lager* according to German Beer Purity Law (the Reiheitsgebot). In South Africa, several new breweries make relatively serious lagers. These include Falcon Crest and Bavaria Bräu (both Johannesburg), Stirling (Durban) and Helderbräu (Cape Town). The old-established Namibia Breweries make a *Maibock* ☆☆▷☆☆☆ (4.8; 6.0) that is tawny, syrupy and slightly iron-ish.

Many African breweries also produce strong stouts. South African Breweries, the national giant, has *Castle Milk Stout* ☆☆▷☆☆☆ (5.0; 6.24) made with lactose. This is light for alcohol, starting firm and smooth, moving to notes of milky coffee, with a grainy, slightly sour finish.

Africa's first micro-brewery was opened in 1984, in Knysna, Cape Province by Lex Mitchell, who previously worked for SAB. He has since opened Mitchell's pubs in Johannesburg and Cape Town. His smooth, firm, malty beers, unfiltered and unpasteurised include *Forester's Draught Lager* ☆☆ (4.0; 5.0), perfumy, with a sweetish middle and late hoppy dryness; *Bosun's Bitter* ☆☆☆ (3.6; 4.5), deep gold, light, fruity and hoppy, with well-combined flavours; the cinnamon-spiced *Old 90* ☆☆☆ (5.6; 7.0), with a Scotch whisky aroma, malty middle and good balance of hop bitterness; and *Raven Stout* ☆☆ (4.8; 6.0), with a rummy aroma, liqueur-ish palate and coffee finish.

INDEX OF BEERS

INDEX OF BREWERIES